IN SEARCH OF GHOSTS

IN SEARCH OF GHOSTS

Ian Wilson

HEADLINE

First published in 1995 by
HEADLINE BOOK PUBLISHING

10 9 8 7 6 5 4 3 2 1

British Library Cataloguing in Publication Data

Wilson, Ian
In Search Of Ghosts
I.Title
133.1

ISBN 0 7472 1183 3

Typeset by Avon Dataset Ltd, Bidford-on-Avon, B50 4JH

Printed and bound in Great Britain by
Mackays of Chatham PLC, Chatham, Kent

HEADLINE BOOK PUBLISHING
A division of Hodder Headline PLC
338 Euston Road,
London NW1 3BH

CONTENTS

PREFACE & ACKNOWLEDGEMENTS

This is a book which would not have been written but for the insistence of my publisher, Alan Brooke of Headline. When he first suggested that I search for the evidence for ghosts, my initial reaction was to decline for what seemed, to my way of thinking, several very good reasons.

First, although in earlier books I have researched and written on the so-called paranormal, for some years I have avoided this field, partly on the grounds that potentially serious findings are too often devalued and drowned out by media sensationalism of the downright spurious. Second, in all my then fifty-two years I had never knowingly experienced a ghost. Third, I had not the slightest intention of trying to change my luck by joining ghost-hunters camping out overnight at some 'haunted' house in search of any ghosts said to lurk there. Even with my then limited knowledge, I had little faith in ghost-hunters' methods, and even less in their success rate. Fourth, I am congenitally night-blind, so that even if I did manage to find a ghost, with or without the aid of a ghost-hunting group, I would probably be the last person able to see what was obvious to everybody else.

Despite my objections, Alan Brooke persisted, and I relented, and for better or for worse, this book is the result. Of course there was method in Alan's perseverance. In recent years British media fascination for ghosts has heightened considerably, with the subject having inspired several popular television documentaries, including one full series, while I was in the course of my research. There has also been a major television drama series entitled *Ghosts*. Radio and television talk shows increasingly choose the subject for debate. Hallowe'en has become much more prominent than it has been for decades. Regular 'ghost walks' provide a popular tourist attraction for several major cities. There has even been a ghost feature in *Hello!* magazine.

But this book will not follow the popular media's presentation of the subject as 'spooky', 'whacky' and ideal for raising a nervous snigger or giggle. Nor is it a volume for the do-it-yourself ghost-hunting enthusiast. As I discovered, this country now has two national clubs for active ghost-hunters. One is the original Ghost Club, led for many years by Peter Underwood, the UK's recognised expert on ghosts. The other is the Ghost Club Society, which Underwood recently formed following a committee-room squabble and departure from the Ghost Club. Although I wanted only to receive their newsletters, daggers are so drawn between the two societies that the rules of each specifically forbid membership of the other. In the event although I had help from individuals representing both, I formally joined neither. Nor have I tailored the book for purist psychical researchers, not least by avoiding their typically near-impenetrable jargon. Rather than describing a person as in the hypnagogic or hypnopompic state, I much prefer to say that he was just going to sleep, or just waking up.

Instead, my whole aim has been to address, as fearlessly and independently as possible, and without courting any particular faction of experts, the key issues of whether ghosts exist, and if so, what they are and why they are. For me, the most potentially rewarding way of answering these questions is not by sitting in a reputedly haunted house armed with camera and tape-recorder, but by listening to those who claim to have had first-hand ghost experiences, and trying to evaluate as fairly and objectively as possible what may be believed and what may not.

Wherever possible I have given people's accounts of their experiences in their own words. I have valued reports by those self-avowedly sceptical towards the subject above those claiming psychic gifts – although, as will be seen, I have accorded serious and sympathetic consideration to the 'sensitive' Eddie Burks. In the case of ordinary members of the public, it had been my aim, with each person's consent, to avoid pseudonyms and to be one hundred per cent open about all facts, since for me any ghost book in which the names and locations have been changed might as well be a work of fiction.

In the event there are some instances in which I have reluctantly used a pseudonym, usually either because of medical ethics or to avoid undue intrusion upon an individual's privacy. These instances are signalled by the words 'whom we will call [e.g. Mrs Armstrong]' or some similar textual indication, such as the name initially appearing in quotation marks. All other names, dates, locations, etc. that appear are real, and wherever possible have been carefully checked with the informants. Although this book can carry no guarantee against any of its cases being hoaxes, I have taken every reasonable precaution to avoid such an eventuality.

The prime purpose of this preface is to record my gratitude to the many people who have freely given of their time to help with my research and/or share with me their experiences in order to make this book possible. These include: John Beauclerk-Robinson, Chelsea, London; Commander Bill Bellars, General Secretary/Treasurer, the Ghost Club Society; Bob and Val Bootle, Cookham, Berkshire; Clive Boreham, Dover Castle, Kent; Eddie Burks, Lincoln; Christopher Calcutt, Calcutt Maclean, Ashford, Kent; Geraldine Charles, archivist, National Maritime Museum; Fr Michael Clifton, St Joseph's Church, Collier's Wood, London; R. J. Comber, Bridgwater, Somerset; Bob Cotterall, Wellington, New Zealand; Miss M. E. Dickinson, Bisham, Berkshire; Professor Arthur Ellison, Beckenham, Kent; Hilary Evans, Blackheath, London; Lady Antonia Fraser; the Venerable Glanville Gibson, Durham; Mrs Peggy Gordon-Russell and the late Dr James Gordon-Russell, Almondsbury, Bristol; Mr R. S. Greenhalgh, Salford, Lancashire; Professor Anthony Hale, Department of Psychiatry, University of Sheffield; Melvin Harris, Benfleet, Essex; Mark Hayward, General Manager, the Theatre Royal, Drury Lane, London; Rodney Hoare, Salisbury, Wiltshire; Commander J. A. Holt, Secretary, the Naval and Military Club, London; Dr Michael Hough, Australian Institute of Parapsychological Research, New South Wales, Australia; Miss Joan Hughes, Salisbury, Wiltshire; John Idris Jones, North Wales; J. M. Kaye, archivist, Queen's College, Oxford; Krystyna Kolodziej, Australia; Doug Lear, Llandrindod Wells, Powys, Wales; Dr and Mrs Kenneth McAll, New Forest, Hampshire; Andrew MacKenzie, Hove, East Sussex; Barbara

McKenzie, Langport, Somerset; Fr Peter Milward, Sophia University, Tokyo, Japan; Ann Mitchell, Basingstoke Library; John Mitchell, York; Rex, Mary and Christopher Morgan, (also Xanthe), Bathurst, New South Wales, Australia; John and Joan Morris, Wye, Kent; the Revd Christopher Neil-Smith, Ealing, London, also his son David; Dr Patrick Ottaway, York Archaeological Trust; Tom Perrott, north London; Canon Michael Perry, Durham Cathedral; Mrs Barbara Peters, archivist, Coutts Bank, Strand, London; Isabel Piczek, Los Angeles; David Rolfe, Burnham, Buckinghamshire; Dr Anne Ross, Aberystwyth, Dyfed; Miss Peggy Spencer Palmer, Bristol; the late Rt Revd Mervyn Stockwood, Bishop of Southwark; Simon Thurley, Hampton Court Palace; Brian Tremain, Longfield, Kent; Dr Tony Trowles, Assistant Librarian, Westminster Abbey; Peter Underwood, Hampshire; Canon Dominic Walker, Rural Dean, Brighton, Sussex; Dean A. Arnold Wettstein, Rollins College, Florida.

I am also particularly indebted, for many favours, to the ever helpful Eleanor O'Keeffe, Secretary of the Society for Psychical Research; also, as usual, to the staffs of the University Library, Bristol, and the Bristol Central Library; also to my editor Ian Marshall of Headline and copy-editor Jane Selley.

By no means least, my most heartfelt thanks are, as ever, due to my wife Judith, who was by my side from the very opening moments of this book, and who helped in innumerable ways, from the typing of manuscripts to the final checking of every dot and comma in this manuscript.

Ian Wilson
Bristol, England
June 1995

PICTURE ACKNOWLEDGEMENTS

The author and publishers wish to acknowledge thanks to the following for use of, or help with, photographs reproduced in this book:

Plates: Rex Morgan & family, pl. 3; the Ghost Club & National Maritime Museum, pl. 4; Brian Tremain and the National Maritime Museum, Greenwich, pl. 6; the J. Paul Getty Museum, pl. 7; Gordon Carroll, pl. 9; *Country Life*, pl. 10; the Naval and Military Club, pl. 11; John & Joan Morris, pl. 12; Auckland City Art Gallery, pl. 17; John Mitchell, pls. 19 & 20; Dr Patrick Ottaway, pl. 21; Doug Lear, pl. 22; Canon Dominic Walker, pl. 23.

Text figures: Duncan & Barbara McKenzie, figs. 1 & 2; Dr Kenneth McAll, fig. 3; Dr Anne Ross, fig. 4; Theatre Royal, Drury Lane, fig. 5.

It had been the author's intention to reproduce National Maritime Museum photographer Brian Tremain's copy of the Tulip Staircase photograph, taken directly from the Revd Hardy's original, and revealing the long exposure cause of the seeming 'ghosts'. However, unresolved legal disputes between Peter Underwood and the Ghost Club prevented this.

Every effort has been made to trace original copyright owners, but anyone inadvertently excepted should get in touch with the publishers.

'I Can't Believe This Is Happening to Me . . .'

'Can you hear what I can hear?'

Disbelieving my own senses, I found myself whispering this question to my wife Judith, in bed beside me, little more than two minutes after she had switched off the light for us to settle down to sleep. It was shortly after midnight on 30 January 1994, and we were in Australia, staying overnight at Abercrombie House [pl. 1], a historic mansion near Bathurst, New South Wales, as guests of the house's owners, Rex Morgan and his family. Judith lay on my right, while from my immediate left came the sound of someone gently but very audibly breathing, as if seeking attention. The sound was utterly distinct and as clear as crystal in the still Australian night.

To my relief, Judith answered with a similarly whispered 'Yes.'

'Can you see anything?' Coming from me the question had particular pertinence because all my life I have been night-blind and am unable to see anything when the lights are turned off.

'No.'

For perhaps a minute more we lay in the darkness listening to the breathing, which continued clearly and insistently. It was coming from right next to me, but at standing height, impossible for any physical person because the floor space beside the bed was already occupied by a large, old-fashioned wooden clothes-airer. Also, although our bedroom door was open, no one could have crept in without our knowledge, because we were separated from the rest of the house by a long passageway along which every floorboard creaked loudly. The breathing seemed to me to be that of a woman, whose presence I seemed to 'feel' standing beside me.

As I continued looking hard in the direction from which the breathing was coming, Judith switched on the light on her side of the bed. One advantage of night-blindness is that no time is lost waiting for one's eyes to adjust to the light, and I saw immediately that no one was there. Furthermore, to my utter astonishment, the breathing seemed almost visibly to fade to silence as we watched.

Another advantage of night-blindness is that the night-sighted partner tends to take charge of investigating night-time disturbances, and so it was Judith, ever practical and down-to-earth, who ventured into the semi-darkness of the passageway to check on possible 'normal' explanations. Could the sound conceivably be coming up through the floor from one of the Morgans' dogs sleeping in the kitchen below us? A short flight of steps just off the outside passageway led down into the kitchen, but Judith found no animal of any kind there, and returned baffled, this time closing the bedroom door behind her.

Already the possibility of a ghost loomed large in our minds. Abercrombie House, large, rambling and isolated, dates back to the 1870s, and earlier that evening, over dinner, the Morgans had matter-of-factly told us that they had experienced occasional ghostly occurrences. These chiefly involved an unknown woman in a long dress who had been seen by guests at parties, and the sound of a bicycle bell heard in the early morning when there was no one around. But there had been no stories about our bedroom, and since the house has over forty rooms, and we were the only guests that weekend, we hardly supposed the Morgans would give us a room they knew to be haunted.

Getting back into bed again, Judith switched off the light, but within half a minute the sound of the breathing was back – as clear and as regular as before. For three or four minutes we lay still, listening and saying together, 'There . . . there . . .' with each succeeding breath, to confirm that we were hearing the sounds at exactly the same time. While neither of us felt threatened or frightened, the presence of something seemingly supernatural so close by meant that there was no question of either of us not being very awake.

Wearily, Judith again switched on the light, and again – and it is impossible to convey adequately the weirdness of the experience – the breathing simply faded on the air as we watched. For as long as the light remained on we could hear nothing. Then, as it was switched off for the third time, the breathing returned almost immediately.

It was by now well after 12.30 a.m., and we were both very tired. We had travelled from Sydney earlier that day, and the two previous days had been taken up with media interviews, a lecture, and participation in the Sydney Writers' Festival, all relating to a book I had written on Shakespeare. Although shortly before leaving England I had reluctantly accepted my publisher's suggestion that I should write a book investigating the evidence of ghosts, I had definitely not come to Australia looking for such material, and was quite unprepared for how to deal with it. My long but by no means close acquaintance with Rex Morgan was through a shared interest in the Turin Shroud, and I had not had the slightest idea until that evening that his home had a reputation for being haunted.

With hindsight I now kick myself that I did not try speaking to the invisible source of the breathing, not least in order to ask who they were and what they wanted – though whether they might have replied I have no idea. However, at the time, partly through shock, partly through sheer disbelief that something of this kind could actually be happening to us, I could only think of a haunting I had once read of suffered by a classics lecturer and his family at Abbey House in Cambridge. After repeated night-time disturbances by the sighing apparition of a robed woman, the lecturer's wife had, more in exasperation than sympathy, pronounced, 'In the name of the Trinity, poor soul, rest in peace.' As she described it, the apparition then almost immediately 'went away to the curtain and I have never seen or heard it since.'[1]

Was it possible that I might be able to cause our 'breathing ghost' to disappear in the same way? Although I have been a practising Roman Catholic for more than two decades, my private prayers tend to be a few simple ones said silently on settling down for the night, and I have never regarded myself as strong on such matters. It was therefore with little conviction, a certain concern for our invisible intruder, but mostly the wish for a quiet night that I composed a very makeshift prayer based on what I could remember of the formula used by the lecturer's wife. Silently, I projected into the darkness: 'Lord Jesus Christ, Son of God:

to whoever is with us in this room please grant eternal rest. In the name of the Father, the Son and the Holy Ghost, Amen.'

To my utter astonishment, immediately upon the 'Amen', the breathing sound ceased. Moments later, still hardly believing that something so simple and so silent could actually have *worked*, I told Judith what I had done. Her response – more in relief than piety – was a heartfelt 'Thank God for that!' She told me that she had heard one final sigh – either unnoticed or unheard by me – then nothing more. Amazingly, just a few moments later we both dozed off peacefully, and slept soundly until the morning.

At breakfast we told our story to the Morgans, provoking the first of many inquests on just how much we could and should believe of our own senses. Indeed, looking back, I still find it difficult myself to credit what I experienced, and would have been rather more reticent about offering it to the opinion of others but for the fact that Judith – very much the feet-firmly-on-the-floor half of our partnership – heard it all alongside me, and vouches for everything that I have described.

Rex Morgan's wife Mary, although she herself had once seen a ghostly figure approach Rex's side of the bed in the master bedroom, suggested that we might have heard a possum. This Judith and I both firmly rejected on the grounds that even if such an animal were able perfectly to mimic the sound of human breathing, it would have to have been right in the room with us, and almost next to my shoulder. We could hardly not have noticed its presence. Furthermore, it cannot be emphasised enough that wherever and whatever the source of the breathing, our minds distinctly located it where someone's head would have been if they had been standing immediately to my left as I lay in bed. As already mentioned, the floor at that spot was occupied by a wooden clothes-airer. Our invisible intruder, therefore, would have had to have been in the middle of this, apparently able to pass right through it. A possum would have had to be hovering in mid-air . . .

Since Rex Morgan had already put on record that he believes his home to be haunted, he was not inclined to be dismissive. Even so, he expressed surprise that our room, known as the Red Room [pl. 2], should have been the subject of such activity. But the Morgans' younger son, Christopher, who works full-time at Abercrombie on its maintenance and restoration, told us that years before he had experienced something

4

similar, though he did not elaborate. We also learned that previous guests staying in other bedrooms had sometimes reported 'feeling' a presence, though in their case they were able neither to see nor hear its source.

So – assuming that my wife and I indeed did experience a ghost at Abercrombie House on the night of 30 January 1994 – who could he or, as I would argue, she have been? Before we left we were shown a small painting from the early years of this century that hangs in the Morgans' drawing room. This features the house in the background, while in the foreground stands a young woman with a bicycle [pl. 3]. Possibly the source of the ghostly bicycle bells? Rex identified her as Miss Rosslyn Stewart, daughter of James Horne Stewart who built Abercrombie House back in the 1870s. But he was unable to suggest why she might have come to haunt the place.

James Horne Stewart was the son of Major General William Stewart, a governor of New South Wales who back in the 1820s was granted 3,000 acres by the British government for his part in opening up the new state. His fortress-like home, Strath, which can be seen from Abercrombie House, has its own reputation for a ghost, which is said to arrive there in a furiously driven carriage, and then moves through the house slamming doors and breaking crockery. At least one person has reported seeing the ghost of a convict at Strath, consistent with William Stewart having been responsible for many convicts during his time as Governor.

But perhaps the likeliest candidate for our Abercrombie House ghost, if indeed this was a woman, is the wife of James Horne Stewart's son Athol. In 1927, while still young, and with a young family, she contracted flu while living at the house and died very suddenly, her husband being so devastated that he abandoned the place within days. The huge mansion lay neglected and empty until the 1950s when another Stewart, William's great-grandson James, took charge of its restoration, passing it on to his son Peter, who in 1968 sold it to the Morgans. Could something of this Mrs Stewart have lingered on at Abercrombie through an inability to come to terms with the untimeliness of her death?

Suddenly we are into the whole field of speculation engendered by any ghost story, giving rise to the key question: just how sure can we be that the breathing that my wife and I so distinctly heard genuinely came from a ghost?; from someone no longer alive? Although our particular story is hardly one of the most spectacular of its genre, the sceptic has every right to subject it to the same critical scrutiny. For instance, assuming that both my wife and I are telling the truth (which we are), could we have indulged in a little too much alcohol when entertained by the Morgans earlier that evening and simply imagined the whole thing? Very definitely no – our total intake was probably only two glasses of wine each, little more than our norm, and we both felt totally sober.

Could the breathing have been simply a trick played on us by one or more of our Abercrombie House hosts – perhaps via a speaker hidden somewhere in our room? We can only respond that the Morgans did not seem to us that sort of family. Indeed, by our own and by most Australian standards they are unusually formal and reserved (Rex, who retains British citizenship, is a Justice of the Peace and very proud of his MBE). If they had indulged in such a ruse, the sudden cessation of the breathing following my impromptu silent prayer – which no living person could have heard – would have been quite a remarkable coincidence.

Even so, in order to address the possibility I asked Rex to write and sign a simple statement formally denying any trickery. The wording is Rex Morgan's own:

Dear Ian,

You and Judith stayed with us at Abercrombie House on the night of 30 January 1994 in what we call the Red Room over the kitchen wing and you reported a ghost experience to us the next morning.

I hereby confirm that neither I nor any member of my family or household played any trick or joke upon you that night in order to cause the sounds you report. Indeed such an idea would not have occurred to us as there are plenty of ghost experiences in my house recorded (and indeed published)[2] by us over the years without any need to contrive them.

Rex Morgan
(Justice of the Peace)[3]

This by no means exhausts the possible explanations for what occurred at Abercrombie House that January night. But whatever the exact nature of our encounter, it is but one of thousands of instances of people from all walks of life having experiences that rightly or wrongly they interpret as ghosts. That is, they see, hear or otherwise sense in a variety of ways the presence of a person who is clearly not there in any normally understood physical form, and who may have the semblance of someone who has died either recently, or a long time before.

In this regard some key questions demand answers. Are such experiences simply illusions, nothing more than the products of overactive imaginations and trickery? Are they real enough, but essentially empty – some sort of recording track that lingers on in certain surroundings and certain circumstances? Or is there really something of someone dead actively there – perhaps trying very hard to make his or her continued existence known in the land of the living?

Hundreds of books have been written about ghosts – all too often thinly researched collections of anecdotes intended to entertain and make the flesh creep. Likewise among the media there tends to be an enthusiastic flurry of interest in ghosts around Hallowe'en, but few working journalists have the time or the inclination to take the subject any more seriously.

Indeed, it is all too easy *not* to take the subject seriously. After all, in the thousands of years during which ghosts have been reported, no one has been able to capture one and subject it to proper independent scrutiny. It is all based on what people *say* they have experienced. And if ghosts are genuinely what they are supposed to be – that is, apparitions of the souls of the dead – how is it that almost invariably they are seen wearing the sort of clothes they would have worn in life? Why aren't they naked? Are we supposed to believe that their clothes somehow survive along with them? Can we really accept the stories that some ghosts go around carrying their own severed heads? How is it that ghosts are reported appearing with accoutrements such as chains, and even items of transport such as coaches and horses? Why are ghosts of animals, such as dogs, cats and even bears, surprisingly commonly reported? It all seems so illogical – sometimes almost ludicrously so.

This book has three underlying aims. First: to try to determine *if* ghosts exist – that is, to try to make the best possible assessment of human experiences of ghosts in order to establish that they really are rather more than just hallucination and make-believe. If our conclusions are positive, then our second aim is to try to determine *what* ghosts are

– that is, whether they are just empty tracings or something rather more real. And our third aim, inevitably arising from the findings of the second, is to try to find out *why* they are – that is, why some people become ghosts, while others do not.

To begin, then, just how good is the evidence for whether or not ghosts really do exist?

Part I

In Search of Whether Ghosts Exist

'Reason says "no", something else says "yes".'
Dr Samuel Johnson

CHAPTER ONE

On Not Trusting Some Ghost Stories

For whatever you may consider it worth, you have just had our Abercrombie House ghost encounter described to you at first hand. Since my wife has checked and approved everything I have written, effectively you have heard it direct from the two people involved in the experience, people willing to identify themselves publicly. You have been given the precise location, and the day and time, almost to the minute. You also have our heartfelt assurance that whatever the source of the breathing we heard that night (and we can only *think* we experienced a ghost), it was so clear, so prolonged and so real that it was certainly not our imagination. In this regard it may be appropriate to say that Judith is a qualified psychologist.

Throughout this book it will be my policy for as many of the cases as possible to derive from named witnesses, and to be given in the witnesses' own words in order to minimise the inevitable errors that creep in with second-hand reporting. But it is important to be aware that every ghost story also depends on the honesty of those telling it, the accuracy of their memory and the reliability of their interpretation of the circumstances. Even the most authoritative and best-attested cases can be found on close scrutiny to have been seriously weakened, if not totally undermined, by some form of human frailty.

Take for instance the case of Canon J. B. Phillips, a highly respected Anglican Biblical scholar whose *New Testament in Modern English* was a major best-seller around the middle years of this century. In his

11

1967 book *The Ring of Truth*, Canon Phillips matter-of-factly described how he had personally experienced, at both a visual and an auditory level, the ghost of the famous writer and scholar C. S. Lewis. In Canon Phillips's own words:

> Let me say at once that I am incredulous by nature and as unsuperstitious as they come . . . But the late C. S. Lewis, whom I did not know very well, and had only seen in the flesh once, but with whom I had corresponded a fair amount, gave me an unusual experience. A few days after his death, while I was watching television, he 'appeared' sitting in a chair within a few feet of me, and spoke a few words which were particularly relevant to the difficult circumstances through which I was passing. He was ruddier in complexion than ever, grinning all over his face, and as the old-fashioned saying has it, positively glowing with health. The interesting thing to me was that I had not been thinking about him at all . . . a week later, this time when I was in bed reading before going to sleep, he appeared again, even more rosily radiant than before, and repeated the same message . . .[1]

It is a matter of public record that C. S. Lewis died on 22 November 1963, so we might reasonably expect Canon Phillips's information that he saw Lewis 'a few days after his death' to mean either late November 1963, or at the very latest the first week in December. Furthermore, since Phillips was only fifty-seven at that time we might logically expect his memory to have been clear on such matters.

However, when, in 1970, researchers from the Society for Psychical Research sent Canon Phillips a questionnaire asking him to provide further details of his experience, he told them that it had occurred 'early on a *spring* evening [my italics] in full daylight'.[2] This is somewhat hard to reconcile with his earlier statement that he had seen the ghost just 'a few days' after Lewis's death, not least since in England in late November, darkness falls around 4.30 p.m.

Furthermore, totally contradicting Phillips's earlier statement that he had not been thinking of Lewis at the time, he now said that the experience had been triggered by a letter informing him 'how he [C. S. Lewis] fared, and indeed, how he died'. Complicating matters yet further, when Phillips was independently interviewed at about the same time by ghost researcher Dennis Bardens, who was assembling material for his book *Mysterious Worlds*,[3] he gave the date as 'early June, 1966' – two and a half years after Lewis's death.

Canon Phillips died in 1982, and in deference to his considerable achievements as a scholar, it ought to be stressed that none of this should be allowed to impugn his honesty or the reality of his ghostly experience. But if even so distinguished and well educated a witness as Phillips cannot be relied upon to get the basic facts right, why should the sceptic be convinced?

Similar considerations apply to a collection of purportedly factual ghost stories recently written by octogenarian consultant psychiatrist Dr Kenneth McAll, who lives near Lyndhurst in Hampshire. McAll has made something of a speciality of 'laying' ghosts, and in his 1989 book about this work, *Healing the Haunted*,[4] he devoted his entire opening chapter to a haunting said to have been plaguing a teacher training college in a certain cathedral close, a college and cathedral that, in line with his policy of non-identification of people and places, he left unnamed and unlocated.

According to McAll's account of the events, often at midnight 'screaming and yelling, loud thuds and noises' would be heard in the close, seemingly emanating from the college's attic floor, apparently located in a residential part of the college constructed on the site of an 'ancient nunnery'. In McAll's words, 'none of the students would sleep in the attic and the atmosphere was cold and eerie'.

But then:

One dark, stormy night two students thought they would brave it out and sleep in the room. They said their prayers and went to bed but naturally both remained alert and expectant. As midnight approached they knelt by their bedsides to pray. Suddenly, without any warning, a tall, dark figure wearing a long black gown and wide-brimmed hat emerged from the wall cupboard beside the fireplace, without the door opening. He simply came through it. The two students, trembling and fearful, stayed on their knees. Then the figure seemed to be fighting with another person for some time. There were screams and yells followed by silence. Stealthily the tall figure then picked up a body, apparently dead, which he carried through the door and down the stairs. On the way down he dropped the body which rolled to the foot of the stairs. It sounded like a bucket of bricks being emptied. The tall figure then trudged off into the night and silence returned.[5]

Naturally this sounds a most dramatic and intriguing encounter, neatly coinciding, according to McAll, with a local legend concerning 'a Cavalier [who] had apparently come over the rooftops and entered a nun's room where he had raped her and killed her and then carried off her body'. McAll states that the two 'absolutely terrified' students alerted the college's principal, who in turn summoned him to get rid of the ghost. McAll, with two Anglican priests and a nurse, arrived at the college and said some prayers, thereby ending a haunting said by him to have taken place 'every night at midnight for over 300 years'.

I have met and interviewed Dr McAll at his Lyndhurst home on two memorable occasions. A veteran of a World War II Japanese prisoner-of-war camp in China, he is a gentle, caring and very Christian individual whose sincerity and integrity are beyond question. But among several features that disturbed my critical sense was his information that the haunting had been going on every night 'for over 300 years'. Any ghostly manifestation occurring so regularly would surely have attracted widespread attention and been the subject of some earlier investigation. Yet from my reasonable acquaintance with the history of psychical research I could find no such case. So where was this teacher training college set in a cathedral close? And what would independent inquiries reveal?

In the event the identification of the cathedral close was almost absurdly simple, not least because Dr McAll had happened to mention that the students had stuck a poster of Salisbury Cathedral on one wall of the haunted attic room. Salisbury is geographically close to McAll's New Forest home, it has a very fine and historic close, and most importantly, from 1851 to 1978, the close included the Salisbury Diocesan Training College for Schoolmistresses, part of which was housed in a historic mansion, the King's House, that is now the Salisbury and South Wiltshire Museum.

Having a Salisbury-resident friend[6] closely associated with the cathedral, I sent him a copy of McAll's chapter in the hope that he had either personally heard of the haunting in the close, or might know someone able to shed light on the story. Within days, he put me in touch with Miss Joan Hughes, a retired warden at the training college, who read McAll's account with what she frankly described as amazement.

She insisted that there had definitely been no three-hundred-year-old-history of ghostly noises in the close. The only noises she could recall during her long residence there were those of the students and an assistant cathedral organist, Mr Humpherson, who once briefly took up practising at midnight only to be swiftly silenced by local protests. There never had been an 'ancient nunnery' in the close, somewhat undermining McAll's story of the murdered nun. With regard to the attic that no one would sleep in, in fact it had been occupied by generations of students without any problem. As for the tale of the Cavalier coming through the wall, this was a near-absurd distortion of the true ghost story, of which Miss Hughes had first-hand knowledge. In her words:

> I think it was in June 1972 that one of my students came to see me with a problem. Two of her friends were in residence in the Audley House [the name at that time given to the part of the college with the attic] on the top floor. This room had been used for students many times before. However, these two students reported being disturbed by seeing a figure in what seemed to be a 'habit' in the room. This happened usually early in the morning before the girls got up. On one occasion, one girl felt a choking feeling on waking, and the figure seemed to be bending over her. This worried them, and whenever one girl went home for a night at the weekend, the other would go over to the Queen's Hostel and sleep on the floor in another friend's room.
>
> I felt that the matter must be approached sympathetically – whether it was a real 'haunting' or just a case of adolescent hysteria (the students were sensible young women, and not the sort to get in a state over nothing). I took Phyllis, the student who came to me with the problem, along to the Maxwell Staff Flat and we talked to my colleague and fellow warden Miss Joan Flarty. She had a daybed in her sitting room, so we arranged that whichever

student was left in college at the weekend when her friend went away should slip along to Maxwell, and we would make her up a bed in the flat. After a while we decided it would be better to tell the Principal, Miss Audrey Ashley, about the whole affair. Miss Ashley took the account sympathetically and got in touch with Dr McAll who had been to the college some time previously to speak to the Christian Union . . .[7]

From that point on Miss Hughes' and Dr McAll's accounts are very broadly similar, Miss Hughes stating that 'After this visit of Dr McAll and his group we had no further trouble.' Miss Hughes also felt at pains to corroborate my own insistence on Dr McAll's basic integrity: 'I do think Dr McAll is a fine Christian psychiatrist and I am sure has helped many people in their psychiatric problems.' In support of the version of the haunting described by the girls, Miss Hughes pointed out that 'before the Audley House (which I think is Georgian) was built, there had been a dwelling for Mass priests for the Audley Chantry in the cathedral.' Was one of these chantry priests the source of the figure in a 'habit' seen by the two students?

The sad aspect of this case, as in that of Canon Phillips, is that what should have been a well-attested example of a potentially genuine haunting has been undermined by McAll's slipshod attitude towards those facts of which he did not have first-hand knowledge. His policy of disguising the locations and identities in his cases made him more prone to this carelessness; hence my concern to be open about identities, locations, etc. wherever possible.

While the Canon Phillips and Dr McAll accounts were both potentially genuine ghost experiences marred by poor attention to detail, far worse errors continue to be perpetrated *ad nauseam* by the compilers of the many popular encyclopaedias of purportedly factual ghost stories published each year in the UK, the USA and elsewhere.

Let us take just one of the four hundred entries in American psychical researcher Rosemary Ellen Guiley's *Encyclopaedia of Ghosts and Spirits*, published by Facts on File of New York as recently as 1992:

Tyrone, Admiral Sir George A crisis apparition[8] of the disting-uished British naval officer, Admiral Sir George Tyrone, appeared on the night of his drowning, astonishing guests who were enjoying a party at his London home.

On June 22, 1893, Admiral Tyrone was in command of the HMS *Victoria*, part of the Mediterranean fleet. For unknown reasons, he gave a command that led to the collision of the *Victoria* with another ship, the *Camperdown*. The two ships were leading columns of the fleet when Tyrone gave the order for the columns to turn inward, even though it would result in a head-on collision between the lead ships. At the last moment, he ordered full steam astern to try to avert the crash, but it was too late and the *Camperdown* struck the *Victoria*. Tyrone's ship went down, and he drowned.

At the approximate time of the accident, Lady Tyrone was hosting an elegant party at their Easton Place home in London. The guests were stunned when Admiral Tyrone, in full uniform, suddenly appeared, walked across the room, and disappeared. It is possible that the emotional distress of the accident, and Tyrone's knowledge of his imminent demise as his ship went down, enabled a projection of himself to appear to his wife and others.[9]

Certain relatively minor slips need to be noted in passing. For instance, the distinguished British naval officer concerned was not 'Admiral Sir George Tyrone', but Vice-Admiral Sir George Tryon. Likewise his London home was not 'Easton Place' but Eaton Place. These comparatively trivial errors aside, it is quite true that Sir George died along with hundreds of other British seamen on 22 June 1893, off Tripoli, seemingly as a result of his miscalculation of his ships' turning circles. Although no one is quite sure how and why it happened, he appears to have become confused about the difference between a circle's radius and its circumference.

Altogether more serious are the discrepancies relating to Sir George's post-mortem appearance at Eaton Place. Rosemary Ellen Guiley, impressively quoted as a member of the American Society for Psychical Research, a member of the Society for Psychical Research (London) and vice-president of the International Society for the Study of Ghosts and Apparitions, gave as her source Daniel Cohen's *The Encyclopaedia of Ghosts*, published by Dodd, Mead & Co. of New York in 1984.

In his turn Daniel Cohen most likely took the story from Peter

Underwood's *Haunted London* (1973), in which it appears in a more elaborate and (at least where Sir George is concerned) more accurate version.[10] Underwood goes so far as to call the case 'one of London's best-authenticated ghost stories' – which it might well have been had any of Lady Tryon's guests that fateful day actually recorded their experience.

But as has been demonstrated by investigations published by British author/sceptic Melvin Harris,[11] when one tries to trace the story back to any truly contemporary eyewitness or second-hand report, the trail ends in a disquieting nothingness. According to estimates, some three hundred distinguished people – 'the cream of Edwardian high society', in Underwood's words, though actually Queen Victoria's reign had another ten years to run – were supposedly 'stunned' at the sight of Sir George's ghost that evening in 1893. Yet there survives not a single known diary entry of this remarkable collective experience, nor a single mention in a letter, nor even a contemporary newspaper report. Compounding suspicions, the times quoted by ghost 'experts' for Sir George's appearance vary widely. And according to Melvin Harris's inquiries, a 'Sir Jasper Hoad' sometimes said to have been a star named witness never even existed.

Melvin Harris believes that the Sir George Tryon story in fact originated as a fictional ghost story, 'A Ghost in a Ballroom', actually published six months *before* Sir George made his fatal miscalculation off Tripoli. In this story, a Mr W. is described walking across a crowded ballroom at 10.15 p.m. only to be found drowned the next morning with his watch stopped at exactly that time. Somehow this would appear to have become muddled with the facts of Sir George's drowning and an unfounded 'factual' ghost story was born.

The lesson for us is that this example is but the tip of the iceberg of cases in which so-called ghost 'experts' have passed stories from one to the other without ever bothering to check their true credentials. Despite the many hundreds of accounts of hauntings and haunted houses that litter the popular ghost encyclopaedias, few are backed by proper first-hand eyewitness reports. As a result, many of these cases cannot be treated with any seriousness.

By way of demonstration, here is yet another example of just how easily a totally bogus ghost can gain wide currency. Elton Holland, retired vice-president of the M. A. Lightman theatrical company in the southern USA, has described how he became the perpetrator of one such story which has now gone into American ghost lore associated with the 2,600-seater Orpheum Theater in Memphis, Tennessee, where Holland was manager during his early years.[12] Having hired an overenthusiastic young technician who showed an alarming disregard for his own safety when climbing around the theatre's balconies, Holland decided as a warning to the young man to invent the story of a little girl called Mary who had appeared in a stage show at the Orpheum during the Great Depression. Holland told his young technician how Mary's mother, watching from the balcony, had been so filled with pride at her daughter's performance that in her excitement she overbalanced and fell to her death. Every once in a while 'when the moon was right' young Mary would come back and look for her mother.

Holland could not have anticipated how, years after he left the theatre, his innocently told story would be picked up by TV stations and newspapers, complete with embellishments from the technician. There were even reported sightings of 'Mary', who was now the one described as killed instead of her mother. Holland remarked:

> Everyone who has written up Mary has talked himself into actu-
> ally seeing her. It's kind of hilarious . . . It comes up about every
> five years, and my wife and I have a big laugh about it.[13]

Such instances do not by any means exhaust the many other human frailties to which claims of ghost experiences can be subject. Another is the 'spooky' practical joke played on a suitably gullible victim – the possibility that my wife and I were concerned to eliminate at Abercrombie House. Students are of course the most likely perpetrators of such pranks, and one particular victim was a young American student whose identity we will in this instance conceal with a pseudonym, 'Kelvin', purely to save him unnecessary embarrassment. All other details are, however, the known facts.

In 1979 Kelvin, by this time a postgraduate student studying philosophy/theology at Southampton University, wrote to London's Society for Psychical Research describing at length, and in all seriousness, a purported ghostly experience that he had had two years previously while studying at Rollins College, Florida. During his graduation year at Rollins Kelvin had written a short book, prompting someone to suggest that he might publicly read selections from this in the college's Knowles Memorial Chapel, a magnificent Spanish Baroque-style edifice built in 1932.

Kelvin, a conscientious sort of chap, made it his habit to go along to the chapel late in the evening to rehearse his readings, initially accompanied by a music student friend who played the organ. On a couple of occasions he was puzzled by a strange droning sound that seemed to be coming from the organ long after his friend had left.

One evening he decided to try his hand on the piano next to the organ. First he seemed to hear a hubbub of unexplained noises all around him. Shortly after that the organ light suddenly went on without there being anyone in the seat. The next moment the organ, all by itself, played an 'otherwordly' chord, lasting for some five seconds. A few nights later, a very similar thing happened, notably soon after three of Kelvin's friends had absented themselves while he was using the chapel's toilet. Adding to Kelvin's conviction that the chapel was haunted, he learned that four years earlier, a girl student had been playing the organ late at night when she had been confronted by the apparition of an elderly man with centre-parted hair who resembled a portrait of one of the chapel's early ministers.

This was a case that I happened personally to investigate very briefly in 1984, simply by writing a letter to the Knowles Memorial Chapel's dean, A. Arnold Wettstein, asking if there was any genuine prior history of such ghostly disturbances at the chapel. Dean Wettstein's well-measured response[14] was that he remembered Kelvin 'very well', that Kelvin's experiences (which had been reported to him) were unique, and that 'if there were students interested in perpetuating a practical joke, they would find no more likely candidate to play it on than Kelvin'. Dean Wettstein also remembered the girl student who had experienced the apparition. She was particularly memorable because she 'occasionally called me at 2 a.m. to report a new revelation of the Holy Spirit'.

Many reported 'ghostly' happenings, sometimes experienced by several people at a time, can be found on careful investigation to derive from simple misinterpretation. Physicist Professor Arthur Ellison, a former president of London's Society for Psychical Research, has described how one morning the society's office was telephoned shortly after it opened with an urgent request:

It was the manager of a small cosmetics factory in Plaistow, east London, to say that his factory appeared to be haunted and, unless something could be done about it fairly quickly, his women workers would go on strike and refuse to enter the factory. They were very frightened indeed. So I went along to the factory and talked to the manager who told me of various incidents which had alarmed his women workers. As is the normal practice, I talked directly to those who had undergone the terrifying experiences. (Second-hand reports, whether hearsay or from newspapers, I have always found to be highly inaccurate.)

So the women who had had the most alarming experiences left their work of pouring mascara into little moulds or filling jars with powder. The stories they all gave to me independently agreed very well. (One might expect this as all the women talked together during their work.)

They said that some time earlier they had noticed various bangs and bumps occurring in the building, particularly on the water pipes. They also said that their radio set was not infrequently switched off then on again unaccountably. In addition they showed me their store of cartons and boxes and informed me that boxes were thrown about when there was no one in the room. They all referred to footsteps walking across the ceiling (the ceiling actually being the underside of the roof space). Several of them referred to a sandy-haired man in a white coat whom they observed to walk through the factory occasionally – but not all of them could see him. They asked me whether I thought that he had been murdered in the building. An alarming experience was described to me by one of the workers who said that she was standing in the cloakroom when her skirt was pulled to one side in an unaccountable manner.[15]

Although Professor Ellison was in no doubt about the women's genuine nervousness, he suspected that there might be a perfectly rational explanation for the phenomena. He carefully inspected the locations where ghostly activities had been reported and the following day delivered his findings to workers, who had been specially taken off the production line in order to hear him. In his words:

> There appeared to be a normal explanation for almost all the happenings of a physical nature. The bangs on the water pipe were probably due to what is called water hammer. The system had been installed many years ago and was probably not well plumbed. There may well have been pockets of air and, in changing direction, the water would hit the pipes and sound exactly like someone striking them from outside. Water hammer is by no means uncommon.
>
> As to the radio being unaccountably switched off and on again the building had not been rewired probably for some thirty years and one could well imagine that intermittent contacts would be quite frequent. The boxes which were apparently thrown about when no one was in the store, on inspection turned out to be by no means stably stacked. There was no mystery there. They were highly likely to fall off the pile and roll about the floor.
>
> And what about the footsteps on the ceiling? The building was old and had wooden roof members. When the temperature changed, especially as it fell during the late afternoon, those long wooden roof members would gradually shrink and, being held by friction and then moving again, would sound exactly like footsteps. This again is by no means uncommon in some buildings. Finally, regarding the skirt being pulled out: I inspected the place where it was reported to have happened and observed a considerable draught coming through a slightly open window. There appeared to be little mystery about the movement of a skirt.[16]

Other Society for Psychical Research investigators have found that hitherto undetected overhead aircraft activity can also be responsible for reported ghostly phenomena. Called to an old house apparently plagued by china falling off the shelves of a mysteriously vibrating cabinet, investigator John Cutten, who shares Ellison's practical skills, found 'that the shaking coincided with a jet plane in the neighbourhood which caused the walls of the house to shake, which in turn made the cabinet vibrate'.[17]

Turning back to the Plaistow cosmetics factory case, despite all Professor Ellison's careful explanations for the various physical phenomena, how could he solve the factory women's most mysterious puzzle, the sightings by some of them of the sandy-haired character in a white coat? In the event, even this presented no difficulty for Ellison:

> It is well known that if someone is in a state of fear and expectancy and concentrating on the possibility of something happening at any moment . . . then they are likely to perceive hallucinations. This is by no means uncommon. The workers in that factory simply did not recognise the underlying reasons for any of the phenomena which they had observed. These phenomena appeared to have led to the full-scale hallucinatory experiences of the more nervous and suggestible of the women.[18]

This state of unconscious hallucination, also known as 'psychological projection', is by no means as rare as might be supposed. Indeed, Canon Dominic Walker, one of those responsible for dealing with ghostly disturbances reported to the Church of England, has insisted that the 'vast majority' of reported ghosts may be explained as 'images . . . from the unconscious mind which are projected by a person under stress or in a state of denial'.[19] Certainly this is an important phenomenon which we will be considering again later in this book.

Before moving on from the different possible explanations for ghost experiences – and we have by no means exhausted the list – we should consider one final scenario: outright fraud. The known examples are comparatively rare, but undoubtedly they exist, one such instance having been conclusively revealed by ghost expert Peter Underwood, until recently President of Britain's Ghost Club. In his autobiography *No Common Task*, published in 1983, Underwood described arriving at a large house in Sussex where the owner, a man living on his own, had reported hearing 'ghostly' music on the ground floor. The music could occur at any time of the day, its composition had not been identified, there was no known background history that might account for the phenomenon, and previous psychical researchers who had visited the house had left baffled.

Indeed, even as he and his host sat opposite each other in a ground-floor reception room, Underwood thought he could hear music coming from another room. He was invited to inspect the room for himself, and as he did so, the music stopped, a pattern which was repeated several times during the ensuing three hours. The music was heard in different rooms over this time, but Underwood noticed that his host always chose to return to the same armchair, seeming to clutch at its padded armrest just before each fresh occurrence.

His suspicions aroused, Underwood snatched a moment when his host was taking the coffee cups back to the kitchen to go and examine the armchair, whereupon he

> discovered a series of small buttons hidden beneath the upholstery at the end of the armrest. I pressed one and heard music! I heard my host hurriedly returning and resumed my seat on the other side of the room. He looked daggers at me . . . He knew the game was up, and admitted that he was something of a gadget maniac and had fixed speakers and recorded muted mixed music under the floorboards. He said he had had a lot of fun with people over about six years, and he insisted that he had never said the music was 'ghostly' in origin: all his visitors had jumped to that conclusion.[20]

Claims of hauntings have certainly been used on several occasions by council house dwellers to try to get themselves rehoused somewhere more congenial. Diocese of Southwark 'exorcist', the late Canon John Pearce-Higgins, stated: 'I have had six cases of "faked ghosts" where the people wanted to be re-housed.'[21] And recently Canon Michael Perry, another of those who deals with ghostly occurrences reported to the Church of England, quoted the following council house example (in this instance anonymous, for obvious reasons) which his Christian Deliverance Study Group investigated at a local authority's invitation:

> Terrifying apparitions were reported [at the council house], as were noises, cold spots, bloodstains which appeared and vanished, threatening voices, and the usual knocks and movements of objects. There seemed to be no reason for all this paranormal activity, and questioning of individuals soon produced wide discrepancies in the stories told. There was a noticeable absence of real dread which

would be expected of a family suffering such psychic persecution, and a mechanical repetition of the stories broke down at the unexpected question. Reference to council records showed that the family had been trying for some time to obtain a transfer to another estate. In view of the fact that the activity was of the sort described in popular fiction and not of the sort normally presented . . . it was finally decided that the 'haunt' was a manufactured one and the council was so advised. At a later date the family was transferred. Subsequent tenants reported no phenomena.[22]

This, then, is an all too perfunctory survey of just some of the possible human frailties that need to be taken into account when investigating reported ghost stories. But what of the ghosts said to show up in photographs and on technical equipment, in which circumstances human frailty might seem to have rather less scope?

CHAPTER TWO

On Not Trusting Ghost Photographs and the Like

For some people the perfect evidence for the existence of ghosts would be a really convincing ghost photograph. It evokes all the old clichés: 'You can't argue with a photograph', 'The camera doesn't lie', 'A picture is worth a thousand words', etc., etc.

Certainly the lure of getting a really good ghost photograph is one that has tantalised Peter Underwood throughout some fifty years of investigation work. On the numerous occasions when he or fellow Ghost Club[1] members have stayed overnight at haunted houses, they have invariably taken with them a variety of cameras, including still, infra-red and video, always hoping that one day they might return with photographs that would really prove the existence of ghosts.

But the blunt fact is that, despite hundreds of such photographic stake-outs, Underwood and his fellow ghost-hunters have never had a single convincing face-to-face encounter with a ghost, let alone got so far as raising their cameras in the hope of recording such an experience on film. I have also yet to hear of even one of the other ghost research organisations around the world which has managed to do any better.

This is not to say, however, that ghost-hunters and psychical researchers do not have a variety of so-called 'ghost' photographs on their files – for what they are worth. Almost invariably these are photographs which were taken casually by ordinary members of the public, and on which a mysterious figure only became visible when the film was developed. Usually neither the photographer nor any others present at the time ever saw this 'ghost' with their own eyes. Nor did they have any other inkling of what might subsequently manifest on their film.

A particularly well-publicised example of this – extolled by Peter Underwood as 'the most remarkable and interesting . . . that I have seen in half a century of serious psychical investigation'[2] – was a photograph [pl. 4] taken by retired Canadian clergyman the Revd R. W. Hardy of White Rock, British Columbia, when on a visit to England with his wife in 1966. As part of an intensive sightseeing itinerary the Hardys visited the seventeenth-century Queen's House at Greenwich, London, part of the National Maritime Museum, where Mrs Hardy was particularly interested to see and photograph the famous Tulip Staircase, the first cantilevered staircase in England. She had a rather spectacular picture in a book back home, and hoped that they could return to Canada with their own similar photograph.

It was actually the Revd Hardy who took the photograph, using an ordinary daylight film and when the couple returned to Canada they had their films developed and made up as slides. Only when they were showing these to a gathering of friends did all present notice unmistakable ghostly figures on the Tulip Staircase. A hooded figure, head bent low, seemed to be clutching with his left hand at the stair-rail at the bottom right of the picture while another figure further up the staircase also had its left hand on the stair-rail. Yet the Hardys were adamant that no one had been on the staircase at the time the photograph was taken.

Alerted by a Ghost Club member who happened to know the Hardys, Peter Underwood became so fascinated by the photo that he and fellow Ghost Club members held a special vigil at the Queen's House on the night of 25 June 1967, complete with a séance in the Great Hall, in the hope that the ghostly figures might be persuaded to appear again. They were to be disappointed in this. Underwood, however, has repeatedly reproduced and discussed the photograph in his books,[3] enthusiastically quoting the exact make of camera the Revd Hardy used, and stating that there could have been no double exposure, and that Kodak and other photographic experts have been 'totally unable to explain the shrouded figures'.

Interpreting the figures as medieval monks, Underwood has pointed out the relevance of information from a historical researcher friend, Dorothy E. Warren, that there was ecclesiastical property on the Queen's House site prior to the Reformation:

> There seems to have been a large medieval house at Greenwich . . . which had an upstairs room grand enough for visiting prelates in the thirteenth century and Miss Warren suggests that this part of the great house may have stood on the site of the later Queen's House . . . The figures do seem to be mounting a staircase extra-neous to the present one; a staircase that may have formerly been the stairway to the abbot's guest room.[4]

Yet although Peter Underwood claims to have given the Revd Hardy's photograph the most careful scrutiny, it is obvious that the figures are clutching a staircase rail known not to have been built until a century after Henry VIII's Dissolution of the Monasteries had put the last monks out of business. Other crucial clues lie in the photograph itself.

Back in 1967 the National Maritime Museum's photographer Brian Tremain made a professional-quality black-and-white print from the Revd Hardy's slide. This is preserved in the museum's archives, together with photographs of the Hardys on a return visit to the Queen's House in May 1967, and letters from the Revd Hardy explaining how he took the photograph. Thanks to the kindness of the museum's deputy director and archivist Geraldine Charles, I was able to examine all this material during a special visit in March 1995.

What immediately became evident as the most important factor in the case is the exposure time that the Revd Hardy chose when photographing the staircase. He did not use flash, and in the low lighting conditions of the house interior, and on the low-speed 64 ASA film that he is known to have used, the camera's shutter necessarily had to be kept open longer in order for the film to capture sufficient light.

Such a long exposure time gives rise to two problems. First, unless the camera is mounted on a tripod, or in some other way held very steady, the slightest movement will create a blur to the eventual photograph. Second, if someone moves across the camera's field of view while the shutter is open, he or she is likely to appear ghost-like two or three times, as if in a slow-motion replay of their movements.

The Revd Hardy was clearly aware of the first problem, and in a letter of 8 May 1967 he told Brian Tremain:

> As tripod or flash could not be used we took a light meter reading, held the camera firmly by hand on a ledge or projection, used probably f8 opening, and guessed at the [exposure] time.

When Hardy revisited the Queen's House he demonstrated how he had held the camera against the edge of a doorway, and the steadiness which he managed to attain is attested by the sharpness of the architectural features in the photograph. Rather less sharp, however, was his memory of the length of the exposure. Although he told Peter Underwood he thought it had been the very considerable time of 'four to six seconds',[5] independent questioning by Tremain produced the more credible estimate of 'no longer than one second'.

The crucial point, however, is the figures in the photograph. Are these really medieval monks? Or are they someone of the present day whose movements were recorded two or three times as he or she ascended the Tulip Staircase during that second or so that the Revd Hardy had his shutter open? One telling feature is the two left hands, each with a ring on their third finger, that are visible at two different levels on the stair-rail. The hands and the rings look rather too alike not to belong to the same person. Furthermore, in medieval times the wearing of rings on the third finger of the left hand was not only unheard of among clergy, it was even unknown among the laity, both bishops and married women wearing their rings on their right hands. It is much more likely that we are looking at someone of a later century.

But what of the medieval-looking shrouded figure in the bottom right of the photograph? In fact, as Geraldine Charles pointed out to me, careful study of Brian Tremain's duplicate of the Hardy picture shows that what seems to be this figure's hooded head is in reality the repeating *shoulder* of someone in the process of ascending the stairs. Furthermore, towards the top of the staircase can just be discerned the actual person making the ascent. The shape of a very twentieth-century-looking head and neck is visible just behind the hand-rail [see reconstruction, pl. 5] – yet is so faint that in secondary copies as reproduced in Peter Underwood's books it has become invisible.

It was Tremain who first suspected that at the time that Hardy took the photograph someone wearing a white coat had simply slipped up the stairs without Hardy even noticing. As long ago as 1967 Tremain tried to replicate the Hardys' photograph by using a long exposure and a staff member in a white lab coat ascending the stairs, producing a result [pl. 6] strikingly similar to the original.[6]

This opinion is not, however, shared by Peter Underwood, who has dismissed Tremain's replication as 'futile'. The Revd Hardy and his wife were similarly less than convinced. They insisted that no one could have slipped past them in the time the shutter was open.

A barrier 'no admittance' was at the base of the stairs and would have had to be removed or climbed over if anyone had attempted the ascent – something which could not possibly have occurred without our notice. Mrs Hardy was specifically watching that no one might intrude into the picture while I operated the manually held camera.[7]

In fairness, there is comparatively little room in the doorway where the Revd Hardy stood to take his photograph, and one certainly might have expected him or his wife to have noticed some intrusion.

However, as was pointed out to me by Brian Tremain, once we discount the illusory 'hooded' head, white coats of precisely the kind that seem to be indicated in the Revd Hardy's photograph were worn by the National Maritime Museum's photographic staff. Furthermore, the figure could well have been one staff member, Ian Larner, who wore a wedding ring. And although neither in 1966 nor today are 'no admittance' barriers normally erected on the Tulip Staircase, even if such barriers were to be put up, staff would automatically slip by them on the understanding that they were intended only for the public.

It also needs to be observed that the photographs that were taken of the Revd and Mrs Hardy on their return visit in 1967 reveal them as a distinctly elderly couple who might well have failed to remember someone briefly slipping by them on the Tulip Staircase, even if they had noticed him at the time. Accordingly, rather than being 'futile', Brian Tremain's reconstruction of the Hardy photograph deserves rather greater recognition as a striking replication of what may well have actually happened.

If this, then, considerably undermines what Peter Underwood has described as the 'most remarkable' ghost photograph that he has come across, what of the rest? Ghost photography goes back a long way, but again beware the Underwood version of its history – as for instance in the following extract from his *Ghosts and How to See Them*, published as recently as 1993:

> Attempts have been made to photograph ghosts since the earliest days of photography. William Mummler, an engraver, was not even interested in ghosts or 'spirit' photographs, but when processing some of his photographs he found faces that should not have been there. Having photographed members of his family he discovered on his plates (so runs the story) the pictures not only of his living family, but also of long-dead relatives. He then carried out what may well have been the first controlled experiment in ghost photography, in 1862. News of his involuntary photography of the dead spread like wildfire through the photographic fraternity worldwide and he made history when his prints were upheld as genuine by the US Court of Appeal Judge, John Edmund, in 1863.[8]

We would be hard put to detect either here or later in the book the slightest hint that Mummler might have been a charlatan. Peter Underwood is not alone in this. His United States counterpart Hans Holzer has adopted a similarly uncritical attitude towards Mummler in his book *Great American Ghost Stories*.[9]

Note now, therefore, the following genuinely authoritative pronouncement on Mummler from Michael Hargraves of Los Angeles' J. Paul Getty Museum Department of Photographs:

> The 'spirit' photograph was created in 1861 by William H. Mummler (1832–1884) of Boston. While attempting to take a self-portrait, Mummler accidentally superimposed his image on top of a previous exposure on the plate inside the camera. He became intrigued with the possibilities of commercial exploitation of his 'discovery' and advertised that he could cause departed loved ones, or some form of spirit, to appear in his clients' photographs. Although he would make the second image somewhat blurry, sitters

often would swear that it was a particular family member or friend. He carried on this chicanery for some time, as did other photographers, convincing the grief-stricken with relative ease that the deceased could 'come back' . . . Mummler was eventually revealed as a fraud when it was found that his 'spirits' were merely double exposures of living people . . . This practice of deception actually continued well into the 1930s.[10]

Included in the J. Paul Getty Museum's collection in Los Angeles is an excellent example of a Mummler-type photograph (the actual photographer is unknown) from the 1880s [see pl. 7]. From this, unconvincing as it is by today's standards, it is easy enough to reconstruct how Mummler and other early 'ghost' photographers worked.

First the photographer would set up in his studio a photograph of his chosen 'spirit', possibly just an old portrait from his collection, blacking out around it so that just the face was visible, and arranging his composition so that the face would appear small, and only in the topmost part of the overall frame. He would then rephotograph it in a deliberately blurry or soft-focus style, knowing that this would create a suitably ghostly effect, and that the more elusive the face the more easily the gullible client would be able to read into it the features of the departed loved one. The partially exposed plate would be left undeveloped to await the client for whom the photographer considered that particular image most suitable.

On the arrival of this client the photographer would then use the same plate for the taking of a perfectly normal studio portrait, with the sole exception that he would deliberately allow a large amount of empty background in the upper part of his composition so that the sitter should not obscure the ghost. When the plate was developed, both the living client and the ghost would be magically seen in the same picture – with the greatest photographic expert in the world genuinely unable to find any sign of retouching. When the sitter was well known, it was even sometimes possible for the photographer to match in a real photograph of the deceased, as in the case of President Lincoln's widow, who was photographed by Mummler with her dead husband's shadowy ghost standing behind her lovingly touching her shoulders.

Peter Underwood displays similar poor critical standards with regard to other ghost photographs too. In his book *The Ghost Hunters*, published in 1985, Underwood reproduces a photograph of a ghostly monk [pl. 8], which, according to his version of events, was taken by an unnamed war correspondent who, with the early ghost enthusiast Elliott O'Donnell, reportedly stayed up 'ghost-watching' overnight at an allegedly haunted manor house, Brockley Court, near Bristol.[11] Unfortunately, as Underwood could and should have checked for himself, the true facts are altogether different.

These are that in 1909 a Bristol University dental student, Arthur Spencer Palmer, borrowed a white sheet from his professor's wife and with his younger brother Charles cycled out to Brockley Court, at that time deserted and already with a reputation for being haunted. Using a variation on Mummler's double exposure technique, Arthur first photographed one of the house's beautifully panelled rooms, then without moving the camera or advancing the film dressed himself in the sheet, stood in front of the lens, and got Charles to open the shutter a second time so that he would appear semi-transparent against the panelling.

The result turned out even better than Arthur had dared hope, and when he circulated the photograph and listened to all the interest it attracted he had not the heart to confess his deception. His escapade soon became all but forgotten amidst the real-life horrors of the First World War, during which Charles was killed in action, while Arthur, now fully qualified in dentistry, moved out to Nairobi, Kenya, to set up a dental practice there.

But among those interested in ghosts and psychical research the photograph had by no means been forgotten, and certainly not by the great Sir Arthur Conan Doyle, who in his waning years had become obsessed by Spiritualism. Conan Doyle made up a lantern slide copy of the photograph and began using this as proof of ghosts in lectures around the world – lectures which in 1929 took him to Nairobi. There, before a packed and attentive audience in the city's main theatre, he began his presentation, with all proceeding smoothly up to the moment when he showed the slide of the Brockley Court ghost. Then suddenly up stood local dentist Arthur Spencer Palmer, loudly exclaiming, 'I am that ghost!' Invited on to the stage, Spencer Palmer matter-of-factly explained exactly how he had carried out his student prank.[12] The story raised headlines even in England, with Conan Doyle's reputation never quite the same again. And yet, fifty-six years after the true facts were revealed, a totally erroneous account of the photograph's creation was being peddled by Peter Underwood.

Few if any of the other ghost photographs repeatedly featured in books have anything more convincing to offer. One such is a photograph of the altar and east window of the church of St Mary the Virgin in Woodford, near Thrapston, Northamptonshire [pl. 9]. It was taken one afternoon in July 1964 by sixteen-year-old shoe factory clerk Gordon Carroll as part of his hobby of cycling round the countryside photographing old churches and castles. Carroll's camera was no more than a simple Ilford Sportsman loaded with the low-speed colour film that was all that was available to non-professionals in 1964. To compensate for the church's low lighting, he set the camera on a tripod and the shutter on a long exposure time, leaving it for what he considered an appropriate period before proceeding to his next shot, showing the church interior from the opposite direction.

Carroll saw no ghost while he was in the church, and indeed had so little inkling that his photograph might have anything special to it that although he had the film developed, he did not even look properly at the results until some eighteen months later, at Christmas 1965. On doing so, he noted with astonishment what seemed to be a figure kneeling at the altar. He felt sure the church had been empty at the time, something he always tried to ensure whenever taking his photos.

To anyone studying Carroll's reasonably good-quality colour photograph, there does indeed seem to be a ghostly-looking figure kneeling at the altar, though to label it a 'monk', as Underwood does,[13] is stretching things rather too far. Fakery on Carroll's part can almost certainly be ruled out – it would be a rare hoaxer who waited eighteen months to find a ghost on one of his negatives. Double exposure is also unlikely – not only does the 1960s Ilford Sportsman have a device specifically to prevent this, but to create a convincing-looking ghost in colour would have demanded far more cunning and advance preparation than Caroll would seem to have had.

Instead, as in the case of the Tulip Staircase, the crucial clue seems to lie in the long exposure time, and the very real likelihood that during the unspecified number of seconds that Carroll's shutter was open some cleaning lady, the vicar, or any other person simply slipped into the church via a side door, dropped to their knees before the altar, and then disappeared again without Carroll even noticing. Dr Stephen Gull and Timothy Newton, who in 1984 examined several purported ghost photographs for *Arthur C. Clarke's Chronicles of the Strange and Mysterious*, concluded that Carroll's contained a whole series of fleeting images of a cleaning lady moving through the church. It would seem that for anyone wanting a ghost photograph that they could place their trust in, Carroll's is yet another non-starter.

Anyone looking for any more inspiring ghost photographs elsewhere is destined to be disappointed. Deserving of mention is the American tanker SS *Watertown* photograph, one of the few examples in which someone is reported to have seen a ghost, photographed it, and obtained a result. As the story runs, two seamen on the tanker were overcome by fumes while cleaning out the ship's tanks, died, and were buried at sea. While the voyage was still in progress, members of the crew began reporting sightings of the two men's ghosts in the form of disembodied heads, sometimes seen by the side of the ship where the bodies had been cast overboard; sometimes alongside the ship in the water itself.

Although there was no camera on board to record these sightings during the fateful voyage, the shipping company provided one for the return journey, whereupon on the sixth of six exposures there appeared the two men's faces recognisable to those who had known them in life. The case was investigated by the eminent and genuinely critical American psychical researcher Dr Hereward Carrington (1880–1958), who is said to have found it quite impressive. As proof of the existence of ghosts, however, the photograph is yet another non-starter, the original having long disappeared.

Similarly worth at least a mention is a photograph claimed to be of the well-known 'Brown Lady' ghost of Raynham Hall, Norfolk [pl. 10], purportedly captured by former Court photographer Captain Provand and his assistant Indre Shira while working on an assignment for *Country Life* magazine in 1936. On the face of it, this particular photograph might seem well attested, the salient details of the day and time it was taken, the location, and the names of those present at the time all being recorded. It is also an all too rare instance of the ghost seemingly having actually been seen at the crucial moment before the film was exposed.

According to Indre Shira's account as subsequently published in

Country Life, he and Provand arrived at Raynham Hall on 19 September. After spending the early part of the day photographing a variety of exterior and interior locations, at about four o'clock in the afternoon they arrived at the foot of the hall's main oak staircase, where they once again set up their equipment.

> Captain Provand took one photograph of it [the staircase] while I flashed the light. He was focusing again for another exposure; I was standing by his side just behind the camera with the flashlight pistol in my hand, looking directly up the stairase. All at once I detected an ethereal, veiled form coming slowly down the stairs. Rather excitedly I called out sharply: 'Quick! Quick! There's something! Are you ready?' 'Yes,' the photographer replied, and removed the cap from the lens. I pressed the trigger of the flashlight pistol. After the flash, and on closing the shutter, Captain Provand removed the focusing cloth from his head and, turning to me, said: 'What's all the excitement about?'
>
> I directed his attention to the staircase and explained that I had distinctly seen a figure there – transparent so that the steps were visible through the ethereal form, but nevertheless very definite and to me perfectly real. He laughed and said I must have imagined I had seen a ghost – for there was nothing now to be seen.
>
> After securing several other pictures we decided to pack up and return to town. Nearly all the way we were arguing about the possibility of obtaining a genuine ghost photograph. Captain Provand laid down the law most emphatically by assuring me that as a Court photographer of thirty years' standing it was quite impossible . . .
>
> When the negatives of Raynham Hall were developed, I stood beside Captain Provand in the dark-room. One after the other they were placed in the developer. Suddenly Captain Provand exclaimed: 'Good Lord! There's something on the staircase negative, after all!' I took one glance, called to him, 'Hold it!' and dashed downstairs to the chemist Mr Benjamin Jones, manager of Blake, Sandford and Blake, whose premises are immediately underneath our studio. I invited Mr Jones to come upstairs to our dark-room. He came, and saw the negative just as it had been taken from the

developer and placed in the adjoining hypo bath . . . Mr Jones, Captain Provand and I vouch for the fact that the negative has not been retouched in any way. It has been examined critically by a number of experts. No one can account for the ghostly figure but it is there clear enough.[14]

Certainly some sort of ghostly shape does seem to be visible on the staircase. And as in the case of the Mummler photographs, we may well be able to accept that the negative has not been retouched in any way. But let us ask ourselves what we are actually seeing as the ghost. If we are frank, it is merely a foggy swirl, the sort of effect that anyone could have created in just a couple of seconds using a dab of grease on a glass filter. If this was introduced surreptitiously, Captain Provand need never even have noticed.

One unavoidably suspicious element to Shira's account is his repeated emphasis on the 'ethereal' and 'transparent' character of what he alone claimed to be seeing – descriptions in marked contrast to the great majority of sightings of ghosts to be discussed later in this book. In these, the word 'ethereal' is rarely if ever used and the ghosts predominantly seem surprisingly solid and normal-looking to their observers, their apparitional quality only becoming evident when they disappear.

Indeed, it is this disparity between the consistently transparent ghosts to be seen in the general run of ghost photographs, and the more substantial ghosts perceived with the eye that, in combination with all the other evidence discussed, sets the largest question mark over the genuine nature of any ghost photograph. We may have to face the possibility that if ghosts truly exist, they may do so at some spectrum which does not normally register on photographic film. No one, for instance, expects to be able to photograph television waves – these need a television receiver, just as a ghost may need a human one.

This notion would certainly have met with some approval from the distinguished mathematician, physicist and former president of the Society for Psychical Research, G. N. M. Tyrrell (1879–1952), who, in a list of nineteen characteristics for what he would adjudge the 'perfect' ghost, listed at number 17 that if a ghost and a living person were photographed beside each other, while both equally visible to some human witness, only the living person would come out in the photo.[15] Tyrrell took the argument further and made the same prediction with regard to sound-recording apparatus: that if the sounds of a living person and the sounds of a ghost were recorded in parallel, again only the sounds of the real person would come out.

However, there exists just a smidgen of evidence that this latter theory might not be totally true. Alongside the cameras and all the other equipment – thermometers, trip-wires, walkie-talkie sets, frequency change detectors, instruments for measuring atmospheric pressure, vibration, wind force and humidity, to name but a few – that Peter Underwood and his fellow ghost-hunters routinely have with them on their stake-outs, they have almost invariably taken tape-recorders as well. And although in the vast majority of cases nothing of any significance has been recorded on these, there is one exception in the form of the sound-track of a night spent at Newark Park in the Cotswolds. As transcribed by Ghost Club member Michael Brett:

Result of 1st blackout session: 2.15 to 2.35 a.m.
(The numbers indicate the position in feet of the recorded sounds on the tape.)

- 2' Dragging/rustling sound.
- 8' Heavy shuffling noise.
- 10' First loud rustling sound heard by Brett, Kiernander, Underwood and Harrison [all members of the Ghost Club].
- 12' Rustling sound.
- 17' Rustling sound.
- 18' Rustling sound and also sound of knocking on stone.
- 20' Heavy metallic sound – almost as though something had been dropped.
- 24' Footsteps on wooden flooring, or someone or something coming down the stairs from the upper part of the house; also rustling and knocking sounds.
- 27' Rustling sound.
- 28' A click, footsteps, and a rustling sound, followed by two distinct and heavy footsteps and very loud rustling and dragging noises, the latter heard by Brett, Kiernander, Underwood and Harrison.

30'   A click followed by two footsteps.
31'   Rustling sound.
34'   Rustling sound followed by what sounds like a sigh.
35'   Rustling sound.

      Result of 2nd blackout sesssion: 4.00 to 4.30 a.m.
 3'   Click.
 5'   Bang.
11'   Rustling and clicking noises.
13'   Voice recorded but unable to distinguish what it said.
15'   Voice recorded . . . : 'Yes, it's looking. Yes.'
21'   Click.
28'   The word 'Yes' recorded, followed by a click.
30'   Very loud metallic sound, followed by a click.
32'   Rustling sound, followed by a click.
33'   Sound of something being dragged, also sound of something heavy being moved.
34'   Clicking sounds.
37'   Very heavy breathing sounds, quite close to the microphone.

Although during the 'active' periods on an Underwood stakeout absolute silence and immobility are asked of everyone, actually obtaining this from a large number of people posted in various positions of discomfort in darkness amidst a clutter of technical equipment is easier said than done, and as the Ghost Club would acknowledge, some of the rustling and other movement sounds noted would have had normal human explanations. The real curiosity is that no one sitting out that night at Newark Park appears to have heard or claimed responsibility for the voice saying, 'Yes, it's looking': they simply somewhat inexplicably found it on the sound-track afterwards. And as a bizarre postscript, it is now said to have disappeared from the tape![16] That aside, however, if this is the best that today's ghost-hunters can offer in the way of auditory evidence for ghosts, why bother to take a tape-recorder to another stakeout?

Sweeping though it may sound, the only sensible conclusion to be drawn from the photographic and auditory evidence so far collected by the ghost-hunters is that if ghosts exist, trying to capture them with any form of technological wizardry is an exercise in futility. Whatever true material might conceivably lie behind the photographic and sound evidence so far put forward in support of the existence of ghosts, as it stands it is pretty useless. Arguably, it is even worse than useless because for too long it has distracted undeniably intelligent researchers from those paths which, had they not been trying to develop more and more ingenious technological gadgetry, might have turned out to be more rewarding.

So, if we can trust neither ghost photographs nor some of the human testimony that we saw in the last chapter, just what paths might be rewarding, and who and what can we begin to trust?

CHAPTER THREE

When a Ghost May Not Be a Ghost

Part I: When It's a Poltergeist . . .

Having already dismissed so much that has been extolled by others as among the best evidence for ghosts, it may now seem doubly perverse to begin the quest for arguably true ghosts with phenomena that are not true ghosts. But a necessary preliminary for any proper perspective on the subject is a better understanding of arguably genuine phenomena often popularly interpreted as due to a ghost, but which careful analysis reveals as probably having more to do with the living. As with so much from the world of the paranormal, the phenomena carry a fancy-sounding label, in this instance reasonably well known: 'poltergeists'.

Any of the Christian clergy working for the Church of England's exorcism service – currently entitled the Christian Deliverance Study Group – will attest that activities that they would classify as 'poltergeist' account for by far the greatest number of cases of so-called ghosts that they are called upon to deal with. In the words of Canon Michael Perry, editor of *Deliverance*, the official book on the service's work:

> In the experience of the Christian Deliverance Study Group, it [apparent poltergeist activity] is the single most frequent cause of appeals to members of the Group for help. The client [i.e. the person reporting the problem] will almost invariably say that there is a ghost in the house which is causing trouble, and would the priest please come in and exorcise it?[1]

* * *

So what is 'poltergeist activity'? And why should we regard reports of it as any more convincing than some of the dubious ghosts and ghost photographs that we have come across?

The term 'poltergeist' derives from the German *poltern*, to make a loud noise, and *Geist*, ghost, i.e. 'noisy ghost', but any loose usage of it in this way tends to lead to misconceptions. The word automatically conjures up a mischievous, invisible little hobgoblin who throws objects around – and certainly the many appeals by 'poltergeist' sufferers for some form of exorcism are a reflection of this misconception. In reality we are dealing with something that might seem to behave in the manner of a hobgoblin, yet is infinitely more complex: long recorded, with a string of repeatedly recurring characteristics; still far from understood, and certainly needing to be handled with considerable sensitivity.

Reports of poltergeist-type phenomena are said to go back to Roman times and certainly a long way before anyone dreamed up the present name for them. In the twelfth century the medieval chronicler Gerald of Wales wrote in his *Itinerary*:

> In this part of Penbroch unclean spirits have conversed not visibly but sensibly with mankind, first in the house of Stephen Wiriet, and afterwards in the house of William Nott, manifesting their presence by throwing dirt at them, and more with a view of mockery than injury.[2]

In January 1772, in the then village of Stockwell to the south of London, a wealthy elderly lady suffered the most astonishing disturbances to her crockery and other household utensils shortly after taking on a twenty-year-old maid named Ann Robinson. At 10 a.m. on Monday 6 January Mrs Golding was sitting quietly in her parlour when, in the words of a contemporary pamphlet:

> She heard the china and glass in the back kitchen tumble down and break; her maid came to her and told her the stone plates were falling from the shelf; Mrs Golding went into the kitchen and saw them broke. Presently after, a row of plates from the next shelf fell down likewise, while she was there, and nobody near them; this astonished her much, and while she was thinking about it, other

things in different places began to tumble about, some of them breaking, attended with violent noises all over the house; a clock tumbled down and the case broke; a lantern that hung on the staircase was thrown down and the glass broke to pieces; an earthen pan of salted beef broke to pieces and the beef fell about.

Supposing that the house had somehow become taken over by an invisible and clearly destructive ghost, Mrs Golding escaped with Ann Robinson and her more movable possessions to the house of a neighbour, only to find that the disturbances followed her there. Even when she fled once more, still accompanied by Ann Robinson, to her niece Mary Pain, who lived near Brixton, the disturbances persisted:

. . . the first thing that happened was, a whole row of pewter dishes, except one, fell from a shelf to the middle of the floor, rolled about for a little while, and then settled, and what is almost beyond belief, as soon as they were quiet, turned upside down; they were then out on the dresser, and went through the same a second time, next fell a whole row of pewter plates from off the second shelf over the dresser to the ground, and being taken up and put on the dresser one in another, they were thrown down again. The next thing was two eggs that were upon one of the pewter shelves, one of them flew off, crossed the kitchen, struck a cat on the head, and then broke in pieces . . .

It was only after the phenomena followed her to a third house that Mrs Golding began to suspect, even though she had already observed that objects could and did move without her new maid being in the immediate vicinity, that Ann Robinson must have something to do with them, particularly as the disturbances had only occurred since Ann had joined her household. And sure enough, once she had sacked the maid, the ghostly phenomena promptly ceased.

Even though the Ann Robinson case occurred more than two hundred years ago, it provides a textbook precedent for other, more recent, astonishing cases. Take, for instance the phenomena that beset the Herrmann family of Seaford, Long Island, USA, in 1958. The Herrmanns were a well-to-do and well-educated family comprising airline executive

Mr James Herrmann (a Fordham University graduate who had served with the US Marine Corps during World War II); his thirty-eight-year-old wife (a trained nurse who had worked as a hospital supervisor up to the time of their marriage); their thirteen-year-old daughter Lucille and twelve-year-old son James Jr.

The first manifestation of their problems came on 6 and 7 February with the mysterious opening and spilling of bottles while Lucille and James Jr. were on their own in the house. Then, at 10.15 a.m. on Sunday 9 February, when the whole family was in the dining room, suddenly popping noises were heard from different parts of the house. Upon investigation a bottle of holy water (they were a devout Catholic family) and a new bottle of toilet water were found opened and spilling their contents in the master bedroom. In the bathroom a bottle of shampoo and a medicine bottle had lost their caps, fallen over, and were spilling. The same was happening to a bottle of starch in the kitchen and a can of paint thinner in the cellar. Quite unable to account for what was happening to them, the Herrmanns called in the police, as a result of which much of what followed usefully became logged in the records of the Nassau County Police Department.

Little more than minutes after the earlier incident, Mr Herrmann saw with his own eyes the now righted bottles of shampoo and medicine in the bathroom begin to move of their own accord – in opposite directions. As entered in the police record:

> Mr Herrmann standing in bathroom doorway, son James at sink brushing teeth, actually saw a bottle of Kaopectate [the medicine] move along the Formica top of the drain in a southerly direction for about 18 inches and fall into the sink. At the same time a bottle of shampoo moved along the Formica drain in a westerly direction and fell to the floor. There was no noise of vibration and no one touched either bottle to move them.[3]

A few weeks later, when the American parapsychologists William G. Roll and J. Gaither Pratt arrived at Seaford to try to help resolve the difficulty, Mr Herrmann gave them the following first-person statement regarding this same incident:

* * *

46

At about 10.30 a.m. I was standing in the doorway of the bathroom. All of a sudden two bottles which had been placed on the top of the vanity table were seen to move straight ahead, slowly, while the second spun to the right for a 45° angle. The first one fell into the sink. The second one crashed to the floor. Both bottles moved at the same time . . .[4]

Patrolman Hughes, the Nassau County policeman first called to the Herrmann's house, was still taking the first statement when he himself was party to an incident enabling him to testify that it could not have been possible for any member of the family to have been responsible for the disturbances by any normal means.

While Patrolman J. Hughes was at the complainant's home *all the family was present with him* in the living room when noises were heard in the bathroom. When Patrolman Hughes went into the bathroom with the complainant's family he found the medicine and shampoo had again spilled.[5]

Another outsider, James Herrmann's cousin Miss Marie Murtha, was likewise able to testify that there had been no visible human interference during an incident which occurred when she was with the children in the living room on Saturday 15 February at 7.40 p.m. Her statement, given to the police two days later, claimed

that she was sitting in the living room of the complainant's home and the two children were with her. The boy was sitting in the centre of the sofa and the girl was standing next to Miss Murtha, who was sitting in a chair in the north-east corner of the living room. Mrs Herrmann went into the bathroom and when she turned on the light in here it caused interference on the television set. The girl started across the room to fix the set and before she got there the picture cleared by itself. The girl came back to where Miss Murtha was sitting and the boy was still sitting on the sofa with his arms folded. At this time a porcelain figure that was standing on the end table at the south end of the sofa was seen to leave the table and fly through the air for about two feet, directly at the television set. The figurine fell to the floor about six inches from the television with a loud noise. The figurine fell to the floor but did not break. Miss Murtha stated that she actually saw the occurrence and there was *definitely no one in the room that was close enough to touch the figurine or propel it in any way.*[6]

Over a period of five weeks some sixty-seven separate disturbances were logged by Roll and Pratt, and by the police. Sixty-four of these involved some form of interference with objects, including the hurling of a small record-player twenty feet across the floor of a basement room; the overturning of a night table; the upending of and damage to a new and prized coffee table; the unboxing of a bottle of Clorox; the hurling of an ink-bottle, and spillage of its contents; the catapulting of a figurine across ten feet; the overturning of a dresser in James Jr.'s room at a time when the room was empty; the explosive removal of a metal screw-top cap from a bleach bottle in the basement when everyone in the house was on the first floor. Just sixteen objects were the focus of two-thirds of the activity, and slightly over one-third of the incidents involved bottles popping. Three incidents took the form of unexplained thumping noises.

Roll and Pratt seem conscientiously to have assessed every possible explanation. Trickery on the part of James Jr. – around whom significantly more of the incidents centred – seemed to be ruled out by the fact that in at least seventeen of the object disturbance incidents James was definitely not physically near the object at the time. Attention-seeking by the whole family also seems highly unlikely – they were risking serious trouble if found to be wasting police time, and all of them seem to have been greatly upset by the destruction of their belongings, to the extent of moving out of the house on four occasions to stay with neighbours and relatives. Mrs Herrmann was particularly distraught, and was keen to have the house exorcised. The local church authorities, however, swiftly and sensibly advised that exorcism was inappropriate for phenomena for which there was no evidence of demonic origin.

The Nassau County police assigned an officer, Detective Joseph Tozzi, to the case full time, and no stone was left unturned to try to find a natural explanation that would enable the department to clear the matter from their books. One early theory was that the disturbances might be due to high-frequency radio waves, but when the only local with a transmitter licence was interviewed, it emerged that he had not used his set for several years. A truck and crew sent out specifically to test for radio frequencies found nothing unusual. The Long Island Lighting Company installed an oscillograph to pick up any abnormal electrical activity, but none was recorded, even though the machine was kept in the same cellar as that in which the bleach bottle incident had occurred. The Building Department checked the house's structural soundness, and found it absolutely normal. The Seaford Fire Department inspected a well in front of the house, but found that the water level had not varied in years. Maps were called for from the local Engineers' Office to check whether the house might have been built over a stream – which proved not to be the case. The local airfield was even asked for a list of planes taking off from the runway facing the Herrmann house, just in case their departure times showed any correlation with the disturbances. They did not.

For Roll and Pratt, familiar as they were with the patterns of prior poltergeist cases, this search for an external physical cause was as useless as we have inferred most of the present-day ghost-hunting activity to be. As they had already established from their careful note-taking, all the happenings were particularised to certain objects, thereby showing selection and, by implication, intelligence. Furthermore:

> Nothing ever happened while all the family were out of the house, when they were fast asleep, or while the children were both at school. With the possible exception of one case, James [Jr.] was known to be in the house during all the disturbances. Other members of the family were frequently absent. Also the disturbances took place nearer to James [Jr.] on the average than to any other member of the family.[7]

Roll and Pratt's tentative conclusion was that twelve-year-old James Jr. was somehow the focus of all the object disturbances, just as Ann Robinson had been in Stockwell two centuries before. There was no suggestion of any conscious intent on his part to move the objects, or awareness that he was doing so; indeed, as already stressed, when the objects moved they did so in ways that James could not possibly have been directly physically responsible for.

So important – and so alien to our present-day science –is this phenomenon of a living person somehow unconsciously moving objects several feet distant from him or her – sometimes even on a different floor level – that further examples demand citing so that the patterns can become clearer. On 10 March 1958 the Seaford poltergeist activity ceased, without any apparent reason, almost as abruptly as it had started. Nine years later Roll and Pratt found themselves investigating a strikingly similar case at the Tropicana Arts warehouse, Miami, Florida, the focus of activity this time being a nineteen-year-old Cuban shipping clerk, Julio Vasquez.

The problem was made unusually acute and expensive in this case by the fact that large quantities of novelty merchandise, much of it glassware, were stored at the warehouse. When, early in 1967, breakages began vastly to exceed those expected in the normal run of things, the Tropicana Arts general manager Alvin Laubheim became understandably alarmed. Here he recalls a marked escalation in events around mid-January 1967:

> . . . everything started to happen. Boxes came down. A box of about a hundred back-scratchers turned over and fell with a ter-rific clatter over on the other side of the room and then we real-ised that there was something definitely wrong here. And for three days we picked things up off the floor as fast as they would fall down . . . We tried to keep it quiet, because we knew it would hurt our business because we are right in the . . . beginning of a season, and it would draw a bunch of curiosity-seekers, etc. So we tried to keep it quiet for about four days. Then finally delivery men saw things happening and people coming in and out would see it hap-pen and word got out and there were more and more people com-ing in. And someone suggested that with the glasses being thrown around and the girls crying in the front from fright we had better notify the police; so I did.[8]

Laubheim's first approach to the police was to say that he thought he had a ghost at the warehouse. The first policeman on the scene, Patrolman William Killam, recalled that he had been told by the duty officer whom

Laubheim had telephoned that the warehouse manager had said:

> that he had a ghost in his place of business . . . going around break-ing ashtrays and he said they were just coming up off the floor and breaking. And I [Killam] told him – I said, 'This guy has got to be a nut.'[9]

While Killam was making a preliminary inspection of the Tropicana Arts aisles he saw a painted highball glass inexplicably fall to the floor and break. This was shortly after followed by the toppling-over of two boxes, then the falling into the aisle twice of a box of pencil sharpeners, then the falling of a box of address books, this latter noted to have been some eight inches from the edge of the shelf only moments before. No fewer than 224 different disturbances of this kind were logged during the overall outbreak, with the pattern emerging that it was Julio Vasquez who was consistently present.

The one note of caution required in the Tropicana case is that it is possible that Julio was practising some sort of trickery. On the night of 31 January 1967 there was a break-in at the warehouse. It was suspected that Julio was involved, and he was dismissed. The stock breakages promptly dropped back to normal levels. That Julio was behind the breakages would therefore seem to be self-evident. The main uncertainty is whether he was genuinely and unconsciously exerting some invisible force, or causing the disturbances by some sleight of hand such as moving distant objects with threads.

Despite signs that Julio was emotionally disturbed, Roll and Pratt insist they found no hint that he was manipulating the breakages. Whatever the merits of that particular case, the genuine nature of the overall poltergeist phenomenon would appear to be supported by a yet more spectacular example which occurred in Germany later the very same year.

In November 1967 a lawyers' office in Rosenheim, Bavaria, began to be plagued by a wave of disturbances that in this instance involved mainly telephone and electrical equipment. Neon lights began failing time and again, and were repeatedly found to have been unscrewed from their sockets by about ninety degrees. There were mysterious sharp bangs. Automatic fuses would blow without apparent cause. The telephones would sometimes go haywire, with four different sets ringing simultaneously. An unusual number of calls were inexplicably cut off. And telephone bills rose alarmingly.[10]

At first, fluctuations in the electrical power supply were suspected, and experts called in from the local generating station indeed detected these. But even when they installed monitoring equipment and an emergency power unit intended to ensure an undisturbed flow of current, the fluctuations continued. As for the high telephone bills, these were traced to hundreds of calls made to the speaking clock – far more than any living person could have dialled within the times registered by the phone company.

As in the previous cases, however impossible it might seem that a living person could have been performing the physical feats involved, there was indeed someone who seemed to be acting as the trigger. The German counterpart of Roll and Pratt, the distinguished psychologist Professor Hans Bender of Freiburg, noticed soon after becoming involved in the case that the phenomena only occurred during the office hours, i.e. when people were present, and also that they seemed specifically to be connected with a certain nineteen-year-old office worker, Anne-Marie Schaberl. In Bender's words:

> When this young girl walked through the hall, the lamps behind her began to swing, light fixtures began to explode, and the fragments flew towards her. In addition, the number of phenomena decreased with increasing distance from Miss S[chaberl] . . . Using an Ampex video-recorder we were able to record on videotape the swinging of the lamps and register the banging.[11]

As Bender homed in on Anne-Marie as the source of the disturbances, the phenomena began to become even more bizarre. Pictures on the walls began to move, occasionally rotating 360 degrees around their hooks and falling off the wall. Drawers opened on their own, and a heavy shelf moved from the wall.

Inquiring into Anne-Marie's psychological history, Bender discovered her to be a country girl with a disturbed, overdisciplined family background who disliked working in town – the sort of emotional tensions common among those at the focal centre of poltergeist cases.

Scene of the author's own ghostly encounter

(Above) **Abercrombie House, Bathurst, New South Wales**, Australia, where owners the Morgan family have repeatedly experienced ghostly occurrences.

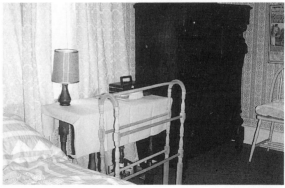

(Top right) **The Red Room, Abercrombie House**, where my wife and I experienced the 'breathing' ghost the night of 30 January 1994. 'She' seemed to be standing in the space occupied by the clothes airer.

(Below right) **Miss Rosslyn Stewart** on her bicycle, from a sketch of 1897. The Morgan family attribute to her ghost their hearing of mysterious bicycle bells.

A 'ghostly' mistake?

(Left) **Revd R. W. Hardy's photograph of purported ghosts** on the Tulip Staircase, the Queen's House, the National Maritime Museum, Greenwich, as commonly reproduced in the books of Peter Underwood and others. The figure seen ascending the staircase at lower right is usually mistaken for a hooded monk.

(Above left) **How a single individual dashing up the stairs** during a long exposure photograph may inadvertently have created the illusion of a hooded monk. The 'hood' is in reality the ascending individual's shoulder. National Maritime Museum photographer Brian Tremain's copy print, taken directly from the Revd Hardy's original, faintly reveals a tell-tale forward-facing head towards the top of the staircase which disappears in published versions. Unresolved legal complications to Peter Underwood's dispute with the Ghost Club prevented publication of Tremain's copy here.

(Above right) **Replication of the Revd Hardy's photograph** by National Maritime Museum photographer Brian Tremain, showing how a member of staff wearing a white coat could be photographically captured at least three times during a single long exposure.

More doubtful 'ghosts' . . .

Faked 'spirit' photograph created by an unknown American photographer, c. 1885, following the methodology of the charlatan William H. Mummler. From a tintype in the collection of the J. Paul Getty Museum, Malibu, Los Angeles, California, USA.

Ghost 'monk' photograph faked by dental student Arthur Spencer Palmer at Brockley Court, near Bristol, in 1909. This fooled even Sir Arthur Conan Doyle, creator of Sherlock Holmes.

Purported 'kneeling monk' as photographed by the then sixteen-year-old Gordon Carroll at the Church of St Mary the Virgin, Woodford, Northamptonshire, in 1964.

Purported 'Brown Lady' of Raynham Hall, Norfolk, as photographed in 1936 by *Country Life* photographers Captain Provand and Indre Shira.

As in the other instances the phenomena stopped when Anne-Marie was not present, and reportedly followed her through a succession of jobs after the one at the lawyers' office, even affecting the electronic scoring equipment at her fiancé's favourite bowling alley. They ceased only when she eventually married.

Such poltergeist-type cases continue to be surprisingly common right up to the present day. We have already remarked that the Christian Deliverance Study Group regard poltergeists as the most common ghost phenomena which they are called upon to deal with. The group's spokesman, Canon Michael Perry, has usefully listed some of the key features most frequently encountered:

A poltergeist attack often begins with small noises such as bangs, rattles, knockings, thumps or clicks. At first they are discounted as normal or coincidental, but then the family notices that something odd is afoot and begins to interpret them in terms of the personal activity of an unseen (and usually unwelcome) guest. They are no longer 'bumps', they are 'knocks', or 'raps', and often 'footsteps' crossing the room or heard through the ceiling and interpreted as sounds of a person in the room or corridor above. After that, the effects rise to a climax and may include any of the following:

(a) Rappings and knockings are very common.

(b) Objects may be seen to move of their own accord and in a bizarre way, defying the laws of motion and gravity, sailing in curved trajectories, or changing course at a sharp angle.

(c) Usually, however, the movement itself is not observed, but only inferred from the results of it, so that the object is suddenly found in an unusual place only a second after it had been seen elsewhere.

(d) Objects appearing from 'nowhere'.

(e) Glass, furniture, crockery being broken – usually not as a direct result of poltergeist activity, but by falling from a shelf to which the poltergeist had moved it. Occasionally, glass may shatter spontaneously.

(f) Doors being opened or closed; curtains billowing when there is no draught causing the movement.

(g) Missiles directed at a person with great speed, but usually narrowly missing, and rarely causing physical harm. Objects may refuse to move when watched, as if 'shy', but will immediately move when the attention of the observer is momentarily distracted.

(h) Water dripping or pools of water appearing.

(i) Rarely, spontaneous combustion.

(j) Cold spots and, rarely, smells.

(k) Sounds of music or the jangling of bells.

(l) Voices, or baby and child-like sounds such as sucking, smacking of lips, occasional crows and chuckles.

(m) Very commonly, interference with electrical apparatus – lights switched on and off, domestic apparatus set in operation, record players and tape-recorders made to fluctuate in speed, electric clocks working in reverse, telephones ringing for no reason, bells going haywire.[12]

These are the now reasonably familiar characteristics of poltergeist phenomena. As further noted by Canon Perry: 'The activity is essentially naughty, childish, a cry for help by demanding attention, and is not experienced as essentially evil or malevolent.' But this still doesn't answer what we are to make of it all. What exactly is happening during a poltergeist disturbance? And what relevance does it have to our better understanding of ghosts?

Although no one can claim to be totally sure, one point of fairly general agreement is that the poltergeist is not a true ghost because no deceased person seems to be involved, the focal source consistently being found to be a disturbed young person exhibiting rather unusual powers. Even so, it is important not to be too dogmatic about this; as always there are exceptions to the rule.

One such exception is a case which occurred during the late 1980s at John and Pat Matthews' mower repair and sales business, Cardiff Mower Services, in Cardiff, South Wales. Ostensibly all the typical signs of a poltergeist seemed to be in play: stones were rolled on the workshop roof; keys went missing, and then were hurled across the room; ball-bearings were thrown about; money in the form of £5 and £10 notes would appear as if from nowhere. For the family who ran the workshop the phenomena became so familiar and so unfrightening that they even labelled their unseen intruder 'Pete the Polt' and indulged in the occasional naming of items – a pen, a plug, old coins – for 'Pete' to conjure up for them.

There are, however, several unusual and disquieting features about the case. First, no obvious *living* adolescent seems to have been involved as the focus of the disturbance. Second, the friendly interplay between the family and 'Pete' is unusual. Third, Pat's brother Fred Cook, who also worked at the business, claimed to have seen three times the ghost of a little boy, who, from the circumstances, seems to have been responsible for the phenomena.

On the first occasion Fred had just opened the workshop one morning when he saw the boy, dressed in short trousers and with a peaked school cap, sitting on one of the shelves close to the ceiling in a corner from which some of the earlier activity had specifically seemed to come. When Fred tried saying brightly, 'Hello! What are you doing here?' a float from a motor mower dropped down and the boy disappeared. The second time was when Fred was working on a piece of machinery with his brother-in-law John. On looking up he saw the boy and shouted out, 'Look behind you!' to John, whereupon a stone came cracking down on the machinery with considerable force. Again the boy disappeared. On the third occasion Fred saw the boy standing in the open door of the washroom waving 'as if saying goodbye'.

All these features do seem to make the case something of an odd man out among the rest and it was conscientiously recorded for the Society for Psychical Research by Professor David Fontana, a University of Wales psychologist[13]. The discrepancies may simply indicate that poltergeist activity on the part of a living young person and similar activity by a dead young person as a ghost are likely to be much of a muchness. Or that the ghosts of dead people may lie behind all poltergeist cases but have simply not been detected elsewhere. However, to draw any such sweeping conclusions from this isolated case would be ill-advised and would expose us to the danger of overreaching ourselves.

If there is one single overall consensus from the hundreds of poltergeist occurrences that have been reported, it is that the living person at the centre of each case seems to have been quite unconsciously deploying a form of energy powerful enough to move and manipulate things at a distance definitely beyond the immediate confines of his physical body. For us to be able to accept that statement in itself demands a huge leap, for it goes against all our understanding of the limits of the human body's potential. Yet unless the often very competent witnesses in each case have been consistently lying or equally consistently duped, it is the only conclusion that seems possible from the available evidence.

Clearly a whole book could be written on this topic. Among other still underexplored areas are the pubertal stage of development so consistently found at the centre of the disturbances; and the clear limitations to the distance at which the mysterious energy can work. Fortunately, however, further research into the poltergeist is unnecessary for our present purposes.

Instead the root question posed by all the poltergeist activity that we have reviewed is this: if there is a ghostly something that can mysteriously and dramatically reach out beyond us while we are still alive – even though we have no conscious control over it – how far may it also reach out beyond us when we are dead?

CHAPTER FOUR

When a Ghost May Not Be a Ghost

Part II: When It's a Passing Caller . . .

Although poltergeist-type cases are the ghostly phenomena that clergy most often get called out to deal with, even commoner (though much less demanding upon exorcistic services) are ghostly experiences carrying yet another fancy name: 'crisis apparitions', or, as we will call them, 'passing callers'. Passing callers do not seem to be true ghosts, but they certainly come much closer to it than poltergeists do. For whereas, as we argued, poltergeists most likely derive from the living, passing callers seem to derive from the newly dead . . .

A single and deceptively simple concept lies behind the passing caller – that around the time of death (and only then) the deceased transmits something of himself or herself to a relative, friend or even mere acquaintance who may be many miles away. The actual form of the transmission may vary from a seemingly ordinary glimpse of the deceased as if he or she were still alive, through a rather more disturbing sighting suggesting that he or she is dead, to a dream or a vision. But the end result is the same: that someone who has just died seemingly breaks the bounds of what has been his or her physical shell and leaps through space to impinge upon the senses of someone still living.

Examples giving validity to this phenomenon seem to cross every cultural boundary. The anthropologist Ronald Rose, a great authority on Australian aborigines, has described how 'Frank', a full-blooded aborigine working on a station managed by a Mr J. Foster, received without benefit of telephone or radio the news of the death of his son

Billie at a hospital forty miles away. As related to Rose directly by Mr Foster:

> Frank's small son was in Kyogle Hospital. He had been there for some time, and as far as I knew was not in any dangerous condition. One morning, a few weeks ago, Frank came to my residence here before breakfast. 'What's the matter, Frank?' I asked, and he told me that Billie had died in the night. There is no way he could have known this – Kyogle Hospital is over forty miles away and my residence is the only place with a phone. I didn't know what to make of Frank's statement; I told him I'd ring the hospital later to reassure him. But before I had done so, my phone rang. It was Kyogle Hospital. They told me that Frank's son had suddenly taken a turn for the worse and had died during the night.[1]

Such sensing of the death of a loved one many miles away seems to be common among Australian aborigines, but is by no means confined to them. From early seventeenth-century England comes a strikingly similar story derived from Shakespeare's great rival Ben Jonson. While staying at Conington, Huntingdonshire, in 1603, in the company of his old tutor William Camden, Jonson reportedly saw in a vision the death of his eldest son over fifty miles away in London from the plague. Jonson recounted the experience in the third person:

> He [Jonson] saw in a vision his eldest son (then a child and at London) appear to him with the mark of a blood cross on his forehead as if it had been cut with a sword . . . Amazed, he prayed to God and in the morning he came to Mr Camden's chamber to tell him, who persuaded him that it was but an apprehension of his fantasy at which he should not be disjected. In the meantime comes there letters from his wife of the death of that boy in the plague . . .[2]

In 1882 the newly formed Society for Psychical Research published as one of its earliest reported cases an account by Captain G. F. Russell Colt of Midlothian of how in the early hours of the morning of 9 September 1855 he saw the death of his elder brother Oliver while the latter was hundreds of miles away serving in the Crimean War as a lieutenant with the 7th Royal Fusiliers at the siege of Sebastopol. As described by Russell Colt, Oliver:

> was about nineteen years old . . . I corresponded frequently with him, and once when he wrote in low spirits, not being well, I said in answer that he was to cheer up, but that if anything did happen to him he must let me know by appearing in my room, where we had often as boys together sat at night and indulged in a surreptitious pipe and chat. This letter (I found subsequently) he received as he was starting to receive the sacrament from a clergyman who has since related the fact to me. Having done this he went to the entrenchments and never returned, as in a few hours afterwards the storming of the Redan [the great defensive emplacement before Sebastopol] commenced. He, on the captain of his company falling, took his place and led his men bravely on. He had just led them within the walls, though already wounded in several places, when a bullet struck him on the right temple and he fell among heaps of others, where he was found in a sort of kneeling posture (being propped up by other dead bodies) thirty-six hours afterwards. His death took place, or rather he *fell*, though he may not have died immediately, on the 8th September 1855.
>
> That night I awoke suddenly, and saw facing the window of my room, by my bedside, surrounded by a light sort of phosphorescent mist as it were, my brother kneeling. I tried to speak but could not. I buried my head in the bedclothes, not at all afraid (because we had all been brought up not to believe in ghosts or apparitions), but simply to collect my ideas, because I had not been thinking or dreaming of him, and indeed had forgotten all about what I had written to him a fortnight before. I decided that it must be fancy . . . but on looking up there he was again . . . The apparition turned round his head slowly and again looked anxiously and lovingly at me, and I saw then for the first time a wound in the right temple with a red stream from it . . . I told others in the house but when I told my father he ordered me not to repeat such nonsense . . . About a fortnight later . . . [my friend] came to my bedroom . . . with a very grave face. I said, 'I suppose it is to tell me the sad news I expect' and he said, 'Yes.' But the colonel of the regiment and one

or two officers who saw the body confirmed the fact that the appearance was much according to my description, and the death wound was exactly where I had seen it . . .[3]

If such a case might seem too long ago to be credible, there is no shortage of similar examples from the present century. Just one of many instances from around the time of the First World War concerns an eighteen-year-old trainee pilot, Lieutenant McConnel, who on the morning of 7 December 1918, while based at Scampton, Lincolnshire, was unexpectedly deputed to fly a Camel aircraft to Tadcaster, sixty miles to the north.[4] Bidding farewell to his room-mate, Lieutenant Larkin, McConnel headed off, only, on arriving at Tadcaster, to find the aerodrome shrouded in thick fog. Becoming disoriented he lost control of the aircraft, and with the engine still at full throttle nose-dived to the earth, his body subsequently being found dead in the wreckage with his watch stopped at 3.35 p.m., the apparent time of the crash.

Meanwhile, back at Scampton, Larkin was reading and smoking in his room when a familiar-sounding clatter along the passageway heralded what he confidently assumed to be McConnel's safe return. Indeed, the door opened and there seemed to be McConnel, dressed in his flying clothes and exchanging pleasantries with his usual good humour before departing with the words, 'Well, cheerio.' Although Larkin was not wearing a watch, the subsequent arrival of another lieutenant, Garner-Smith, at a quarter to four suggested that McConnel's visit had been at around 3.30 p.m. The point of Garner-Smith's visit was to ask if McConnel had returned, prompting Larkin to respond, 'He is back. He was in the room a few minutes ago.' Garner-Smith thereupon went off fruitlessly to search for McConnel, and it was only later that evening that Larkin heard that his room-mate had died in Tadcaster, and thus realised that he must have seen McConnel's ghost.

Best-selling novelist Wilbur Wright has described a strikingly similar experience from the Second World War relating to an Aircraftsman Stoker, whom he had known only casually while he was stationed as a ground engineer at RAF Hemswell, Lincolnshire. In Wright's own words:

In early 1941 . . . I returned from leave by bus late one Sunday evening completely out of cigarettes, and all the canteens were closed. But I remembered I had left some cigarettes in the hangar and walked down in the black-out, entering the hangar through the central steel doors at the front. The aircrew room was on the right, where flying personnel of 61 Bomber Squadron kept their flying clothing. I heard a noise from the crew room and opened the door to investigate it. It was in total darkness and I switched on the light. The black-out curtains were in position and I saw a figure in uniform groping in one of the lockers. He was wearing a flying helmet, a leather fur-lined jacket, black knee-length flying boots, and I recognised him as Leading Aircraftsman Stoker, a mid-upper gunner on the Hampden bomber, who had to fly with the hood open to look for attacking fighters . . .

I said, 'Hey Stoke – what are you doing?'

He replied irritably, 'I can't find my bloody gloves.'

'Well, that's your problem,' I said. 'Put out the lights when you go.'

He made no reply to that, and I entered the hangar, found my cigarettes and went back to my billet. Next morning I went to breakfast, and as always happened, I asked the man next to me what had been happening during my week's absence.

'Very dodgy two nights ago,' he said. 'They went mine-laying in the Dortmund Ems Canal and we lost McIntyre and his crew, hit at low level by flak, rolled and went straight in. The mine went off – they had no chance.'

'My God,' I said. 'That chap Stoker had a lucky escape then!'

'Stoker? Oh, he went in with the rest. There was trouble before they took off – he couldn't find his flying gloves and he could have frozen to death with the rear gun hatch open. He was moaning all the way out to the transport.[5]

As Wilbur Wright freely admitted, the experience shook him so badly that he actually reported sick to the Station Medical Officer, and it took him a while before he got properly back to normal. As he particularly recollected:

Looking back the most remarkable aspect was that the air gunner looked perfectly normal to me. His clothing creaked as usual when he moved, his face was worried but in no way remarkable, and it was only later that I realised that he had been groping round in his flying-clothing locker in pitch darkness.

It may be difficult to believe that the dead Aircraftsman Stoker somehow 'flashed' this impression of himself across four hundred miles from where his shattered body lay in Dortmund, but this is by no means the furthest distance over which such transmissions seem to have travelled. In 1986 a health visitor of Polish parentage, Krystyna Kolodziej, described to me how five years previously she had seen her father Kazimir at the time of his death – even though she knew he was eleven thousand miles away in Australia.

On the night of 21 March 1981 Krystyna was with a friend in her flat at Hackney, east London. She had not seen her father for some twelve or thirteen years, and indeed their relationship had never been close because throughout most of her life he had had a chronic drink problem. But when Kazimir knew he was dying he had written to tell her, and he even sent her the money to fly to Australia to visit him for the last time, an offer that with mixed emotions she declined because it would have meant her missing the B.Sc. examinations for which she had been studying during the last three years. Then, in Krystyna's own words:

> My friend had been with me a few hours and . . . she and I were sitting on my sofa talking at about 11 p.m., and she was describing to me some clothes she had bought recently . . . Suddenly, and while still attending to her, my father's face appeared high on the wall to my left, just next to a large mounted picture. Indeed part of it occluded the picture. I saw it out of the corner of my eye, because my face was actually turned toward my friend, and the face imprinted itself on to my awareness in a way so real that I shook my head and looked away, as if trying to shake off the vision in disbelief. This time, I looked directly at the place and saw the face again, after which it disappeared almost instantly. The entire episode lasted only about ten seconds and my friend, absorbed in what she was saying, noticed nothing in my expression. I told her of it the next morning. My father did die within hours of my seeing

him, and I woke spontaneously just before the phone rang to tell me . . .

What I remember most was the expression on my father's face – there was no expression . . . If I had to describe the feeling the apparition imparted to me, it was as if seeing me, and perhaps being seen, was a duty my father had to perform.[6]

If Krystyna's experience of a dying father transmitting to his daughter is dramatic enough, another example goes one further, involving a dying father of two children seemingly transmitting to both of these near-simultaneously. As related by one of those children in Aniela Jaffé's *Apparitions and Precognition*, published in 1963:

It was in Zurich in 1940. I took my usual way back to work after lunch. As I walked along towards my office, I suddenly saw my father. Strange, I thought, he's been away for the last fortnight, why has he come back so unexpectedly? I hastened my steps and called out, 'Hello, Father!' The words were hardly out of my mouth when he disappeared. I looked around on all sides, wondering whether I had been dreaming. My father was nowhere to be seen. Deeply perplexed, I went on to my work. No sooner had I arrived than I received a phone call from a relative, telling me that my father had died of a stroke in the night. I immediately rang my sister to give her the bad news, and told her about my eerie experience. What did she tell me? I could hardly believe my ears. At that very time Father had appeared to her in the Bahnhofstrasse, and had suddenly disappeared.[7]

Examples such as this, striking as they are, can often be undervalued because they occur within a family, giving rise to accusations that they are mere psychological projections, or figments supplied by the imagination to give comfort to someone recently bereaved. Also, although in some of the above-quoted cases the bereaved persons cannot have known of their relatives' deaths, it is well recorded that those left behind often do experience feelings of closeness to their dead loved ones during the months immediately after their loss.

Other cases, however, as we have already seen from the two RAF examples, crucially show that the same phenomenon can also occur between individuals who have no known blood relationship, and this is supported by many more examples of this type.

For instance, the former Roy Jenkins, now Lord Jenkins of Hillhead, recorded in his diary for Saturday 19 February 1977 how when he was newly arrived in Rome in the early hours of that morning he had, as if in a dream, a passing caller-type transmission relating to the death of his old friend and fellow-MP Anthony Crosland, whom he knew to be seriously ill back in England. Jenkins recollected:

> I awoke about 6.30, having had a vivid dream about Tony [Crosland] being present, and his saying in an absolutely unmistakable, clear, rather calm voice, 'No, I'm perfectly all right. I'm going to die, but I'm perfectly all right.' Then at about 8 o'clock we had a telephone call from the BBC saying that he had died that morning, curiously enough at almost exactly the same moment that I awoke from my dream about him.[8]

It may be a dying or newly dead favourite teacher who transmits himself or herself in this way. Diana Norman, wife of the BBC Television film critic Barry Norman, relates how a 'smart, intelligent' secretarial friend once told her:

> I was at school at a convent. My favourite teacher was a nun called Sister Bridget. Then I got ill and had to spend some time in the convent infirmary. One day I looked up to see that Sister Bridget had come into my room. She smiled at me and I smiled back. Then she turned away and just walked through the wall. I began to scream at that, and the nuns came running to see what was the matter. I told them that I had seen Sister Bridget and that she had disappeared. Then they told me that Sister Bridget had been taken ill and had died – a few minutes before I saw her.[9]

The transmitter may be an employee, even a humble cleaning lady. Joan Hughes, who earlier helped with the ghost incident at the Salisbury teacher-training college, recalls:

* * *

We had a cleaning lady, Mrs Dobbs, who looked after the Chapel and the tutorial rooms in Old Deanery. She was a Downton woman, a strong Church woman, and a very pleasant person. She used to chat to me a lot as my tutorial room was in Old Deanery. I knew she had to have a serious operation, and on the afternoon it was to take place, mentioned it to my colleague Miss Flarty. She said Mrs Dobbs had just greeted her as she passed the Chapel door on her way back to the Hostel. I told her that Mrs Dobbs was at that moment probably on the operating table. In fact she was – and had died there.[10]

Arguably one of the most fascinating and illuminating scenarios of all is one in which the dying transmitter and the person on the receiving end are unknown to each other at the time of the experience, their connection not becoming clear until some weeks into the future. In 1935, the highly respected Roman Catholic priest Fr Walter Cooksey related the following to the psychical researcher Sir Ernest Bennett, then compiling a series of case histories of hauntings for his book *Apparitions and Haunted Houses*:

On 3 December 1908 I was living with the Roman Catholic Bishop of Southwark, in St Georges Road, London, SE1. One other priest lived in the house, but at this date was away from home, so that the bishop and I were alone except for the servants, whose quarters were in the semi-basement. This being the bishop's official residence a number of people came and went in the daytime, and occasional visitors came and stayed. On the evening of the 2nd the bishop and I dined together alone, and after dinner he went to his room and I to mine on the third floor.

At about 6.30 a.m. on 3 December I got up and proceeded downstairs to the bathroom. As I turned the corner of the stairs from my room on the third floor and was proceeding down the flight of steps which led to the landing on the second floor, I saw an elderly man standing at the foot of the stairs. He was a stranger to me and wore a cassock and white cotta or short surplice. This man, who had grey hair and a very long straight upper lip, stood with his hands joined and his head on one side looking up at me in an enquiring sort of way. I thought that he was some priest who had come on after dinner overnight and that he was looking for the bishop's oratory, and was just about to speak to him when he vanished completely. I still thought he had gone into one or other of the passages and looked for him in both. Till I failed to find him I had no idea but that he was a living man. I then went upstairs again a couple of times and came down in the same way as I had done at first to satisfy myself that it was not some trick of light shining in from the street, but nothing more happened and I saw no more of the figure.

At breakfast later I asked the bishop if anybody had stayed in the house overnight and he said, No. I then went about my usual work and at luncheon the bishop told me that he had had a telegram to say that a Father Ford of Bromley, Kent, had died that morning at 6.30 a.m. As I did not know Father Ford even by sight this information did not affect me at all. About five or six weeks later I was appointed to take the place of this Father Ford at Bromley. When I got settled in and began to visit my parishioners I went into a house and in the parlour I saw a large framed photograph of an elderly priest, without a shadow of doubt the man I had seen on the stairs on 3 December. When the owner of the house came in I asked, 'Whose portrait is that?' She replied, 'Why, don't you know, that was dear Father Ford.'[11]

As Cooksey emphasised, he was only thirty-eight at the time of the experience. He had never knowingly seen a ghost before, and what most struck him, as it had struck Wilbur Wright in respect of Aircraftsman Stoker, was the extraordinary clarity of what he saw, as if it actually was the real-life Father Ford (had he known what the priest looked like) standing there before him. Cooksey insisted: 'Although the only light was through the window's front street lamps, I saw every detail of this apparition quite clearly.'

When one embarks upon any serious study of ghosts, it quickly becomes apparent that not only are the apparitions very frequently perceived as looking solid and alive, but also that this passing caller variety of ghost is particularly common. Almost all of us seem to know someone who has had an experience of this kind. In my own case my mother, who made no claims to being psychic, woke up at 6 o'clock one morning in 1963 profoundly conscious that my step-grandfather, who lived in an old people's home three miles away, was calling out to her. An hour later the matron of the home telephoned to say that my grandfather had died at 6 a.m. of a sudden heart attack – calling out as he did so. His death had not been expected; he had been our guest for Sunday tea only a few hours before. In a survey carried out between 1978 and 1981 among one thousand inhabitants of the Tyrolean town of Bolzano, on the border between Italy and Austria, nearly fifty per cent reported some similar strange coincidence at the time of the death of a relative or friend.

A key feature of this particular variety of ghost experience is that the transmitter – the dead person – seems much more real than the sort of empty recording track that some suppose ghosts to be. Even if the passing caller is not heard to speak, or if they are heard but say nothing meaningful, the prevailing impression is that the dead person has quite deliberately willed himself or herself to make the appearance, albeit for no immediately obvious reason.

For instance, in the case of cleaning lady Mrs Dobbs seen by Salisbury warden Miss Flarty, there is no suggestion of any particularly strong connection between the pair, yet for some reason it was to Miss Flarty that Mrs Dobbs appeared. Likewise Aircraftsman Stoker appeared to Wilbur Wright, even though the two were not particular friends. And most strikingly of all, although at the time of his ghostly appearance no one could have known that Father Ford's successor would be Father Cooksey, the former appears to have specially sought out the man who would walk in his footsteps in his beloved Bromley parish. For the sake of curiosity? Or just to wish him well? Who knows?

Among other features of the passing caller is that there seems to be nothing prolonged or repetitive about the sightings, hence, unlike in the poltergeist cases, the absence of any calls for exorcism. Each appearance is just a fleeting one-off, never to recur. While the transmitter can reach anywhere in the world – even from as far away as Australia – having done so they just disappear and mostly never trouble the living again.[12] For this reason alone I have chosen not to regard this type of manifestation as a true ghost – *because it doesn't haunt.*

Inevitably many questions are left unanswered, not least whether the passing callers make their dramatic transmissions just *before* death, at the very *moment* of death, or shortly *after* death. The evidence is unclear and should not unduly trouble us. There is also the question of whether such occurrences may have a link with the 'near-death experiences' of people who clinically 'die' and then recover, and who report having been able invisibly to drop in on friends and relatives. This, however, demands in its turn a far closer study of near-death experiences than is possible here.

Whatever, the overriding feature of the passing caller seems to be that it is a free soul, which may only manifest with extraordinary brevity, like a short-lived firefly, yet which nonetheless appears able, during that time, to whisk effortlessly anywhere in the world. And that, as we will see, represents a fundamental difference from that which we are at last about to tackle directly: the ghost proper.

CHAPTER FIVE

Ghost Stories Age-Old and Worldwide

If we look back through time at ghost stories as they have been recorded by the world's ancient cultures, what immediately strikes us is their broad similarity. Peoples across the world have differed widely in the gods they have worshipped, from the exotic animal-headed pantheons of ancient Egypt to the austere monotheism of present-day Islam. But with regard to true ghosts – that is, to the dead who purportedly make nuisances of themselves by haunting the living – people's perceptions have largely been the same, whether they were born in Tooting or Timbuktu, whether they lived thirty or three thousand years ago, and whether they believed in heaven and hell or in some form of reincarnation.

From ancient Egypt, for instance, there survives from the 19th/20th Dynasty period (*circa* 1200 BC) a text describing how a high priest of Amun was repeatedly haunted by the former chief treasurer to the Middle Kingdom King Rehotep, who lived sometime around 1700 BC. It seems that the treasurer was concerned about the neglect and dilapidation which had befallen his tomb, the location of which had been lost. As a result of his ghostly pressure, the tomb was apparently rediscovered and given appropriate renovation.[1]

Among the ancient Assyrians those who died in battle, were murdered, or were in any other way deprived of proper burial rites were thought to become greatly feared ghosts called *ekimmu*. A surviving Babylonian divination tablet, apparently prepared for a man defined as 'in the grip of a ghost of one who lies in the open country' (i.e. someone who had never received proper burial rites), prescribes how if a proper ceremony is carried out this troublesome ghost will be 'consigned to the wind' and the man cured.[2]

The ancient Greeks certainly believed in ghosts. The site of the Battle of Marathon, in which ten thousand Greeks under their general Miltiades heroically defended their country against invading Persians in 490 BC, was said to be haunted for centuries afterwards by ghostly sounds of battle. Even five centuries later the classical geographer Pausanias wrote of it in his *Atticis*: 'At this spot every night you may hear horses neighing and men fighting.'

The Roman author Plutarch, in his biography of Miltiades' son Kimon, wrote how the people of the Chersonese region of northern Greece slew a notoriously murderous captain called Damon while he was bathing at their local bath-house, resulting in the bath-house ever after becoming so plagued by the sounds of Damon's sighing and groaning that it had to be closed down. The Roman biographer Suetonius, reporting on the assassination of the tyrannical Roman emperor Caligula, and his subsequent makeshift burial in a shallow grave in the Lamian Gardens, likewise described how until Caligula's sisters were able to return from exile and give him a proper funeral,

> all the City [i.e. Rome] knew that the Gardens had been haunted until then by his [Caligula's] ghost, and that something horrible appeared every night at the scene of his murder . . .[3]

Probably the most remarkable of the Roman era's ghost stories derives, however, from the pen of the very down-to-earth and scientifically minded Pliny the Younger (*circa* AD 61–113), who in one of his typically informative *Letters* wrote of a 'large and spacious' house in Athens where

> frequently a noise like clanking iron could be heard at the dead of night, which if you listened carefully seemed more like the rattling of shackles. At first it seemed to be far off, but it steadily came nearer and nearer, whereupon a ghost appeared in the form of an old man, extremely thin and tattered-looking, with a long

beard and bristling hair, rattling the fetters on his feet and hands. The poor people who lived in the house understandably suffered sleepless nights filled with every imaginable fear . . . Inevitably the house eventually lost all its occupants, for everyone regarded it as impossible to live in, so it was entirely abandoned to the ghost. However, in the hope that a tenant might be found who did not know what had befallen it an advertisement was posted offering it either for sale or for rent.

According to Pliny thereupon there arrived in Athens a philosopher from Tarsus called Athenodorus, who although needing accommodation for himself and his household, immediately became suspicious of the low price being asked in the advertisement. Even so, on learning the true reason, rather than being deterred, he decided to rent the house, and after moving in, duly settled to await whatever ghostly encounter the first night might bring.

When darkness fell he [Athenodorus] asked for an easy chair to be prepared for him in the front part of the house; and after further requesting a lamp, together with his pen and notepad, he advised everyone with him to go to bed . . .

The first part of the night passed without incident, then began the clanking of fetters. However, he neither glanced up, nor laid down his pen, completely ignoring the distraction. But the noise grew louder and nearer, until it seemed at the door, and at last in the room where he was. Looking round, he saw the ghost exactly as it had been described to him. It stood in front of him, beckoning him with its finger. Athenodorus indicated with his hand that it should be patient, and turned again to his writing, but as he did so the ghost rattled its chains over his head, and when he looked round again he saw it beckoning as before. At this he immediately took up his lamp and followed it. The ghost slowly stalked along, as if burdened with its chains, and having turned into the courtyard of the house, suddenly vanished.

Having been thus left alone, Athenodorus marked the spot with a handful of grass and leaves and then the next day went to the city authorities and advised them to have the spot dug up. Upon doing so they found a human skeleton enmeshed with chains, the body itself having completely rotted away due to the time it had been in the ground, leaving just the bare bones, discoloured by the fetters. These bones were collected up and buried at public expense, after which, the ghost having been duly laid, the house was haunted no more.[4]

Of course Pliny's story is a hoary old one, he did not describe it at first hand, and whatever the original true circumstances, some of these will almost certainly have become distorted during the retelling. But when we turn to nineteenth-century Japan, and to a culture very far removed from that of the Greeks and Romans, we find a strikingly similar story among several told to British diplomatic attaché A. B. Mitford shortly after Japanese ports had begun to be opened up to the West during the late 1860s. According to the story as transcribed by Mitford:

About thirty years ago there stood a house as Misumé, in the Honjô of Yedo [Tokyo], which was said to be nightly visited by ghosts, so that no man dared to live in it, and it remained untenanted on that account. However a man called Miura Takéshi, a native of the province of Oshiu, who came to set up in business as a fencing master, but was too poor to hire a house, hearing that there was a haunted house, for which no tenant could be found, and that the owner would let any man live in it rent-free, said that he feared neither man nor devil, and obtained leave to occupy the house. So he hired a fencing room, in which he gave his lessons by day, and after midnight returned to the haunted house.

One night his wife, who took charge of the house in his absence, was frightened by a fearful noise proceeding from a pond in the garden, and thinking that this certainly must be the ghost that she had heard so much about, she covered her head with the bedclothes and remained breathless with terror. When her husband came home, she told him what had happened, and on the following night he returned earlier than usual, and waited for the ghostly noise. At the same time as before, a little before midnight, the same sound was heard – as though a gun had been fired inside the pond. Opening the shutters, he looked out and saw something like

72

a black cloud floating on the water, and in the cloud was the form of a bald man. Thinking that there must be some cause for this, he instituted careful inquiries, and learned that the former tenant, some ten years previously, had borrowed money from a blind shampooer and being unable to pay the debt, had murdered his creditor, who had begun to press him for his money, and had thrown his head into the pond. The fencing master accordingly collected his pupils and emptied the pond and found a skull at the bottom of it; so he called in a priest, and buried the skull in a temple, causing prayers to be offered up for the repose of the murdered man's soul. Thus the ghost was laid, and appeared no more.[5]

Like the Athenodorus story this one has similarly not come down to us at first hand. Again, therefore, we are right to be cautious about accepting every detail. But the important point is that although this latter story is some eighteen centuries and seven thousand miles removed from the Athens of Athenodorus, even so it is strikingly similar in its understanding of what ghosts are, namely:

(1)   that what appears to be the ghost of someone dead has manifested in and started to disturb one specific location, a private house.

(2)   that the ghostly disturbances have taken visual and auditory form, and have mostly occurred at night.

(3)   that as a result of living people being frightened by these disturbances, the house has become near unacceptable for normal habitation.

(4)   that with the coming of a tenant not frightened by the disturbances the source of the haunting has been determined as a person who has seemingly died in violent circumstances and has not been laid to rest.

(5)   that with the discovery of that person's mortal remains, their removal to a more suitable location, and the conduct of an appropriate funerary rite, the hauntings have been duly terminated.

Aside from Greece, Rome and Japan, when we look elsewhere around the world, and throughout the centuries of recorded history, it is again often some violent or unhappy death combined with an unsatisfactory mode of burial that seem to give rise to the conventionally understood ghost. Among the Chinese, we find Chu Hsi, a follower of Confucius, writing in the fifth century BC:

> if a man is killed before his life span is completed, his vital spirit is not yet exhausted, and may survive for a while as a ghost.

Likewise, as noted by the great authority on Chinese culture Arthur P. Wolf, the Chinese regard ghosts as:

> discontented souls . . . forced by their circumstances to prey on the living. They include the neglected dead . . . also those hateful souls who . . . remain at the scene of death seeking revenge – murder victims, suicides and the unjustly executed.[6]

So deeply ingrained in the universal human psyche are such ideas of ghosts that many cultures have embodied in their funerary procedures special rituals to try to ensure that the dead person will not try to become a ghost. Tibetan Buddhists specifically instruct the deceased not to haunt, while among the native Indians of South America the Barama River Caribs of Guyana are said to put thorns in a dead person's feet to prevent his or her ghost walking.

Although this latter practice might sound like just another quaint superstition of a primitive people, there is a wealth of archaeological evidence to suggest that our early Celtic and Viking ancestors went to even more elaborate lengths for apparently the very same reasons – particularly when they believed that the dead person was likely to return to haunt.

Thus in 1835 at Haraldskjaer Fen, Denmark, near the ancient Danish royal seat of Jelling, there was found, well preserved by peat, the body of a young woman who had died back in the Iron Age. The particularly chilling feature of the discovery was that she had been deliberately and carefully pinned down by wooden crooks driven tight over each of her knees and elbow joints, in addition to which strong branches had been fixed like clamps over her chest and lower abdomen, again fastened at each end by wooden crooks. A local antiquarian quickly pointed out:

> Every countryman will immediately recognise in this corpse the
> body of someone who when living was regarded as a witch and
> whom it was intended to prevent from walking again after death.
> Many of us have either ourselves seen, or have heard old people
> speak of, stakes standing here and there which have been driven in
> in earlier times . . . by those who . . . thought that by this means
> they could get the better of the ghosts. Our forefathers believed
> that so long as the stakes stood the ghost remained pinned in the
> ground. If the stakes were removed, however, trouble would start
> all over again.[7]

For those who might feel inclined to dismiss such an interpretation as
just another piece of quaint superstition, the great twentieth-century
Danish expert on such 'bog bodies', Professor P. V. Glob, has provided
an example from his own direct experience in which such pinning down,
pagan as it might seem, demonstrably worked. In Professor Glob's own
words:

> There used to be an absolute plague of ghosts at certain times on a
> hill at Dynved, in the north-west of the island of Als [Denmark].
> As luck would have it, about fifty years ago there lived on the
> other side of the straits of Als, on the Jutland mainland, a clergy-
> man strong enough to cope with this state of affairs. One day he
> appeared on the hill with a heavy oak stake and a hammer, walked
> around for a while on the hillside and finally drove in the stake at
> a spot where there was nothing in particular to be seen. From then
> on peace reigned on the hill. Forty years later a museum official, J.
> Faben, from Sønderborg Castle, undertaking an investigation of
> the hill for quite different reasons, came upon a thousand-year-old
> Viking grave. The Viking's breast was still transfixed by the point
> of the stake which the clergyman had driven in. When the stake
> was planted it had, of course, been long forgotten that a Viking's
> grave existed on the hill, yet it was the clamour of this heathen
> soul which had been disturbing the sleep of the good Christian
> folk of the neighbourhood down to our own century.[8]

* * *

Similarly, in 1936 Swedish scholar Dr Albert Sandklef uncovered the well-preserved, fully dressed body of a medieval man in a peat bog at Bocksten, Halland, on the west coast of Sweden. From a variety of clues, including coins in the man's pocket, Sandklef deduced that the man had been murdered and thrown in the bog by local people around the year 1360.

> To stop the dead man 'walking' his murderers had driven a birch stake through his back just above the buttocks and another at his side, though this last had only gone through his clothing. Finally, a stake of oak cut from a piece of building-timber had been driven through his heart, so that the ghost might not harm the murderers.[9]

Even the spot where the man had been buried, at the meeting point of four parishes, had been carefully chosen with ghost folklore in mind, for it was believed that burial at a crossroads prevented a potential ghost from choosing any direction for its ghostly activity.

This sort of lore was not confined to Scandinavian cultures. In Yorkshire, during the reign of Richard II, a monk of Byland Abbey cheerfully filled several blank pages of a manuscript of Cicero with his own highly individual collection of ghost stories, the evidential quality of which might well cause raised eyebrows among the more critical members of the present-day Society for Psychical Research.

When the monasteries were abolished during the Reformation, to be replaced with the more scientific-minded attitudes of the Renaissance, it might have been expected that the old superstitious beliefs relating to ghosts would be swept away in the process. After all, it had been clearly written into the new Protestant theology that there was no Purgatory, the belief that had led to monks and nuns spending much of their lives saying prayers for those dead who had left them money to do so. According to the new way of thinking, when men died they either went straight to Heaven or to Hell. Since there was no intermediate state of the kind in which ghosts seemed theoretically to hang around, ghosts simply could not exist, and anyone retaining a belief in them was likely to invite ridicule for clinging to the superstitious past.

Somewhat to Protestant discomfiture, however, the experiencing of ghosts did not simply tail away into nothing, as they might have felt entitled to expect. Instead thoroughly honest devout Protestants continued to be troubled by hauntings, as a Swiss Protestant minister Lewes Lavater felt obliged to admit in a book published in Zurich in 1570:

No man can deny . . . the many honest and credible persons . . . as well men as women, of whom some are still living and some already departed, which have and do affirm that they have sometimes in the day and sometimes in the night seen and heard spirits [i.e. ghosts]. Some man walks alone in his house, and behold a spirit appears in his sight. Yes, and sometimes the dogs also perceive this, and fall down at their master's feet, and will by no means depart from there, for they are sore afraid themselves too. Some man goes to bed and lays him down to rest, and by and by there is something pinching him, or pulling off the clothes. Sometimes it sits on him, or lies down in the bed with him, and many times it walks up and down in the chamber. There have been many times men seen, walking on foot, or riding horseback . . . known to divers men, and such as died not long before.[10]

Lavater also noted the incidence of what we would now describe as poltergeist-type activity:

It is reported that some spirits have thrown the door off from the hooks, and have troubled and set all things in the house out of order, never setting them in their due place again, and that they have marvellously disquieted men with rumbling and making a great noise.

To find such ghostly phenomena being reported back in the sixteenth century, hundreds of years before the term 'psychical research' had been invented, is fascinating enough. It is doubly compelling when we realise it was being reported by people whose contemporary theology, like our contemporary science, told them that it was impossible. Shakespeare, through the various characters in *Hamlet*, reflected the different attitudes towards ghosts of his own time, ultimately settling on traditional Catholic theology with his view that Hamlet's father's ghost was a soul needing saving from Purgatory through the intercession of the living.

Experiences of ghosts continued to proliferate in the seventeenth century, and particularly dramatically following the first major conflict of the English Civil War, the Battle of Edgehill on 23 October 1642, as a result of which three thousand dead were left on the battlefield. According to contemporary pamphleteers, a whole series of ghostly replays of the battle seem to have been experienced, along the lines of what had happened after the Greek Battle of Marathon two thousand years earlier.[11] Apparently the opening occurrence, experienced by a group of local shepherds, was 'on Saturday – which was in Christmastime, between 12 and 1 o'clock in the morning', and took the form of 'first, the sound of drums afar off, and the noise of soldiers, as it were giving out their last groans'. Then the ghosts went on to re-enact the battle, during which 'the King's forces seemed at first to have the best, and afterwards they were put into apparent rout'.

Reportedly the experiences were not fleeting, but lasted some three hours, after which those who had shared them 'made with all haste' to nearby Kineton. There they called on the local JP William Wood and to him and the local minister Samuel Marshall swore 'upon their oathes' the truth of the ghostly happenings they described. The next night, which was the Sunday before Christmas, Wood, Marshall and others went out to Edgehill and experienced exactly the same, prompting Marshall to make a special journey to impart the news to King Charles, then staying in Oxford.

Early in 1643 there was issued a further pamphlet, 'The New Yeares Wonder',[12] detailing fresh disturbances around Edgehill. In the middle of the night of 4 January residents were woken in Kineton itself by 'the doleful and hideous groans of dying men'. These were accompanied by the noise of trumpets and drums 'as if an enemy had entered in their town to put them to a sudden execution and plunder all their estates'. Those brave enough to look out of their windows saw 'armed horsemen riding one against the other, and so vanished all'. Some pregnant women were so disturbed that they miscarried.

Senior officers sent by King Charles to investigate, among them Colonel Lewis Kirke and Captains Dudley and Wainman, were said to have experienced the phantom battles, even recognising some of the dying men, including the royal standard-bearer Sir Edmund Verney, who had reportedly fought without armour, having had a premonition that he would die on the battlefield. The best suggestion at the time was that the apparitions might have been due to the fact that the bodies of some who had died in the battle still lay unlocated and unburied. This certainly appears to have been the case, for once these were given proper burial the disturbances seemed to end.[13]

A generation later, at the time of the accession of King William III, similar circumstances seem to have pertained to a ghost reported by the London merchant Sir James Houblon, then in Cork, to the famous diarist Samuel Pepys. According to Houblon the ghost of a man who had been murdered and his body hidden had appeared to an English serving-girl in Cork, and as a result of the ghost showing the girl where to dig for his bones, these were found and the ghost thereafter duly laid.[14] The parallels with the Athenodorus case, the Japanese barber case, and others are all too apparent.

Although it is impossible to apply the same critical standards to such old cases as we would to present-day ones, the key factor is that throughout as many centuries as anyone can remember, and right across the world, ghosts appear to have manifested in the same way, have originated for the same reasons, and have created the same disbelief among those experiencing them – all as if there really is a common substratum of serious truth to the phenomenon.

In first-century China, the naturalist philosopher Wang Ch'ung expressed his puzzlement that ghosts were reported wearing clothes when all reason suggested that even if a man's soul somehow lived on after death, his clothes would surely not become ghosts as well. As Wang Ch'ung expressed it:

If the earthly spirit [ghost] is really the spirit of a dead man, then it ought to be nude . . . because garments have no spirit.[15]

Yet defying all reason, ghosts throughout time, right up to the present day, have been reported as wearing clothes. It is just one of many illogicalities that has to be faced by anyone attempting to come to terms with ghosts.

Similarly, consistently across the world, the prime factor that seems

79

to cause a ghost to manifest is some traumatic form of death, usually accompanied by irregularity relating to burial. In the early 1980s, Dr Charles Emmons, Professor of Sociology at Gettysburg University, conducted a major survey on belief in ghosts in Hong Kong, in which he uncovered what he called 'stunning similarities' to Western beliefs:

> Specifically in Chinese terms the factors most likely to produce a troubled spirit [i.e. a ghost] are death as a young child, death before marriage, suicide or other violent or unpleasant deaths, [and] improper burial.[16]

We have seen the same in our English historical cases. And as my wife and I discovered in the case of the Abercrombie House ghost, even though we did not know what background problem had caused the haunting, the simple offering of a prayer for the repose of that ghost's soul was what seemed so dramatically to halt the haunting.

So if there really is a long and convincing historical and cross-cultural pedigree for the existence of true ghosts – that is, those of the repeatedly haunting variety – just which present-day cases of these should we now be looking at in all seriousness?

CHAPTER SIX

Ghost Stories Needing to Be Taken Seriously

It is one of the ironies of the subject that people so often associate ghosts with historic old houses. In reality, any ghostly goings-on that may have transpired at such old houses usually took place so long ago that any hard information about them has long been forgotten.

The royal palace of Hampton Court, where a regular part of the standard tour is the so-called Haunted Gallery just outside the royal apartments on the first floor, is a classic example. Here tour guides have long entertained visitors with stories of how the ghost of Henry VIII's wife Catherine Howard runs shrieking down the gallery and disappears through a door at the far end. Catherine's ghost is supposedly re-enacting her real-life last-ditch appeal for Henry's mercy, while he was at prayer in the nearby Chapel Royal and she was awaiting the arrest that would lead to her execution.

But quite aside from some historical doubts as to whether this appeal ever happened – for instance, Hampton Court's comptroller Simon Thurley has pointed out that the rooms through which Catherine would have had to pass would have been locked and guarded[1] – I have yet to come across any first-hand description of Catherine Howard's ghost. The story originated in the second half of the last century with a Mrs Cavendish Boyle, who apparently occupied a grace-and-favour apartment near the Haunted Gallery, and whose story is said to have been corroborated by a Lady Eastlake, who often stayed with her. But although according to Peter Underwood Catherine's ghost 're-enacts the grisly event on the night of the anniversary',[2] no one appears to have reported actually seeing this extraordinary happening for at least a century.

Altogether more credible, by contrast, are cases in which hauntings are authoritatively reported in relatively recently built properties. And in which the concern is not so much to stake out the house in the hope of seeing the ghost, but to do whatever is necessary to restore normal order.

One such case concerns a well-respected Bristol architect, who we will call Peter Taylor, who in 1984 was appointed by an international bank to complete the construction of a major new office development where the original developers had gone into receivership. Although unfortunately the precise location, along with the real name of the architect, cannot be given for reasons that will become clear, the crucial information is that it was on the site of a cinema that had been left derelict for some years. As Peter Taylor told me in an interview at his offices:

> When we were brought in we found that the building was 90 per cent complete. But unfortunately it did not comply with the building regulations. Nor did it have a valid planning consent. And many hundreds of thousands of pounds had to be spent in order to get it back in good order.
>
> We appointed a very reputable contractor, but after a few weeks of our involvement their workforce began to complain that strange things were happening. Lifts would go up and down by themselves. Lights would go on and come off. Workmen's tools left in one place at night would be in a different place in the morning, etc.[3]

Initially, Peter blithely dismissed these occurrences as what he called 'typical contractors' excuses for not getting on with the job'. But then the happenings assumed an eerie and mystifying point of focus:

> It became apparent that there was a problem with the third floor ladies' toilet. The building at this time was almost complete. The air conditioning was working. The ceilings were in. Obviously the light-fittings were on. However in this particular area, condensation, i.e. moisture, was flowing down the walls and in this particular toilet there was a nasty smell. We tried to locate this in a sen-

sible manner by taking the whole thing virtually apart. It was not solvable. There was no apparent logical reason for either the moisture or the smell or the feeling of coldness that you had when you went into the room.

Yet for Peter there had to be some logical explanation:

I went back to the office thinking about this and got out the old drawings of the original cinema and plotted on the section plan where the third floor ladies' loo was. It coincided precisely with the projection room.

And, to his astonishment, when he mentioned this to the senior estate agent for the development he was told: 'But that's where the projectionist of the old cinema hung himself back in the 1920s!'

An immensely practical individual, Peter Taylor went back to both sets of plans, carefully overlaying those of the new office block upon those of the old cinema with its projection room. But there could be no mistake. Where the projection room had been was exactly where the inexplicable damp and smells were occurring in the new construction. Bizarre though it seemed, the only logical explanation was that somehow the dead projectionist was reacting adversely to the new development. However, even if this was the case, what could be done about it? Peter Taylor went on:

I informed the client, i.e. the bank, and the agents. They said: 'For God's sake don't tell anybody. We mustn't allow this to get out to the market.' But what the heck could we do?

In no little desperation the Bishop of Bristol, the Rt Revd John Tinsley was consulted, and with his help a special 'laying to rest' ceremony for the projectionist was very quietly and unobtrusively held at the affected location over one weekend. Although Peter Taylor declined to attend, to his astonishment it worked where all else had failed. The terrible smell, the condensation problems, and all the mysterious happenings with the workmen's tools ceased as abruptly and mysteriously as they had begun.

What is so important about this case is that a particular ghostly manifestation happened, the ghost and his apparent problem were identified, specialist help was called for, and the problem was made to go away. In other words, a result was obtained, exactly as was achieved in my experience at Abercrombie House.

Even more spectacular from this point of view is our second case, one that happens to have been first reported in Peter Underwood's autobiography. Although, as in our projectionist case, Underwood felt obliged to cloak some identities with pseudonyms, thankfully in this instance the crucial true identity of the ghost can here be given for the first time.

The location was the pleasant village of Hook, Hampshire, the year 1968, and the setting a modern and spacious four-bedroomed chalet-style house that had been built only five years earlier on the site of what had been an old farmhouse, Hayden's Farm, and its outbuildings. The proud new occupiers of this property were Mrs Barbara McKenzie, her husband Duncan, their three daughters and their three dogs. As recalled by Mrs McKenzie:

We felt it was a good move. The rooms were large for a modern house and the garden big enough for us to have a large kennel and run built for our three dogs to live out-of-doors. The four bed-rooms enabled our three daughters to have a bedroom each. For the first few weeks I was kept pretty busy and the only unhappy occurrence was that one of our dogs, a beautiful two-year-old Sealyham Terrier, suddenly and unaccountably went completely beserk. He had shown no previous signs of temperament and was a beloved pet who had won many prizes, but without warning he bit one of the children badly and I had no option but to have him destroyed. The veterinary surgeon later told me that a post-mortem examination had revealed no physical reason for such an aberration.[4]

Later in this book we will give some consideration to the sensitivity of dogs and other animals towards ghostly phenomena, this being one possible interpretation of the above incident in the light of what follows. Our first concern here, however, is the nature of the ghostly disturbances themselves, occurring as they did in what was a thoroughly modern house. In Barbara McKenzie's words:

> I began to notice strange noises round the house. I knew I was alone in the house at the time so I decided they must be due to the oil-fired central heating system. One evening, however, after the noises had been particularly loud and puzzling, I said to my husband, as casually as I could: 'You know, I think this house is haunted.' He grinned at me, and said, 'Oh, is it?' and went on reading his book.
>
> The noises continued, most often sounding like footsteps coming downstairs. They always occurred in daylight and usually between 10.30 a.m. and 9.00 p.m. but Thursdays somehow seemed to be a favourite day. However the noises were spasmodic and didn't worry me unduly at this stage; I was still convinced that there must be a logical explanation, although the heating system had been examined and I couldn't think what the answer might me.

Already noteworthy here is the daylight occurrence of the ghostly phenomena. As we will discover in a later chapter, this is by no means as rare as might be supposed. But more important for what happens next is that so far Barbara McKenzie and her husband had quite deliberately made no mention to their children of the disturbances – a perfectly understandable precaution. The McKenzies' eldest daughter, however, now returned from boarding school for the Christmas holidays. She had hardly been in the house for more than a few hours before she had so baffling an experience of her own to report that the earlier happenings could no longer be ignored. Barbara McKenzie recalls:

> She came to me in the kitchen with a dead-white face, saying, 'Mummy, something funny is going on here.' . . . This particular daughter has a down-to-earth, practical approach to life, and is certainly unimaginative; so I asked her what funny things were going on. 'I was just about to go upstairs,' she replied, 'when I heard someone coming down, so I stepped back and waited, but no one came . . .' I was trying to think what I could say to her without frightening her any more when she suddenly grabbed my

arm and said: 'But Mummy, the footsteps coming downstairs – they weren't coming down where the stairs are, but behind me!'

This really puzzled me for until then I had never actually thought about where the noises were coming from, but had simply accepted that they were associated with the existing stairs – if not the heating system! The next time I heard the footsteps I ran to the foot of the stairs and listened closely as they approached. Yes, my daughter had been right, the footsteps came from a place and position where there were no stairs; in fact they seemed to come from the doorway leading into the lounge. Another thing I noticed: when people walk down our stairs, three of the treads squeak, but the 'phantom' footsteps didn't cause any creaking at all.

Barbara McKenzie asked one of the villagers who had known the old farmhouse where its staircase had been.

He soon drew a rough plan which we hastened to superimpose on the plan of our existing house, and of course we found that the original stairs had occupied the position of the present door from the hall to the lounge.

Mrs McKenzie has kindly provided me with sketches showing the superimposition of both sets of plans, [figs. 1 and 2] from which it can clearly be seen that the ghostly footsteps derived from where there definitely had been a staircase in the old farmhouse, but where there was no longer one in the present-day property. The sound of the footsteps even extended beyond the boundary of the modern house. Seemingly the ghost was moving in the house as it had existed in his or her own time.

But who could this ghost be? When Barbara McKenzie next met the villager who had drawn her the plan, she asked him directly, on her own admission 'very much with tongue in my cheek', if he knew whether the farm had been haunted.

He laughed. 'Never,' he said. 'Although of course young Robin did shoot himself there . . .' I was full of questions: who was young Robin? When did he kill himself? And why? But all the answers I

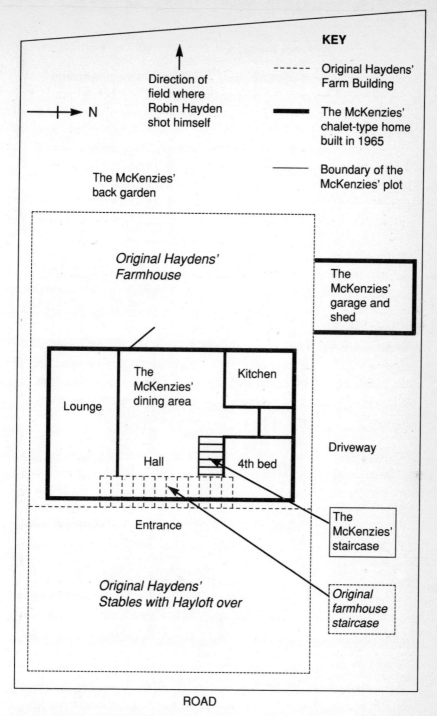

KEY

------ Original Haydens' Farm Building

▬▬▬ The McKenzies' chalet-type home built in 1965

─── Boundary of the McKenzies' plot

N

Direction of field where Robin Hayden shot himself

The McKenzies' back garden

Original Haydens' Farmhouse

The McKenzies' garage and shed

Lounge

The McKenzies' dining area

Kitchen

Hall

4th bed

Driveway

The McKenzies' staircase

Original farmhouse staircase

Entrance

Original Haydens' Stables with Hayloft over

ROAD

Fig. 1 Approximate Ground Plan of the Original Haydens' Farmhouse (shown dashed rule), Hook, Hampshire, with the McKenzies' chalet-type house, built in 1965, superimposed over. For detail of the McKenzies' upper floor, with path of the ghostly footsteps, also the disparity between the Hayden and McKenzie staircases, see next page. *From rough plan supplied by courtesy of Duncan and Barbara Mckenzie.*

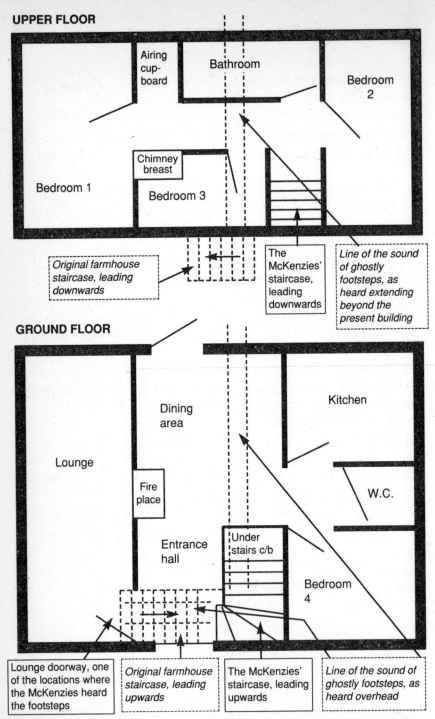

UPPER FLOOR

Airing cup-board

Bathroom

Bedroom 2

Bedroom 1

Chimney breast

Bedroom 3

Original farmhouse staircase, leading downwards

The McKenzies' staircase, leading downwards

Line of the sound of ghostly footsteps, as heard extending beyond the present building

GROUND FLOOR

Dining area

Kitchen

Lounge

Fire place

W.C.

Entrance hall

Under stairs c/b

Bedroom 4

Lounge doorway, one of the locations where the McKenzies heard the footsteps

Original farmhouse staircase, leading upwards

The McKenzies' staircase, leading upwards

Line of the sound of ghostly footsteps, as heard overhead

Fig. 2 **Approximate Plan of the Upper and Ground Floors of the McKenzies' house,** showing location of the original farmhouse staircase (dashed rule) and the track of the ghostly footsteps. Note that because the McKenzies' home was designed chalet-style, the upper area is smaller than the ground floor and set centrally over the latter. *From rough plan supplied by courtesy of Duncan and Barbara McKenzie.*

could get were that he was the farmer's son and it had happened in the 1920s . . .

With unanswered questions buzzing in her head Barbara McKenzie was frustrated to find the ghostly phenomena now actually intensifying:

Two days after Christmas the noisiest period we had known began. Even my husband, who had been sceptical up to this point (even though he had heard the footsteps), then became convinced that it wasn't mere imagination. We had guests and they too heard 'him' not only coming downstairs, but also pacing to and fro upstairs, and they said they sometimes heard the sound of two shots, one immediately after the other. We had been hearing these for months but had thought someone was rabbit shooting; on reflection we realised that these shots were always heard several minutes after the sound of the footsteps.

Although Mrs McKenzie on her own admission experienced only sounds, and never actually saw anything ghostly, this was not the case with everyone who was at her house that Christmas. Her mother-in-law:

said that she saw a young man 'in Teddy-boy's clothes' in the kitchen while I was there; and one of the children once called me to see a floating white light 'like the shape of the high-speed flame on the TV commercial' but I saw neither of these things.

Even so, the persistence and sheer noisiness of the ghostly sounds alone were more than enough to drive her to distraction. As she recollected:

One Thursday at the end of January I had been out most of the morning and when I returned home about 2 o'clock I heard such heavy, stamping footsteps above my head that for the first time I really became frightened. I telephoned a friend, a sensible, level-headed doctor, and even over the telephone she could hear the stamping, so I knew it wasn't my imagination running away with me.

* * *

At her doctor friend's urging, Barbara McKenzie now sought outside help, receiving the soundest advice from a local author, Alasdair Alpin MacGregor, whom she knew to have a special interest in psychical matters. His recommendation was that she try to find out more about the young man called Robin who had shot himself.

In fact, on leaving MacGregor's house, Mrs McKenzie happened to meet up with an elderly villager called Rose who remembered Robin very well, not least because she had attended the village school with him. He had been the son of Fred Hayden, the farmer whose house had stood on the site of the McKenzies' home. Rose's strongest recollection of Robin was that although he was a most gentle individual, he had, in her words 'the biggest feet I've ever seen. When he was eight he had larger feet than most men.' Indeed, it was her impression that the teasing Robin had received from other children about his feet might well have contributed to his suicide.

For Barbara McKenzie this information was in itself quite fascinating enough, given that the haunting involved heavy footsteps, as of someone with big feet and wearing farm boots. But adhering to the advice she had been given by Alasdair MacGregor, she pursued her inquiries into Robin and his death by looking at back copies of the local newspaper, the *Hants and Berks Gazette*.

She soon discovered that Robin's death had not been in the 1920s, as the villager had supposed, but instead on 27 December 1912 – causing her to recall that the ghostly activity had been at its most intense two days after Christmas Day 1968. She also remembered her visitor's sighting of a young man 'in Teddy-boy's clothes', just the sort of fashion that would have been prevalent around 1912.

But it was the personal details of the tragedy, as reported in the *Gazette* of 4 January 1913, that she found most illuminating, as well as deeply touching. Under the headline 'Young Man's Suicide' she read:

It is with the deepest regret we have to chronicle the tragic death of Robin Ernest Hayden, the second son of Mr F. Hayden, farmer and contractor, of Hook, who on the morning of Friday, December 27, was found dead in a field called Stable Close, adjoining Sheldon Lane, with a revolver at his side. Following immediately after the

Christmas festivities the sad news cast quite a gloom over the whole neighbourhood. The deceased, who was eighteen years of age, was always of a bright and happy disposition. He was well known in the village and had made a great many friends, and it seemed impossible to believe that the news could be true. He had been in his usual health with the exception of a slight influenza cold, and although he seemed a little depressed there was nothing to cause any suspicion that he was in any way troubled or worried . . . He retired to bed as usual on Thursday the 26th about 10.50 and rose again the next morning just after five o'clock with his brother Charles, who last saw him alive. About 10.30 on the morning of the 27th Mr Walter Wearing, baker, was coming down Sheldon's Lane when he saw a body lying in the field adjoining the lane. He proceeded to the spot, and found it to be that of Robin Hayden. He at once informed the deceased's parents and Mr Charles F. Hayden identified the body as that of his brother. Dr Davison, of Odiham, was telephoned for, and PC Phillips arrived in a few minutes. The doctor examined the body and found a wound over the right eye. The constable ordered a conveyance and the body was taken to the parents' home.

A formal inquest into Robin Hayden's death was held the following day at the local public house, the White Hart, presided over by the coroner, Spencer Clarke. This established that although the revolver found next to Robin's body had five chambers, only one of these had been discharged to fire the fatal shot. On reading this, Barbara McKenzie recalled the two distinct shots, one immediately after the other, that she and others had heard. Could these have been both the original shot and its echo?

The *Gazette*'s report continued:

PC Phillips said he searched the deceased and found on him several notes which were handed to the coroner, and the father Mr F. Hayden identified the writing as that of his son. In these notes the deceased expressed his intention to end his troubles and wished his parents, brother and sisters goodbye.

* * *

Barbara McKenzie's next quest was to look up the original files from Robin Hayden's inquest. From these she learned that Rose's impression that Robin's suicide might have been because of teasing about his big feet was mistaken. As the suicide notes revealed, Robin had fallen in love with the daughter of the landlord of the old White Hart pub. He knew his family would be against this, as the Haydens' employers, the wealthy Burberry family of the raincoat empire, were extremely puritanical and his father and mother had gone along with this, to the extent of milking cows before midnight on a Saturday night in order not to work on a Sunday. Robin had therefore seen no other recourse than to take his own life.

For Barbara McKenzie no further explanation was needed for the alarming ghostly footsteps. However, her whole attitude to what had been happening was now imperceptibly changed. Instead of feeling that she was the victim of a ghost, with all the concomitant fear and uncertainty that that word conveys, Barbara had come to realise that what had been disturbing her home was a real person, an individual who had provided her with sufficient clues to establish who he was and that he needed help. In her words:

Instead of an annoying and embarrassing ghost, he [Robin Hayden] had now become to us a soul who could not rest, and I felt we had to do something about it.

So do something the McKenzies did. Although they were active Anglicans their own rector proved none too sympathetic or helpful. Indeed, when Barbara told him she thought she had a ghost he bluntly suggested that she should 'take more water with it'. However, she persisted in trying to find someone prepared to help lay Robin to rest, and was eventually put in touch with the then Rural Dean of Farnborough, the Revd Ben Hutchinson. Hutchinson visited the house 'in civvies' one Saturday afternoon, and, in Barbara's words:

we all said prayers in every room of the house, commending the soul of Robin to rest; and believe it or not, we have had no noises, no walking downstairs sounds, no gunshots, no stampings from that day to this.

92

* * *

For anyone brought up on horror films Barbara McKenzie's experience might not seem very special. After all, the phenomena were almost entirely auditory rather than visual. Even Peter Underwood seems to have had little interest in the case, for although he published Barbara's account verbatim, with Robin Hayden's true identity disguised under the pseudonym 'Chris', he gave the matter no serious investigative follow-up. Perhaps he felt that because Robin Hayden's ghost had been persuaded to stop haunting, it could be of no further interest to him or his Ghost Club.

For us, however, the case is different, for two important reasons. The first is precisely because we *do* know Robin Hayden's identity. Whereas so many hauntings consist of, if anything, a phantom who remains notoriously elusive, in Robin Hayden we confront a ghost who, though he may have expressed himself only by sounds, emerges as a *person* with whose plight we can identify. Indeed, if we accept that everything happened the way Barbara McKenzie described it – and as we know, the case has a plethora of corroborative witnesses – then from the very fact that we are aware of Robin's identity and the circumstances surrounding his death, we are almost automatically forced to accept that ghosts genuinely do exist. The really interesting questions then become what ghosts are, and why they are.

The second reason that this particular case is significant is that when something was done to try to help Robin Hayden – i.e. the Revd Hutchinson's ceremony of 'laying to rest' – *a result was achieved*, that is, the haunting was made to stop, firmly and decisively. As in the cases described earlier, this point is of paramount importance, for the unavoidable implication is that for such a result to be achieved these ghostly manifestations cannot have been mere empty 'recording tracks', as some have supposed ghosts to be. There have to have been real people behind them, people genuinely released from the site of their haunts: the projectionist in his projection room, Robin Hayden on his father's farm, etc. If we can begin to accept this, then whatever views we may have held about life and death suddenly need to be taken that bit more seriously.

Clearly, the Robin Hayden type of ghost is one that will be at the forefront of our further inquiries. It offers the potential to open up a

93

host of key questions about why ghosts may take some of the forms they do, and, not least, why people become ghosts at all. But before we consider some of these questions, is there any other approach to the phenomenon of ghosts that might help us understand a little more clearly exactly what it is that we might be dealing with?

CHAPTER SEVEN

Ghosts Difficult to Deny

No one should underestimate how difficult it is to accept that ghosts might exist. Not least of the problems involves trying to equate ghosts with the highly materialistic attitudes of our present-day theories of what we are. Typifying these is a book widely used in British schools, *How Your Body Works*, in which the 'I' in charge of our bodies is represented as a high-powered executive sitting in an office on the top floor of the brain, manning a desk crammed with phones, computer terminals, etc. According to this model the real 'I' is a little someone who sits contained inside our brain space, the implication being that when the phone lines from the body downstairs stop ringing at the time of death, our little executive simply goes out of business, and that's the end of him.

As we have already seen from the examples of poltergeist phenomena, there do seem to be instances of individuals even in life who can affect objects at some distance from themselves. This is one of our first indications that the containerised super-executive model may not be quite right. Furthermore, since such object-moving is not done consciously, it would appear that it is not the conscious 'I' sitting up in the brain space who is responsible, but instead perhaps some form of second self, operating at the level of our unconscious minds, and which can move beyond our bodies.

Immediately, of course, we are into scientific heresy – not least because decades ago twentieth-century psychology decided that the unconscious mind was too nebulous to be considered a proper subject of study. Traditional religious belief all over the world, however, is firmly on the side of the non-containerised rather than the containerised model, holding that there is a second self which is of the whole body, not just the brain, which even in life can in certain circumstances travel outside the body, and which survives death. The ancient Egyptians believed in such a second and even third self with their concepts of the *ba* and the *ka*. But even in our own time there have been too many instances of people experiencing being able to move beyond their bodies for the idea not to be taken with some seriousness.

One example which has long impressed me is an account by the German cancer specialist Dr Josef Issels of what he was told by a woman dying of cancer at his famous Ringberg Clinic in Bavaria:

One day I experienced a remarkable happening. I was doing my morning round on Ward One, the ward reserved for the acutely ill. I went into the room of an elderly woman patient close to death. She looked at me and said: 'Doctor, do you know that I can leave my body?' I knew approaching death often produced the most unusual phenomena. 'I will give you proof,' said the woman. 'Here and now.' There was a moment's silence, then she spoke again: 'Doctor, if you go to Room 12, you will find a woman writing a letter to her husband. She has just completed the first page. I've just seen her do it.' She went on to describe in minute detail what she had just 'seen'. I hurried to Room 12, at the end of the ward. The scene inside was exactly the same as the woman had described it, even down to the contents of the letter. I went back to the elderly woman to seek an explanation. In the time I had gone she had died. It was the first, though not the last, time I experienced unusual happenings with seriously ill patients.[1]

People who clinically 'die' and are then resuscitated often report similar 'near-death experiences', the striking feature of which is the apparent separateness of the physical body from a second self, a self that seems to embody the real 'I' and which moves around invisible to those still in the land of the living. One of the earliest authoritatively reported cases of a near-death experience is that of Dr A. S. Wiltse of Skiddy, Kansas, who 'died' of typhoid fever in the summer of 1889. He recalled:

> I . . . discovered that I was still in my body, but the body and I no longer had any interests in common. I looked in astonishment and joy for the first time upon myself . . . with all the interest of a physician . . . I watched the interesting process of separation of soul and body.[2]

In the manner that ghosts are reported passing through walls and people, so Wiltse discovered that he seemed able to do the same. He recalled, for instance, seeing a man standing by the door of the room where he had just 'died':

> To my surprise his arm passed through mine without apparent resistance . . . I looked quickly up to see if he had noticed the contact but he gave me no sign . . . I know I attempted to gain the attention of the people with the object of comforting them . . . I passed about among them . . . but found that they gave me no heed.

Similar feelings were reported by a saleswoman from North Florida who in July 1964, when aged only nineteen, was struck and nearly killed by a car as she was hurrying across a pedestrian crossing. As she recalled to the American cardiologist Dr Michael Sabom, who has made a special study of near-death experiences, immediately after the moment of impact she found herself viewing the accident scene as if separate from her physical body and feeling 'emotionally detached from the whole situation'. She went on:

> I remember seeing the car being dented. And I saw my body. My attention was called to my body when the attendants put it on the stretcher . . . I saw myself in profile . . . I was viewing my body as they picked it up and put it on the stretcher. It was from a distance away, actually.[3]

Intriguingly, this particular woman found that after her recovery from the accident she seemed to retain the apparent ability to leave her body at will.

* * *

This would occur at night and I would simply get out of it and see it lying in bed. My husband was working for the forest service and was gone at night. But it seems like I could just get out of my body and see it lying there and go check on everything. We were living in a house trailer at the time. The first time it happened, it was just a matter of weeks after my accident . . . It was a spontaneous thing. I was very concerned because I was hearing noises . . . it was late at night . . . I left my body . . . I just walked back and forth within the trailer looking out the windows and everything to make sure everything was all right . . . I routinely started doing this to check on things. The next time it happened I realised I was unlimited . . . I went down the street and came back . . . It was just a deserted neighbourhood at night . . . [but] it scared me to leave the body unattended there [in the trailer].

Quite independently, a woman whose case came to the attention of out-of-body experiences researcher Robert Crookall described a hospital ward experience strikingly like that of Dr Issels' cancer patient, except that she lived to tell the tale. Lying ill in a hospital bed she reportedly felt something detach from her and travel to the middle of the ward, whereupon:

there it seemed to unravel itself into another version of me. I looked down at my body. I thought I was dead. I went into the corridor and saw my husband. I wondered where my daughter was, and the next instant I was standing beside her in a gift shop. She was looking at some 'Get Well' cards. I could 'hear' her read the verse. She decided it would be disrespectful and bought another. Then I was back in my body. When my daughter came with the card, I repeated the verse she had read.[4]

While the floating double or second self of the people who have these experiences seems in a variety of ways to behave like a ghost, it is important to note that unlike true ghosts they are not seen by the living. Also they appear able to move around more freely than the sort of place-bound ghosts that we have come across. Notable in this regard is how the Florida saleswoman described herself as feeling 'emotionally detached' from her real surroundings and her physical body, something that would not seem to be the case with the true ghost.

Cases of this kind at least give some credibility to the idea that we might have some form of second self that could in certain circumstances become a ghost. One step further than this is a whole branch of medicine in which ghosts are recognised as existing by patients and doctors alike, even though rationalising them is altogether more difficult. This area concerns the many thousands of people who have had limbs and other parts of their bodies amputated, and who continue to feel the parts they have lost, even though all reason tells them they are no longer there. One famous example of this was Horatio Nelson, who had his arm shot away during a land engagement in 1797, and who specifically described the sensations he continued to have of the lost limb as proof of the existence of the soul.

This might be rationalised away as just the nerve endings continuing to send messages from the original limb to the brain, though, as has been argued by the biologist Dr Rupert Sheldrake,[5] the 'ghost limbs' phenomenon does seem rather more complex and interesting than this.

First, from the study of hundreds of thousands of people who have suffered amputations it would seem that nearly all of them experience the sensation of the limb's 'ghost' – trying to scratch a foot that is no longer there, or reaching out to answer the telephone with a missing arm. And although time eventually lessens the physical pain of the amputation, all too often the feeling that the limb is still there continues. As Sheldrake was told by a Mr Herman Berg, who had a leg amputated in 1970:

> I can always feel the missing leg as being there. At first it seemed to hang through the bed or stick straight up. That's stopped, but it's always there . . . Right now as I scribble this I'm sitting at my desk in my shorts and the missing limb is where it should be over the chair in position, and the toes have some feeling too.[6]

Likewise American Leo Unger, a World War II veteran who in November 1944 had both his legs amputated below the knees after he trod on a landmine, wrote:

* * *

From the very first day I have always had the feeling that my legs and feet were still in place. Early on I had severe phantom pains that felt like balls of fire going down my limbs and off my toes. After twenty years I seldom got that feeling, but I do often feel the bones in my feet were just broken, just as they were when I was wounded.

Such ghost limbs can reportedly be made by their owners to pass through solid objects like doors and walls. According to some pet-owning amputees, their animals can be sensitive to them. George Barcus of Toccoa, Georgia, told Rupert Sheldrake that his pet dog 'will not enter the area of my missing leg. She refuses to lay in the space vacated by the leg.'[7]

And just as a ghost seems to be frozen in a moment of trauma, so amputated body parts may feel as if fixed as they were at the moment of their loss. A *British Medical Journal* report has described the case of a sailor who accidentally cut off his right index finger; for decades afterwards he claimed to feel the finger rigidly extended just as it was when it was severed. When, for example, he moved his hand towards his face in the course of eating, he felt he was in danger of poking his eye out, even though all reason told him this was impossible.

One even weirder aspect of ghost limbs is a belief among amputees that whatever has happened to the severed part may continue to haunt the person to whom it once belonged. Following a survey of nearly two hundred amputees carried out in the 1880s, the American psychologist William James reported this conviction as 'very widespread'. It has continued into the present day.

American William Craddock, one of those who responded to Rupert Sheldrake's appeal for experiences regarding amputated limbs, wrote of his father, who worked as a maintenance man at a hospital in Jacksonville, Illinois:

In the 1940s I used to stop at the boiler-house on my way home from school. One day my father had something wrapped in cloth on the workbench and he tried to hide it as I came in. I could see the cloth had blood on it, and when I asked my father what it was he said never mind. He later told me it was an amputated limb and he had just wrapped it to make sure nothing was bent in an unnatural way. He told me he knew a man who was suffering great pain with an amputated arm and they finally dug it up and straightened his fingers. His pain left.[8]

In another story reported to Sheldrake, a man had his finger amputated and preserved in a jar:

The man was OK for several years. Then he went back to his doctor, who had amputated his finger, complaining of a feeling of extreme cold in the missing finger. The doctor wanted to know where the jar with the missing finger in it was. The man told him it was in his mother's heated basement where it had always been. The doctor told the man to call his mother and check the jar. The mother didn't want to but found a broken basement window a few inches from the jar. As soon as the finger was warmed up the pain left.

In 1970 the American psychiatrists Frazier and Kolb reported the case of a fourteen-year-old boy who had had his leg amputated and the limb incinerated. He was subsequently deeply troubled with continuing burning pains to his ghost leg. The psychiatrists discovered that a year earlier, the boy had attended a lesson in which the teacher had told a story of a man suffering from unbearable stinging pains in his ghost leg. When the leg was unearthed from where it had been buried ants were found to be burrowing into it, and when they were removed and the leg reburied, the stinging pains ceased. Rightly or wrongly, the boy blamed the incineration of his leg for the burning pains he was experiencing.[9]

If we are prepared to accept at least some legitimacy to these cases – and as Dr Sheldrake has insisted, the phenomena reported lend themselves to, and merit, proper research – what we appear to be glimpsing is something very interesting indeed: namely that that which once belonged to the body may somehow be able to remain in touch with it in a way that might legitimately be described as haunting.

The same principle might well lie behind the 'sympathetic magic' used in witchcraft: obtain a lock of hair or a fingernail clipping from the object of the magic and that detached and seemingly now inanimate object can become a vehicle for harming the whole person. Sheldrake recalled:

> I first encountered this way of thinking when I was living in Malaysia. One day I was staying in a Malay village, a *kampong*, I was cutting my nails, throwing the parings into a nearby bush. When my hosts saw this, they were horrified. They explained that an enemy might pick them up and use them to harm me by witchcraft. They were amazed that I did not know that bad things done to my nail clippings could cause bad things to happen to me.[10]

If we are prepared to accept this magic, perhaps we can begin to understand why ghosts are consistently reported wearing clothes. It is possible that in whatever dimension we may be dealing with, the garments and other belongings that they had in life continue to be as much a part of them as their arms and legs.

Whatever significance there may be in these ideas, we cannot even begin to understand them properly in terms of some overall theory. But the undeniable fact of ghost limbs, and the phenomenon's striking parallels with ghosts as they are conventionally understood, surely serve to make at least a little more credible and worthy of serious study the contention that there really is *something* out there that people call ghosts. If we are prepared to accept this, then we are ready to proceed to the next stage of our odyssey. That is, that if ghosts exist, what can we determine, from everything reported of them, of *what* they are?

Part II

In Search Of What Ghosts Might Be

'Ghosts now – well they are just people who have died and bound themselves, because of great happiness or great tragedy, to a spot on earth.'

Tom Corbett

CHAPTER EIGHT

Ghosts and the Senses

If we are prepared to accept that some people genuinely experience ghosts, it is important, from the point of view of trying to understand what they are, to consider carefully how they perceive them. All too often, for instance, a ghost is assumed to be the same as an apparition – that is, something which appears, or makes itself visible – when in many cases the experience is entirely auditory.

Even some of the more scientific psychical researchers have produced misleading statistics by too glibly assuming that most ghosts are visual. For instance, Celia Green and Charles McCreery of Oxford's Institute of Psychophysical Research have maintained that 84 per cent of the ghost experiences reported to them involved a sighting,[1] the problem being that since their publicised appeal for cases specified that they were looking for apparitions, they received what was almost certainly a disproportionate number of visual cases, even though they added that they were looking for experiences 'involving any of the senses'. In a survey of one hundred examples collected among Icelanders by the Iceland University researcher Dr Erlendur Haraldsson, only 42 per cent of the cases were visual, and this may be nearer to the true proportion.

Sight, by general agreement, is the most powerful of our senses, as a result of which those cases involving the *seeing* of a ghost are inevitably of the greatest interest. And *how* ghosts are seen can be as important as what is seen. Even a hundred years ago, Mrs Eleanor Sidgwick of the recently founded Society for Psychical Research, from an analysis of more than three hundred available case histories, shrewdly observed of visually experienced ghosts:

> The ghost is usually either seen on looking round, as a human being might be, or seen to come in at the door. Sometimes it forms gradually out of what at first seems a cloud-like appearance. I do not think there are any cases of its appearing suddenly in a spot which the percipient was actually looking at and perceived to be vacant before. It disappears suddenly in this way sometimes, and sometimes if the percipient looks away for a moment it is gone. Sometimes it vanishes in a cloud-like manner, sometimes, retaining its form, it becomes gradually more and more transparent till it is gone. Frequently it disappears through the door, either with or without apparently opening it, or goes into a room where there is no other exit, and where it is not found.[2]

A particularly good example of a ghost being seen upon the percipient looking round is one which appeared on 8 March 1994 to a night-porter at the exclusive Naval and Military Club in Piccadilly, London. Although the porter, fifty-two-year-old Trevor Newton, was the only witness and so far the apparition has only appeared once, the sighting is in all other respects very well attested. According to Newton, described by his colleagues as 'a very steady man', he was standing at the fireplace in the Egremont Room, on the club's second floor, operating the punch-card timing mechanism which is used to prove that he actually makes his rounds (from this we know that the sighting was at exactly 3.07 a.m.). As he turned round:

> It was then I saw it. About six foot tall. White hair swept back, brown coat. I can't recollect any face whatsoever. I moved over toward the wall. I froze for a second. Then I got out of there – quick, to be honest. It was all over in a matter of seconds.[3]

The figure was clearly male, and from Newton's description of his height, his hair, and particularly the fact that his coat was an ankle-length First World War trenchcoat, retired steward Peter Brabbs, who worked for the club for fifty years, has confidently identified the ghost as deceased

Naval and Military member Major William 'Perky' Braddell [pl.11].
After distinguished service with the Royal Dublin Fusiliers during the
First World War Major Braddell was transferred to the Northumberland
Fusiliers, and then seconded to the Royal Artillery as an anti-aircraft
battery commander during World War II. One night, while he was dining
at the club, it was hit by a German bomb at a moment when he had been
called away to take a telephone call. When he returned to his table it
was to find his two dinner companions dead in the rubble. He himself
had only a few days more to live, for on the night of 19 May he was
killed when the Kensington anti-aircraft battery he was commanding
received a direct hit.

It is particularly significant that Trevor Newton described the figure
he saw as '. . . very solid indeed. I could not see through it in any way
whatsoever'.[4] He has also remarked on the subject of ghosts in general:

> If anyone had said to me there's such a thing – never, no way
> would I have believed it. But I know what I saw . . .

From across the Atlantic comes a similar sighting of a ghost by Mrs
Coleen Buterbaugh, a very level-headed secretary at the Nebraska
Wesleyan University, Lincoln, Nebraska. On the morning of 3 October
1963 Mrs Buterbaugh was taking a message from her boss, Dean Sam
Dahl, to a professor whose office was in the nearby C. C. White Building.
She reached this building at about 8.50 a.m., and after walking through
its hall entered the professor's suite. At first everything seemed quite
normal until, in Mrs Buterbaugh's words:

> Something drew my eyes to the cabinet along the wall in the next
> room. I looked up and there she [the ghost] was.

Note the similarity of the latter phrase to Trevor Newton's account of
how he first saw Major Braddell; also to the descriptions of those
reporting passing caller ghosts, as discussed in Chapter 4. Mrs
Buterbaugh continued:

> She had her back to me, reaching up into one of the shelves of the
> cabinet with her right hand, and standing perfectly still. She wasn't

at all aware of my presence. While I was watching her she never moved. She was not transparent and yet I knew she wasn't real. While I was looking at her she just faded away – not parts of her body one at a time, but her whole body all at once.[5]

Like Trevor Newton, Mrs Buterbaugh was able to give a clear and convincing-sounding description of the figure she had seen. The woman was very tall, probably six feet to Mrs Buterbaugh's own diminutive five. The cabinet she was reaching into was an old music one with high shelves, and whatever she was looking for was on one of the topmost shelves, way beyond Mrs Buterbaugh's own reach. She had a 'bushy bouffant' hairstyle, the sort that was fashionable around the time of the First World War. Again consistent with this period she was wearing a long-sleeved white blouse and a long dark brown or black skirt reaching to her ankles.

Like Major Braddell, this ghost also proved identifiable. From inquiries made among older members of staff, Mrs Buterbaugh's description seemed to correspond with a spinster music teacher, Clarissa Mills, who worked at the university between 1912 and her death in 1936. In a photograph of Miss Mills in an old yearbook she was wearing a bouffant hairstyle. An elderly member of the university who had known Miss Mills remembered her as tall, thin and black-haired, with music and choral group singing as her main passions. Significantly, the filing cabinet which Mrs Buterbaugh saw Miss Mills reaching into contained choral group arrangements dating mostly from Miss Mills's time at the university.

Another very solid-looking ghost was one experienced by Lady Carson, widow of the Ulster leader Lord Edward Carson, at a house she and her husband had purchased in 1920, the ten-bedroom Cleve Court, near Minster, Kent, part of which dates back to Elizabethan times.[6] In December 1949, when she was sixty-eight, Lady Carson was sleeping in an upstairs bedroom when she was woken at 1.30 a.m. by her spaniel, Susan, apparently wanting to be let out for a canine call of nature. Going out on to the landing, she switched on the light, but while descending the stairs with the spaniel she happened accidentally to brush a switch, plunging her back into darkness.

As she turned the lights on again, the spaniel ran whimpering back up the stairs, and Lady Carson suddenly became aware of a youngish-looking woman coming down from the room she herself had just left. The woman was wearing a full-length grey skirt, a shoulder-cape, and a white lace head-covering. Instinctively, Lady Carson first assumed her to be an intruder, only to realise that no sound was accompanying her movements. The woman who, according to Lady Carson, walked rather than floated, quickly disappeared into the Elizabethan part of the house. Lady Carson remarked of this 'Grey Lady': 'I thought that ghosts were transparent but this one looked quite material in every way.'

The same ghost had been experienced by different people over several decades, including a former maid at Cleve Court who described seeing her in 1905. Her likeliest identity is the wife of a notorious rake, Josias Fuller Farrer, who in 1762, having inherited a considerable fortune, turned Cleve Court 'into a scene of riot and extravagance almost incredible'. According to local legend Farrer's wife was often kept locked up – a story substantiated at least a little by a strange, old-fashioned bolt fitted on the outside of one of the house's rooms.

It is worth noting the contrast between the solidity of all these ghosts just described, and the transparency of the purported ghosts we saw earlier featured in ghost photographs – arguably further weakening the latter's remaining credibility. At the same time, however, one other point repeatedly remarked on by percipients, even in the case of well-observed ghosts, is an apparent lack of definition to the facial features.

In the case of the 'Grey Lady' Lady Carson simply described her face as 'averted' while Clarissa Mills seems to have been facing away from Mrs Buterbaugh. But Trevor Newton, it may be recalled, remarked quite spontaneously of Major Braddell: 'I can't recollect any face whatsoever.' In the case of the little boy seen three times in the Cardiff 'Pete the Polt' case (see pp. 54–5), Fred Cook reported being able to see just an oval shape but no face under the boy's school cap. Similarly Brian Nisbet, a conscientious investigator for the Society for Psychical Research, quoted a father who in November 1975 reported how his four-year-old daughter had been disturbed by the ghost of a woman in a full-length white dress:

No features were visible. All I saw above the collar of the dress was a light brown, almost gingerish, blur that didn't seem to have a solid substance. It was as if I could see into it but not through it.[7]

This is all the more surprising given that this particular figure was seen by the father for about five seconds at 9 p.m. fully illuminated by a hundred-watt lamp on the landing of his house. And in marked contrast to the indistinctness of the woman's facial features, the stitching on her dress, which was embroidered with small blue and red flowers, was apparently exceptionally clear:

> With regard to the stitches being so plain in the flowers on the dress – it was a detail that stood out most clearly, and although I can't give a reason for it, my concentration upon this was that they seemed so bright and the colours so intense.[8]

A similar description was given to me by a Mrs Joan Morris of a ghost she saw not long after she and her husband had acquired an old house in the village of Wye, near Ashford, Kent. In the spring of 1985 Mrs Morris was sewing under a light at one end of the long sitting room when she looked up – again a classic way in which ghosts are seen according to Eleanor Sidgwick – and there was a girl standing at the other end of the room, dressed in a mob cap and a tight-waisted garment, looking quite solid and lingering for several minutes, yet with no face distinguishable. As Mrs Morris later discovered, the same mob-capped ghost had previously been seen and sketched [pl. 12] by a Miss Cox, of the Cox's apple family, while living at the house back in 1948.

Another common factor linking Major Braddell, Clarissa Mills, the Grey Lady and the Mob Cap Girl is the soundlessness of each. This may seem fairly consistent with how ghosts are imagined, yet as we have already seen, ghosts can not only be noisy, they can also, not uncommonly, be sensed only as sounds, among the commonest of which, as in the Robin Hayden case, are footsteps. These were a major feature of one case reported to British psychical researcher Andrew MacKenzie by a Devon schoolmaster, Eric Williamson.

In the late 1960s Williamson worked as a teacher at a boys' school in south Devon, where his classroom was on the first floor of the school's two-hundred-year-old Warden's House. His first indication of something odd simply took the form of light knocks on his door. When he opened the door in answer to the tapping there would be no one there. Occurring on premises frequented by schoolboys this could of course simply have been due to resourceful pranksters. But altogether more difficult to explain were footsteps occurring around midday, when the boys were all at lunch in a separate building. These footsteps, seemingly of someone ascending the stairs, Williamson would hear as he worked alone in the classroom preparing the afternoon's lessons. Stopping just outside his door, little more than inches from him, they:

> bore no resemblance to the clod-hopping of lively boys; indeed I would say they were slow and measured and gave no impression of urgency. From the sound I would say that the foot-wear was of leather and would be heel-less: there was never any click as would come from a built-up heel. Each foot seemed to be placed carefully upon each stairtread and on the boarded landing, and in moving each foot sounded as if it were sliding along. I would sit in my room and wait for the steps to progress up to my door, where they stopped. Then there would be a slight pause and then a very light 'knock, knock, knock,' on the middle panel and nothing more.[9]

That this was neither imagination on Williamson's part nor the undetected work of schoolboy pranksters was recently reinforced by a visit to the Warden's House by Andrew MacKenzie. The school has been closed down for some years, and when MacKenzie made his unannounced call he found that the Warden's House is now a private residence. A young woman opened the door to him, and after MacKenzie explained that he had written about ghostly knockings and footsteps at the house thirty years previously, he asked her if she or others had experienced anything similar. She responded:

> 'Not knockings, but the rest, yes . . . Come in.'
> She led me down a corridor into a room where there were two young men. It was sparsely furnished. Indeed, there was a general feeling of desolation. Then they told their story. From where they had their rooms on the floor above, where the classrooms had been, they had heard the sound of soft footsteps on the stairs and loud bangs below. When they investigated, no one was ever there.

Visitors who had heard the footsteps and the noises had asked them to check if anyone was there but their inevitable reply was that there was no point in this as checking on the noises produced no result.[10]

MacKenzie learned that no one had informed these latest occupants that the house had any reputation for being haunted. He was also aware that they could not have known about the occurrences from reading his book, since in it he had deliberately omitted the location.

From his research, together with that of Eric Williamson, MacKenzie had discovered that the school had been built on the site of a monastic college founded in 1335 by the notable Bishop of Exeter, John Grandison (1292?–1369). Were the footsteps those of one of the college's long-deceased monks? The carefully measured tread heard by Williamson strongly suggested this to be the case.

Ghostly sounds attributed to medieval monks, this time in the form of chanting, have also been reliably reported at Beaulieu Abbey in Hampshire, now part of the estates of Lord Montagu. Beaulieu was one of the many monastic establishments closed at the time of Henry VIII's Dissolution of the Monasteries, and Michael Sedgwick, a curator of Lord Montagu's famous motor museum, is among several who believe they have heard the long-departed monks' chanting. Just before Christmas 1959 Sedgwick was smoking and typing late at night in his cottage on the east side of the abbey's now ruined former church, and had just opened the window to clear the air of tobacco smoke when, in his words:

I heard it quite distinctly. It was definitely chanting, and very beautiful chanting. It came in uneven waves, as if from a faulty wireless – sometimes quite loud and then fading away. It was just as if a Catholic Mass was being played on the radio in the next flat, but I thought it was curious that someone should have the radio on at that time of night. Anyway it was so beautiful that I tried to find it on my own wireless. I tell you, I went through every blessed programme there was – French, Italian, everything – and I couldn't find it. Later I was told it was just a common or garden supernatural phenomenon.[11]

* * *

Sedgwick heard the chanting again another night when he was working late. So did the wife of film director Fred Zimmerman during the filming at the house of *A Man For All Seasons*. And Lord Montagu's half-sister Miss Elizabeth Montagu, now the Hon. Elizabeth Varley, has acknowledged several times hearing the sounds, on the first occasion when she was eighteen and living in Palace House, also in the abbey's grounds:

> It was a hot summer's night, very late, and I was sitting on my window seat looking out with my Pekinese beside me . . . I was so deep in my thoughts that it [the singing] had been going on for quite a while before I became conscious of it. What first made me aware of it was the frissons of cold that started to run up and down my back. It was the sound of many voices in repetitive singing, which faded and strengthened like the sound from a primitive wireless. At first I thought it was a wireless in the servants' hall. But the sound wasn't coming from there. I couldn't tell you where it *was* coming from. The next morning . . . an archaeologist friend . . . asked me to sing the tune to him. It was pretty well carved in my memory, so I sang it. He told me it was a well-known Gregorian chant . . .[12]

It is interesting to note that as observed by both Michael Sedgwick and a former catering manageress at Beaulieu, Mrs Bertha Day, who has also heard the chanting, it seems specifically to happen when someone local to Beaulieu has died.

Curiously, while ghosts making noises of all sorts are comparatively common, reports of ghosts speaking – and certainly talking in a responsive way to those experiencing them – are quite rare.[13] A widespread folkloric belief has it that ghosts are not allowed to speak unless spoken to first, a conviction reflected in an anecdote concerning Dr Samuel Johnson, who was in the habit of sitting reflectively in silence for long periods. A friend apparently once told him teasingly: 'Sir, you are like a ghost: you never speak until you are spoken to.'

According to the same folklore, the way to get a ghost to speak is to say to it something to the effect, 'In the name of God, why are you troubling me?'[14] However, I have yet to come across any authoritatively reported case in which this formula has been used at all, let alone successfully. So far as can be determined (and mediumistic communications aside), responsive dialogue with ghosts either does not occur, or is as near nonexistent as makes no difference.[15]

Smell is not a sensation popularly associated with ghost experiences, yet 8 per cent of the Celia Green/Charles McCreery sample involved smell,[16] as did 3 per cent of Erlendur Haraldsson's Icelandic cases, as did our already mentioned case of the cinema projectionist who committed suicide. Another instance of a particularly unpleasant ghostly smell was described to me in all seriousness by retired NHS senior psychiatrist the late Dr James Gordon-Russell of Almondsbury, Bristol. This experience occurred during a week's holiday in the 1960s spent by James, his wife Peggy and their three children, Martin, Fiona, and Elspeth, in a wing of an old house in North Devon owned by a retired colonel.

The problem arose the very first evening, and was heralded by baby Elspeth, who was sleeping in the same room as her parents, uncharacteristically refusing to stop crying. Then, as James and Peggy at last tried to settle down for the night, suddenly James was aware of the room becoming filled with an overpowering smell of rotting leaves or graveyards. Simultaneously the temperature seemed to plunge, causing him to shiver violently. Next, the bedclothes were sharply pulled away, dropping to the floor. Curiously Peggy, right next to James, experienced neither the smell nor the temperature drop. But she too felt the strong tug on the covers. Yet when the two older children were checked, both were sleeping soundly in their rooms at the end of a long corridor.

James, a down-to-earth individual professionally trained to be alert to delusions in others, felt deeply disturbed by the experience, and insisted that the family should all leave the very next morning. He derived some comfort, however, from the fact that even without his telling the owner why they were checking out so early, the latter simply commented: 'Oh, so you've experienced it too.' Clearly they were by no means the first to have experienced the hotel's smelly ghostly visitant.

Yet another instance of an unpleasant ghostly smell was reported by Nebraska University's Mrs Buterbaugh, associated with her sighting of Clarissa Mills:

*　*　*

114

About four steps into the room [where Clarissa Mills's ghost was seen] was when the strong odour hit me. When I say strong odour, I mean the kind that simply stops you in your tracks and almost chokes you. I felt that there was someone in the room with me . . . I looked up and there she was.[17]

But by no means are all ghost smells unpleasant. As well as (but not synchronous with) the ghostly monastic chanting associated with the grounds of Beaulieu Abbey many, including Lord Montagu himself, have experienced at Beaulieu a strong and inexplicable odour of incense.[18] Among other instances of pleasant ghostly smells, the Blue Room at Bovey House, an attractive country-house hotel near Beer, East Devon, is said to be haunted by a tall, headless lady dressed in rich blue brocade who signals her presence with the smell of fresh lavender. Peter Underwood and his wife Joyce thought they smelt this 'faint but distinct' lavender odour one morning at 4.30 when they stayed in the Blue Room a few years ago,[19] though the hotel's present proprietors tend to attribute such phenomena to their chef's aftershave.[20] Bramshill House in Hampshire reputedly has a Grey Lady who appears around 3 a.m. wafting an often out-of-season scent of lilies.[21] Similarly, cleaners at the eighteenth-century Manor House at Bury St Edmund's, owned by the Marquess of Bristol, have at certain times noticed a mysterious and attractive fragrance that they have attributed to a ghostly Scented Lady.[22]

Touch hardly rates as one of the senses involved in ghostly experience, ghosts mostly being reported passing right through living people rather than actually being felt by them. But even so, some very real 'feelings' of a different sort must be included among ghostly sensory experiences, not least as attested to me by Bob Bootle, a level-headed former producer of BBC science documentaries, and his wife Val.

In 1971 Bob and Val travelled to a school at Hayle in Cornwall which was featured in a 'Young Scientists of the Year' television programme on which Bob was working. Hayle is a small port at the mouth of the estuary in St Ives Bay, and one of the school's teachers, Edward Wigley, being an enthusiast for the area, took the Bootles on an impromptu walking tour of the surrounding north Cornish coast and countryside.

In the course of their walk, during which Bob and Val became thoroughly disoriented, they noticed several old tin-mine workings. Then suddenly, as they were walking down a track bathed in sunshine, Bob felt a powerful gooseflesh sensation, accompanied by an equally powerful chill oddly at variance with the warmth of the day. Even more curiously, as he moved further down the track the sensation disappeared as quickly as it had come, prompting him to retrace his steps back to where he had felt the gooseflesh. To his astonishment, the feeling returned as powerfully as before, and when he moved away it again vanished. Intrigued, he called Val over, and without telling her what to expect, found that she experienced exactly the same.

When they described their feelings to Edward Wigley, he immediately told them that they were by no means alone in having had such an experience at this particular spot. Pointing to a small depression in the ground a short distance away, he told them that it was the site of the great Levant Mine disaster of 1919, the second worst in the long history of Cornish tin-mining accidents. On 20 October of that year, as a whole shift of men was on the man-engine that transported them up and down the 1,600-foot shaft, a rod snapped, plunging the engine, its human cargo and tons of rubble down into the darkness below.[23] News of the disaster brought rescue teams hurrying from hundreds of miles away, but access was so difficult that it was four days before the last of the miners' bodies was recovered, thirty-one being found dead and twelve seriously injured. It would seem that what Bob and Val, along with unknown others, had experienced was a kind of ghost of the emotions generated by the tragedy, even though neither had previously even heard of the disaster.

Something rather similar, except that it was at sea, was reportedly experienced by Midlands company director the late Alexander (Alec) Gracie, while he was serving as an officer-cadet on board the Merchant Navy vessel, *Poplar Branch*. In about 1920, when Gracie was just twenty years old, he was standing on the *Poplar Branch*'s bridge with the captain and chief officer as they were sailing off southern Ireland when, as recounted by his widow Margaret:

Suddenly Alex (who had never been ill in his life) felt extremely ill and depressed, and was convinced he was about to die. At the same moment the Captain suddenly said, 'God, I feel terrible! I think I'm going to die!' Immediately the Chief said: 'So do I, sir!'

Two 'very solid-looking' ghosts

(Top right) **Major William Braddell**, whose 'very solid-looking' ghost, identifiable by his distinctive trench-coat, appeared to porter Trevor Newton at the exclusive Naval and Military Club, Piccadilly, London (above), at 3.07 a.m. on 8 March 1994. A staunch member of the Naval and Military Club, Major Braddell was killed in 1941 commanding an anti-aircraft battery in Kensington, just a few days after losing two of his friends to a direct hit from a German bomb while they were dining at the club.

(Right) **Girl in a mob cap** whose ghost appeared in 1948 in the sitting room of an old house in Wye, Kent, as sketched by eyewitness Miss Cox of the Cox's Orange Pippin family. This same girl, again very solid-looking though lacking distinguishable facial features, appeared in the same place to Wye resident Mrs Joan Morris in the spring of 1985. Very recently, local estate agent Christopher Calcutt's electronic measurer inexplicably failed when he tried to use it in the same location.

Ghost and 'Receiver'?

(Left) **Thomas Howard, fourth Duke of Norfolk**, identified by Catholic priest Fr Francis Edwards, S.J., as the most likely candidate for the ghost in Elizabethan costume reported by switchboard operators at Coutts & Co.'s Bank headquarters in London's Strand. From a contemporary portrait.

(Above) **'Ghost-sensitive' Eddie Burks of Lincoln**, who claims to be able instinctively to 'tune in' to ghosts whom others experience only at rare intervals. At Coutts Bank he said of what he could 'see' of Thomas Howard: 'He drew my attention to . . . the gold or silver chain suspended from his neck. At the end of the chain was a disc with delicate tracery worked in gold or silver.'

Unlikely setting for a haunt . . .

(Above) **The Garden Court at Coutts & Co**. The magnificent first floor reception hall at Coutts' headquarters in London's Strand. The ghost identified as Thomas Howard was seen by Coutts' switchboard operators in an office just off this.

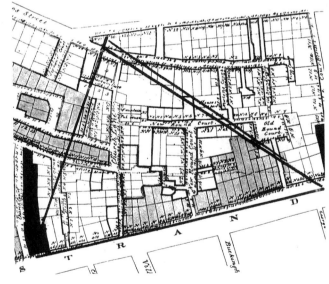

(Right) **The Coutts Site in the West Strand**, before the company acquired the site, from a street plan of the early nineteenth century. The connection of the Elizabethan Thomas Howard with this particular location remains a mystery.

Alec did not speak, he was so junior. He looked at the time out of curiosity. After a moment he felt quite normal again, and so did the Captain and Chief, who left the bridge, both remarking how odd it was.

As soon as Alec was relieved, he went into the chart room and working back from the time and speed of the ship, took an exact reading of their position at the time of the occurrence. When they returned to Liverpool he asked a friend in the shipping office to check whether there was any known significance attached to the spot. He found that they had in fact been passing over the exact location of the wreck of the *Lusitania*, sunk in 1915 with loss of all hands, the bodies never having been brought up from the sea-bed.[24]

A sudden feeling of cold is a commonly reported accompaniment of ghost experiences, so much so that ghost hunting enthusiasts routinely carry thermometers among their equipment. However, whether the sensation is purely subjective, or derives from a real localised drop in air temperature remains as yet undetermined.

It is quite evident, then, that with certain limitations and curiosities, ghost experiences can involve nearly the entire spectrum of human senses.

But this only raises fresh questions. For instance, does everyone have the same capacity to sense ghosts? Or are some people – and even animals – rather more sensitive to them than others?

CHAPTER NINE

Who and What Senses Ghosts?

From even casual study of reported ghost experiences it becomes apparent that people can have surprisingly varied degrees of sensitivity or perceptiveness towards ghosts.

For instance, Icelander Erlendur Haraldsson's research showed that in the 43 per cent of his cases in which more than one person had been present at the time of the ghost experience, only one-third of these described experiencing the same as the main witness. As we noticed in the case of the 'smelly' Devon ghost reported by James and Peggy Gordon-Russell, James alone experienced the smell and the sharp temperature drop, but both felt the bedclothes sharply tugged away.

This variation between one person and another towards the same ghost is by no means unusual. In the well-attested case of the nun-like ghost persistently experienced by classical scholar J. C. Lawson and his wife at Abbey House, Cambridge – the very case which inspired my impromptu prayer for the Abercrombie House ghost – while both Mr Lawson and his wife would see the nun (whose facial features, typically, were never fully distinct), only Mr Lawson would hear the heavy, almost policeman-like footsteps which heralded her approach. And only Mrs Lawson would see the door open and close.[1]

A similar pattern pertains to sightings of a cloaked, tricorn-hatted horseman experienced on two different occasions by late-night rally drivers on a road south of Denton, near Grantham, Lincolnshire.[2] On the first occasion, the early hours of the morning of 29 January 1967, engineer John C. B. Watson of Mapperley, Nottingham, rounded a left-hand bend to see the figure to his right, seemingly about to move directly into the road. Fearing a collision, he braked sharply, prompting his two passengers, his navigator and his mother Mary, to ask what was wrong. It transpired that neither had seen anything of the horseman. A few weeks later, after Watson had driven on the same road during a second rally and seen nothing, finishing competitor Peter Shenton told him that he had just seen the same ghostly horseman riding, in his own words 'the biggest horse I could ever remember seeing'. The location was the same as where Watson had his experience. Like Watson, Shenton braked sharply, startling both his navigator, John Haslam, and his wife Barbara. Yet, just as in the case of Watson's passengers, neither Haslam nor Barbara Shenton saw anything.

Although in this instance the disparity may have been due to different states of consciousness on the part of the two drivers, there are some definite indications that children can be more sensitive than adults to ghosts. For instance, some of the children who stayed at Cleve Court in Kent reportedly experienced its Grey Lady ghost well before Lady Carson's dramatic encounter with her in 1949 (see pp. 108–09). According to Lady Carson her then six-year-old son Edward, who had his bedroom in the Elizabethan part of the house, told her that he did not like the lady who walked in the passage from which his door opened. When she inquired what the lady looked like, he replied: 'I don't know. She only walks away.' Lord Carson's great-niece Patricia Miller, who stayed at Cleve Court when she was four, similarly astonished Lady Carson by talking about 'the lady' who was with her in her bedroom. When Lady Carson asked who she meant, she responded: 'The lady who stands by my bed. There she is.' She pointed to a corner of the room, and became quite indignant when Lady Carson said she was unable to see anyone there. Diana Colvin, who also stayed at Cleve Court when very young, likewise spoke of 'The poor lady who walks in and out. No one speaks to her and no one tells me who she is.'[3]

Later in this chapter we will come across a two-year-old child showing special sensitivity towards a ghost, but meanwhile, in the same vein, it is worth noting that some domestic animals, particularly dogs, can be more sensitive than their owners to ghosts.[4]

As but one example, in the case of the lily-perfumed Grey Lady reported at Bramshill House, staff member Fred Cook had originally scoffed at the idea both of ghosts in general and that Bramshill House in particular might be haunted. Then one evening while he was routinely patrolling the house with his Labrador:

I opened the door of the Long Gallery (now used as part of the Library and twice the length of a cricket pitch) and there was the Grey Lady – seemingly staring at me. If I was mistaken, my dog wasn't. She gave a howl of terror and fell over backwards in her hurry to get away. There was no stopping her, she raced out of the house – and I wasn't far behind![5]

Although Fred Cook managed to summon the courage to revisit the Long Gallery, only to find the ghost no longer there, apparently nothing would persuade his dog to do so again. In other cases later in this book we will find dogs exhibiting similar fears.

When we return to adult human sensitivities to ghosts, there are extreme instances in which just one or two among a large group of people see a ghost, while the rest of those present notice nothing unusual. For example, guides at Dover Castle who take parties of tourists through 'Hellfire Corner' – some three and a half miles of tunnels beneath the castle that were carved out for defence purposes during the Napoleonic period, and extended in World War II – have reported occasions when certain individuals have seemed to see and even enter into conversation with presences invisible and inaudible to the rest of their party.[6]

On one such occasion guide Leslie Simpson was taking a group of twenty through the old Defence Telecommunications Network Centre, and was standing at the barrier of the repeater station when a woman in the group became agitated and fell down on one knee. Afterwards she told him that she had seen a man in naval uniform tinkering with the equipment. This man had walked towards the group, straight through the barrier, and then through her . . .

Another time guide Karen Mennie was taking a group through the same area when she saw two of her party, a father and a daughter, seemingly seeing and, in the case of the girl actually in conversation with, someone whom no one else could see. Although the father was quite casual, the girl seemed very agitated. When Karen mentioned that the area had a reputation for being haunted, the father promptly told her that he and his daughter had just seen the ghost, who had given his name as Bill Billings, and had told the girl that he had been killed while assembling an amplifier rack.

This is a rare instance of reported conversation with a ghost, and obviously when only one person in a large group claims such an experience the chances have to be fairly high that that person is hallucinating. Yet it is possible that some people may genuinely be considerably more sensitive to ghosts than others, and certainly there is no shortage of people who have claimed such sensitivity.

One such is the Revd Christopher Neil-Smith, who made a speciality of laying ghosts during the 1960s and 1970s, and who now lives in retirement in Ealing, London. He has claimed that he can sense ghosts by special 'vibrations'.

> I was looking round an old country house on holiday with a guide, when I suddenly felt a vibration and the guide subsequently mentioned that there had been a ghost where I had felt it . . . Once when I was asked to lay a ghost at a London flat, I went round the room first and told the occupant that I felt vibrations in five of the rooms but not in the other three. Then they told me that the ghost have been seen or felt in the five rooms I mentioned, but not the other three. This was a clear indication that my vibrations related to the evidence from independent statements made by three other people who had seen or felt the ghost.[7]

Neil-Smith has explained his 'gift' thus:

> A doctor I know takes sensitivity tests – acknowledging ghosts may well be a matter of sensitivity. Two people of differing sensitivity might enter a room; one would be conscious of the ghost, the other not.[8]

Another Anglican cleric, the late Canon John Pearce-Higgins, vice-provost of Southwark Cathedral, who dealt with ghostly disturbances reported in the diocese of Southwark, had on his own admission no special perceptiveness towards ghosts. In order to overcome this disability he controversially used Spiritualist mediums to put him in touch with whatever ghost might be troubling the premises to which he had been called. One medium whom he used frequently, a Mrs Ena Twigg, was involved in the following case:

> This was in a vicarage where the young new incumbent, with a wife and four children, urgently invoked my help to get rid of the terrible atmosphere of depression in the house, there were also footsteps going up and down the stairs, and the eldest boy flatly refused to sleep in the late vicar's bedroom. Mrs Twigg came with her husband, and together with the vicar and his wife we sat one evening while Mrs Twigg relayed to us what she said she saw and heard, correctly describing this sad unhappy middle-aged bachelor, who said he was tied to the place by the sense of what he had left undone. We tried to comfort him. We also told him he was upsetting the children. 'But,' he said, 'I come for the children. I am fond of them. Children were the only people I could really communicate with when alive ...' Through Mrs Twigg he then correctly described alterations in the vicarage itself and in the church – in neither of which places either she or I had ever set foot before ...[9]

Another Anglican clergyman who has openly used both sensitives and Spiritualist mediums is the Revd J. Aelwyn Roberts, retired vicar of Llandegai, near Bangor, north Wales. Roberts's chief sensitive is the near identically named poet and crowned National Bard of Wales, Elwyn Roberts, while among several mediums he has particularly favoured the Spiritualist minister Winnie Marshall. Although the Revd Roberts has set many of his experiences down in an entertaining and intriguing book, *Holy Ghostbuster: A Parson's Encounters with the Paranormal*, he has so indiscriminately fictionalised the names of both the people and the places involved that it is difficult to regard them as having any evidential value.

Worthy of much more serious attention is Irish-born sensitive Tom Corbett, who has for many years lived in Chelsea, London. He has described people's varying sensitivities to ghosts, and his own special gift, with considerable precision:

123

* * *

I can see ghosts. I haven't got any power over them, like exorcising them, or telling them to go away. But if there's a ghost around I can tell you where, and sometimes, what it looks like. Other people have this gift in varying degrees. Some, like me, see them, some hear them, others just sense them. Most people, of course, aren't psychic at all, so they won't ever see a ghost – even if it's standing right next to them.[10]

In the early 1960s Corbett, together with journalist Diana Norman, wife of the television film critic Barry, toured several of Britain's stately homes, among them Longleat in Wiltshire, seat of the Marquess of Bath. Diana Norman relates how Lord Bath's second son, Lord Christopher Thynne, who along with Longleat's librarian Dorothy Coates showed them around, set a special test for Corbett. Taking them to an upstairs corridor Lord Thynne told them it was where the ghost of Longleat's famous 'Green Lady' was said to walk. Whereupon:

Tom Corbett walked slowly up the passage, while we stood watching him and shivering. His hands were behind his back and his head cocked a little to one side, like a farmer trying to gauge the weather.

'No,' he said, slowly. 'No.'

He came back and led the way into another passage that was yawning on our right. As far as I could see it was indistinguishable from the first . . .

'There's something here,' he said. 'Something dreadful happened here. This is your corridor, not the other one.'

There was a silence.

Miss Dorothy Coates, who has been Longleat's librarian for a long time, looked at Lord Christopher. Then she spoke up. 'You are quite right, Mr Corbett. This is the "Walk". Christopher showed you the wrong corridor.'

Tom was the only one of us who remained quite unmoved. He was used to being tested. He was also used to being right . . .[11]

One English churchman who was highly impressed by Tom Corbett was the late Bishop of Southwark, the Revd Mervyn Stockwood. In the 1960s, Bishop Mervyn's official residence was a large house in south London, where on two occasions he was startled to be confronted in his bedroom by the ghost of an elderly, sad-looking woman. Deciding that this was an opportunity to test Corbett's gifts, the bishop invited him to visit his residence. Stockwood recalled in his autobiography that immediately upon Corbett's arrival he

> described the woman as I had seen her, told me she had come from overseas, and pointed correctly to the room in which she had appeared to me. When I mentioned this in a newspaper article, an elderly woman in Dublin wrote to tell me that during the First World War she had lived opposite my house and had got to know a Polish refugee who used to live there. She added that the refugee was a woman who longed to return to her country and was unhappy in London.[12]

Tom Corbett is no longer active in such ghost-sensing, and his place has been taken in recent years by Eddie Burks of Lincoln [pl. 14], who claims a similar gift. Born in London in 1924, Eddie Burks had a near-death experience during a tonsillectomy operation at the age of five, an occurrence which may have had something to do with awakening his sensitivities, even though these did not manifest until much later in life. Eddie went on to a thoroughly down-to-earth career – going to university, marrying, becoming an engineer specialising in airfields and roads, culminating in a Civil Service post as a Principal Scientific Officer. It was not until 1970, when his wife unexpectedly dropped dead at the age of forty-eight, that something of Eddie's special gift began to manifest.

He and his wife had been very close and his first and very understandable reaction to her death was devastation. The very day after she had died, however, as he was in the kitchen getting a piece of chicken from the fridge, he suddenly found himself laughing uncontrollably. For he became aware that his wife was with him in the room. As he matter-of-factly told me when I visited him at his home, without his in any way trying to make contact with his wife, she simply appeared to him, not only this first time but on numerous subsequent occasions, including in the passenger seat of his car while he was driving home from Norfolk. When she was with him they were able to converse freely, but there were also long periods when she did not appear, during which Eddie made no attempt to try to contact her.

In 1975 Eddie began to find he could sense other presences, to the extent of even being able to talk to them in the same way as he conversed with his wife. As he describes it:

> When I sense a spirit, my level of consciousness changes, not unlike the way you feel when someone is standing behind you. Then it develops into communication. I don't know who they are at first.[13]

In 1983 he became involved in his first proper haunting, at a house in Leicester.

> A local vicar called me, because a young couple in his parish thought their house was haunted. Soon after moving in, they heard footsteps on the landing, a woman crying, and their two-year-old daughter started talking to someone they couldn't see.
>
> When the vicar and I went to the house, the daughter was asleep downstairs, in the spare bedroom, and her uncle was baby-sitting. We knew that the previous occupant of the house was an elderly lady who had died from a fall down the stairs. As soon as we went into the child's bedroom I sensed a woman, who was crying. 'What's happened to my house?' she moaned. 'What are these people doing here? I can't use my own bedroom now.'
>
> I said to the vicar that I thought she hadn't realised she was dead. 'Ask her about the fall down the stairs,' he said to me. Then I turned back to the ghost. Her reply was, 'That was a narrow squeak, wasn't it?' I continued with her, until she understood that she was in the next life. It was difficult to persuade her until two people came towards her, and she recognised them as having passed on. The little girl was asleep while we were there, but when she woke up the following morning, she told her mother that she had said goodbye to the lady. She must have seen the old lady in her dreams. It happens quite often with children, because they are much more aware than adults.[14]

* * *

This is immediately notable as another example of a young child seemingly having a greater sensitivity than adults to ghosts. It is also significant that, according to Eddie Burks's interpretation at least, the ghostly encounter was partly via a dream, an assertion that would find support from folkloric traditions all over the world.

Even more intriguing, however, are some of the insights Burks gives us into ghosts – particularly the old lady's apparent lack of realisation that she was actually dead. This finds an echo in remarks by others claiming such sensitivities, as for instance a medium used by Canon Pearce-Higgins in the case of an ex-vicarage in the Midlands built on the site of a pre-Reformation priory and haunted by two monks from early Tudor times:

> The monks . . . had continued to perform their daily offices and although the Priory had been dissolved in AD 1536 still imagined themselves to be carrying out the daily monastic routine in field and church. I had a most interesting time trying to persuade them that they were dead.[15]

Without doubt Eddie Burks's most intriguing experience – and the one which has brought him most to public attention – was in sensing and coming to an understanding with an even more historic ghost – and at none other than the head office of exclusive Coutts & Co Bank in London's Strand. For anyone visiting this bank, which stands almost opposite Charing Cross Station, the overwhelming impression is one of light, airy modernity. Behind a glass-fronted exterior an escalator sweeps visitors up to a spacious, plant-filled and marble-clad first-floor reception hall, the Garden Court [pl. 15], that seems light years away from the world of ghosts.

Yet in August 1992 one of Coutts'switchboard operators reported to her superiors that during the afternoon, and therefore in full daylight, she had seen a dark figure cross the office, accompanied by a chilling drop in the temperature. At about the same time there was a malfunction to the computers and lighting. Three other staff reported seeing the same figure on separate occasions, both during the day and in the early evening. The figure seemed to be male, and according to at least one impression, headless, and was always seen going into one particular room. Barbara

Peters, Coutts' archivist, was asked whether she knew of any precedent for the sightings, and it was as a result of her contacting the Spiritualist College of Psychic Studies that Eddie Burks was called upon.

Burks visited Coutts in the early afternoon of 14 August 1992. He was met in the reception hall by Barbara Peters and introduced to three of the staff who had seen the figure. As they talked in a small office close to the switchboard, Eddie, in his own words, felt that he 'could feel his [the ghost's] presence almost at once'. He quickly asked the staff to take notes of what he was about to say, and immediately began to give a description of the man he was seeing and feeling.

> He is a man of considerable pride who had some social standing in his time. I feel his impatience. He was not a criminal.

Burks then went on to relay what he could hear the man saying to him:

> I have been waiting a long time, yet you continue to keep me waiting needlessly. I practised the Law. I would not bend to the Queen's command conveyed to me through her servant, who held the Great Seal. By this time I knew too much. Did I become indiscreet I could threaten Her Majesty, so when it was discovered that I would not be amenable a case of treason was trumped up, and I was beheaded not far from here on a summer's day, which made me loath to depart. I have held much bitterness and I am told that if I am to be helped I must let this go. In the name of God I ask your help. I cannot do this alone. The memory is still strong.

Sensing this clearly high-ranking ghost walking up and down, Eddie accompanied him, and was thanked for this, while Barbara Peters and the others watched in some astonishment, unable on this occasion to see or hear anything of Eddie's companion. Eddie now tried to focus on giving some account of the ghost's appearance:

> He was wearing doublet and hose. The doublet was dark red or black with puffed upper sleeves and lace around the cuffs. It was taken in around the waist and slightly flared below. He wore a ruff around his neck. His shoes were dark with silver buckles . . . He

was tall and fairly slim. He had a thin face and aquiline nose.

As he was dictating these details, he was astonished to hear his Elizabethan companion breaking in to remark approvingly:

That is a fair description, but you have not mentioned my ornaments.

Eddie explained:

He drew my attention to the jewelled rings on his left hand and the gold or silver chain suspended from his neck. At the end of the chain was a disc with delicate tracery worked in gold or silver.

In Elizabethan times 'ornaments' could indeed refer to personal jewellery. Even more interesting was the ghost's next statement:

At my execution I took off my ruff for I did not wish them to be spoilt. They were to be given to my son. I put around my shoulders the black mantle which was part of my accoutrement in Law. I did not mind if this were stained, for it was stained already through this injustice! . . . I wait upon you.

According to Eddie:

I then sensed, half saw, his [the ghost's] daughter approaching . . . She was dressed in Elizabethan costume, but entirely in white, and she radiated light. She took both his hands . . . They turned, walking towards the Light . . . He then looked back for a moment to thank us for helping him.

Obviously it is very difficult for anyone of sceptical disposition to know how to adjudge such impressions, given over the space of forty-five minutes in the surroundings of a twentieth-century commercial premises. Despite the length of his ghostly encounter, Burks, for his part, left Coutts that day without any idea of the actual identity of this executed Elizabethan.

However, an article which Eddie wrote for the Spiritualist magazine *Light* was spotted by journalist Gillian Cribbs and on 21 February 1993 retold in a front-page story in the *Sunday Telegraph* – 'Haunted Coutts calls in the Ghostbuster' – ending with the information that 'an archivist is trying to trace the Elizabethan through historical records'. This in turn was read by the erudite Father Francis Edwards, archivist of the English branch of the Jesuit order and a member of the Royal Historical Association, who immediately recognised that even from the relatively sparse details that Eddie had gleaned, the Coutts ghost ought to be identifiable.

For Fr Edwards a crucial clue lay in the fact that this mystery Elizabethan had been beheaded. He knew that although executions among all classes were plentiful during Queen Elizabeth's reign, the great majority of these were by public hanging. Beheadings, by contrast swifter and more discreet, were reserved for a mere handful of the highest classes. Most of these were well recorded and could be easily eliminated. Elizabeth's favourite, the Earl of Essex, for instance, might have matched the Coutts ghost's physical description, but Essex's beheading had been on a chilly 25 February, not 'a summer's day'. Mary, Queen of Scots was trebly eliminatable. Like Essex she had been beheaded in February; the location was Fotheringhay, Northamptonshire, by no stretch of the imagination 'not far' from Coutts; and not least, she was a woman.

Putting all the details together Fr Edwards felt that there was really only one logical candidate: Thomas Howard, fourth Duke of Norfolk [pl. 13], whose biography, *The Marvellous Chance*, Edwards himself had written in 1968. As he suggested in a letter published by the *Sunday Telegraph* the week after Gillian Cribbs's article:

I do not know what the archivist at Coutts Bank will come up with, but the apparition that appeared in the Strand seems to correspond remarkably well with what we know of Thomas Howard, fourth Duke of Norfolk. Born in 1536, he was executed on a trumped-up charge of treason on Tower Hill on 2 June 1572. He was tall and slim, with aquiline features that were beautifully drawn by Lukas de Heere, around 1569. He is yet another character waiting in the wings of history for a fairer deal from historians. Although he technically disobeyed Queen Elizabeth I by persisting in a project to marry Mary, Queen of Scots, then in captivity in England, he had no evil design on Elizabeth. He was a devout Anglican to the last. He really owed his death to Sir William Cecil, who feared him as a rival for power . . .[16]

It is hardly every day that a sensitive's insights on a ghost get such authoritative historical endorsement. Even more unexpected is that this should come from a Catholic priest – a group usually implacable in their opposition to anything mediumistic. On its own, therefore, Eddie Burks's sensing of the Coutts ghost – Thomas Howard or otherwise – might seem very convincing indeed.

But considerable caution is needed. It is more than a little puzzling, for example, that Thomas Howard should haunt the Coutts site, which before the bank acquired it was a maze of small alleyways and courts [pl. 16] with no known connection with Howard or his family. The duke's main London residence, Howard House, formerly the Charterhouse, lay in Smithfield a mile away. Arundel House, another Howard property, lay a good quarter-mile to the east. And Norfolk House was likewise some distance removed. As already noted by Fr Edwards, the site of the duke's execution was Tower Hill, a good mile and a half eastwards. And his corpse, including his severed head, was buried in the Tower of London's Chapel of St Peter ad Vincula.

Furthermore what might, despite this difficulty, still seem a good evidential case has been further weakened, in the wake of the press interest aroused by the Coutts case, by Eddie Burks going on a whistle-stop tour of dozens of haunted locations around England and Wales. At each, in exactly the manner of Tom Corbett before him, Eddie did his best to impart his impressions of what he sensed and these have been recorded in a recently published book written in partnership with Gillian Cribbs.[17] However, all too often lacking throughout this are clear identifications with specific historical characters.

The need for caution when considering the claims of sensitives, mediums and similar psychics is further underlined by research from America conducted by the respected psychical academics Dr Michaeleen Maher of the New York New School of Social Research, Gertrude Schmeidler of the City University of New York, and others. In 1973 while Maher was studying psychology at City College of the City

University of New York, a family friend called Kathleen told her that she, her sister Peggy and her mother Margaret had all experienced what seemed to be a ghostly dark figure moving along the hallway of her apartment near Washington Square Park in New York's Greenwich Village. The figure invariably turned into the bathroom or the master bedroom before disappearing.

Making a floor plan of the apartment Maher carefully marked on this where Kathleen, Peggy and Margaret had seen the ghost. She then invited four sensitives and eight sceptics, all of whom had been told nothing of the haunting, to visit the apartment. The sensitives were asked to mark on blank copies of the floor plan where they sensed a ghost to be. The sceptics, for their part, were asked to indicate where they thought someone with an overactive imagination might see a ghost. Sensitives and sceptics alike were also given copies of a carefully prepared check list and asked to circle on this any entries that they thought might correspond with the ghostly phenomena as reported by Peggy, Kathleen and Margaret.

When Maher studied the results, only one floor plan, that of a sensitive called Phyllis Woodbury, showed a significant correspondence to what had been described by the three women – even though another of the sensitives, Ingo Swann, specifically described seeing the ghost advancing towards him. As for the check lists of ghostly phenomena, again only one, that of the sensitive Ingo Swann, showed a significant correlation with what the women had reported. While the sensitives undeniably did better than the sceptics – who produced nothing of significance in either case – their results were hardly a triumph.[18]

In a similar, more recent study, following ghostly disturbances in a residential building in New York City reported by eight separate witnesses, Michaeleen Maher found that only two out of four sensitives achieved a significant correspondence on the floor plan, and just one with regard to the check list. Even in the case of the two who were successful with the floor plan, one described the ghost as a malevolent entity, and the other as a happy woman.[19]

Overall, then, we must conclude that while some people genuinely have a greater sensitivity than others in perceiving ghosts, any sweeping claims of special sensory powers need to be regarded with considerable caution. However impressive we may find Eddie Burks's sensing of

Thomas Howard, to assume that he is reliable in all cases may well be wide of the mark. Nonetheless if we do accept at least some of the sensitives' insights as valid, then it is to be inferred that ghosts may be much more sentient, and more potentially communicative, than might have been supposed from the experiences of ordinary percipients.

If people vary so widely in their ability to sense ghosts, is there any inanimate instrument that may do better? The straight answer seems to be no. Despite all the wonders of modern technology, no one has yet succeeded in developing a reliable ghost-detector; if they had, no doubt all the ghost-hunting groups would have been clamouring for it by now.

But this is not the same as saying that certain technological equipment and instruments are not affected by ghosts. In the case of the Coutts Bank haunting, the computers crashed synchronously with the appearance of the figure in the reception hall. And when Major Braddell appeared at the Naval and Military Club, all the external floodlights came on, completely out of phase with the time switch which controlled them. No less remarkably, when Kent estate agent Christopher Calcutt was measuring the main room in the house at Wye where Joan Morris had seen the ghost of the girl with the mob cap (see p. 110), his electronic measurer failed at precisely the spot where the ghost had been seen, even though he had no idea of the significance at the time. He could only get it to work again when he moved to the other end of the room. So instruments would seem, on occasion, to exhibit a significant response to ghosts, even if they cannot yet detect them.

We may now be at least a little wiser about who and what senses ghosts, but what of when they are seen? And where? How accurate is the conventional idea that ghosts are creatures of darkness? And what can we determine of the extent to which they may be rooted to any one location?

CHAPTER TEN

Ghosts and Time

Can exploring the question 'Why do ghosts appear when they do?' help us to understand any more about what ghosts are? Certainly grappling with it can dispel some popular misconceptions.

One of the prime misconceptions, for instance, is that ghosts are necessarily creatures of darkness. Undeniably our Abercrombie House ghost manifested after midnight, and her breathing was only audible when the electric light was off, becoming inaudible when it was switched on. The ghostly nun experienced by the Lawsons at Abbey House, Cambridge (see pp. 3 and 119) was only seen at night, and generally between the hours of midnight and 4.00 a.m.[1] Lady Carson saw Cleve Court's Grey Lady around 1.30 a.m. Rally-driver John Watson saw his ghostly horseman 'at about 2 a.m'. The Naval and Military Club's 'Major Braddell' appeared at precisely 3.07 a.m. The Gordon-Russells experienced their 'smelly' ghost at night. And in a rather similar case described to me by BBC radio researcher Liz Clark,[2] it was around 2 a.m., while she and her family were staying in an Edwardian house in Port Isaac, Cornwall, that she woke up to see a figure in a stripy gown bending over the cot of one of her daughters:

> The reason I woke up was because one of the babies was crying. By the time I looked across to the cots, the crying had settled down to a sleepy whimper, and I saw someone I took to be my husband, Mike, tucking the baby in. Mike had a stripy dressing

gown which this figure appeared to be wearing . . . It wasn't until this figure negotiated the gap between the cot and the wall in a smooth, almost gliding fashion to come towards me that I suddenly questioned whether it was Mike. I felt across the bed to make sure – and then dived under the covers when my hand brushed up against him . . . For a couple of years [afterwards] I had to keep the light on overnight if Mike was away.[3]

Against these 'hours of darkness' ghosts (although it should be observed that the Grey Lady and Major Braddell were seen in full electric light), there is no shortage of examples from the daytime. It may be recalled that Mrs Buterbaugh of Nebraska Wesleyan University saw Clarissa Mills at 8.50 a.m., when it was full daylight and there were plenty of people already at work. Barbara McKenzie specifically noted that Robin Hayden's footsteps 'always occurred in daylight and usually between 10.30 a.m. and 9 p.m'. Thomas Howard was seen by the Coutts Bank receptionists during the daytime and early evening. According to Commander Bill Bellars, currently General Secretary of the Ghost Club, the ghosts that he and his wife experienced, back in 1957 when he was attached to the British Joint Services Mission in Washington DC, manifested only in daytime. From soon after their arrival in their rented house in Veazey Street, downtown Washington, Bellars's wife Jane and the children's nanny Marley

> heard footsteps, firm footsteps going upstairs: always in the daytime and never later than 6.30 p.m.

Jane Bellars repeatedly saw the ghost of an old man when driving into the garage during daylight hours.

Then Bellars himself, arriving home 'early one Saturday afternoon' on a brilliantly sunny Washington day,

> let myself in through the front door . . . [and] saw out of the corner of my eye a woman in a green period dress sitting in an armchair in the sitting room on my right. I realised instinctively that she couldn't possibly be there.[4]

* * *

W. Macqueen Pope, historian of the Theatre Royal, Drury Lane, reported the theatre's ghostly 'Man in Grey', whom he claimed to have seen 'on numerous occasions', and that this ghost was:

> . . . a daytime ghost . . . He has never been seen at night, or later than six in the evening. All the recorded accounts of his appearance are between nine a.m. and six p.m.[5]

This surprisingly high incidence of daytime hauntings is reflected in Erlendur Haraldsson's quantitative survey of ghost experiences studied by him in Iceland:

> . . . forty-four of our [hundred] respondents reported experiencing apparitions in daylight or in full electric light, twenty in semi-darkness and only nine in darkness.[6]

So we may accept that ghosts show comparatively little preference for daytime or night, light or darkness. There remains, however, the question 'At whatever time they appear, why do they choose that particular occasion anyway?' Are they reflecting some anniversary, of hour, day or year, that may be significant to them? Or is their timing connected with the particular circumstances of the living to whom they are appearing? Perhaps there are a variety of factors in play.

One common idea about ghosts deserving the firmest note of caution is that they appear cyclically, that is, on special anniversary days. According to a recent book by Peter Underwood:

> Well-known cyclic ghosts in England include 'a white shape' in the vicinity of the Bloody Tower at the Tower of London each 12 February, the anniversary of the execution of Lady Jane Grey . . .; a drummer boy seen on Hickling Broad, Norfolk, each 15 February; the annual appearance of 'Juliet', who hanged herself on 17 March in the vicinity of the Ferry Boat Inn, Holywell, Cambridgeshire; the ghostly form of Lady Blanche de Warren each 4 April at Rochester Castle, Kent, where she was killed by an arrow that day in 1264; a phantom coach which drives towards Blickling Hall in Norfolk each 19 May and then vanishes; another phantom coach

which crashes into the old bridge at Potter Heigham in the same county at midnight each 31 May; a phantom sailor who is seen in Ballyheigue Bay, Ireland, each 4 June; a ghost Cavalier who visits Hitchin Priory in Hertfordshire each 15 June; the famous ghost nun who walks each 28 July at Borley Rectory in Essex; the ghost of Sir Walter Raleigh who returns to his old home, Sherborne Castle, each 28 September; Constania, Lady Coleraine, who manifests each 3 November at Bruce Castle, Tottenham, in London, where she committed suicide; and a 'grey lady' who walks at the Royal National Orthopaedic Hospital, Stanmore, London, each 13 November. In December, Christmas Eve and the last day of the year are positively bursting with ghostly activity . . .[7]

With respect to Peter Underwood, to present such anecdotal material as a serious calendar, as he does both in this recent book,[8] and in his Ghost Club Society's newsletter, does a positive disservice to any genuine attempt to come to some sort of understanding of ghosts. When we consult Underwood's own *Gazetteer of British Ghosts*, for instance, the most we hear about the Sir Walter Raleigh sighting is that Sir Walter's ghost 'is said to walk round the old castle garden on Michaelmas Eve and to disappear in the arbour . . .' No mention even of a single first-hand sighting within living memory. Yet Underwood would have us believe that Sir Walter's ghost appears 'each 28 September'. Similar reservations apply to the rest of Underwood's list. If he genuinely believes that there is any likelihood of the ghosts he has named actually appearing at the specified sites on the specified dates, then there can be no doubt that he would be there staking them out with a group of ghost-hunters.

In fact, as Peter Underwood is undoubtedly aware but fails adequately to acknowledge, there are all sorts of calendrical problems about a ghost reappearing on one particular day of the year. For instance, if the traumatic event responsible for the haunting originally took place on a Sunday, would the ghost elect to appear on the nearest equivalent Sunday or stick to the exact calendrical date? Would he or she adjust the day of his appearance during leap years?

A major difficulty for anyone who died before 1752 is that their calendar would have been up to eleven days out of synchronisation with ours. This is because of errors that had accumulated in the old Julian calendar, as used in Catholic Europe up to 1582 and in England up to 1752, and which were only adjusted by literally moving the date forward. Lady Jane Grey's 12 February would therefore be our 22 or 23 February. If the ghosts cited by Underwood were genuinely well attested as appearing on the dates he cites, then we would have to accept that ghosts of several hundred years ago have adjusted themselves to our twentieth-century calendar. But as they are not well attested, the issue does not arise.

Having said all this, it may be recalled from the Robin Hayden haunting that the ghostly footsteps, after having been 'spasmodic' earlier in the year, did manifest more strongly at Christmastime, reaching a particular peak 'two days after Christmas', and thereby seeming to echo the anniversary of Robin's suicide. However, they were also extremely strong one month later, at the end of January, which seems to negate any rigid application of an anniversary argument.

Equally pertinent in this same case is Barbara McKenzie's observation that 'Thursdays somehow seemed to be a favourite day' for the footsteps. She had mistakenly formed the impression from newspaper reports that it was 'a Thursday morning' that Robin had shot himself. In fact 27 December 1912 was a Friday. If there was any sort of cyclical or calendrical pattern to the recurrence of the footsteps on Thursdays, we can only surmise that they reflected the pitch of Robin's emotions the day before his suicide, rather than the day itself.

If it could be believed, the case that would be most demonstrative of a synchronicity element to ghostly phenomena, in this instance a minute by minute one, is the so-called Dieppe raid case. Well documented in the archives of the Society for Psychical Research, but irritatingly cloaked by pseudonyms, the case involved two Englishwomen, thirty-three-year-old 'Dorothy Norton' and her sister-in-law 'Agnes Norton', vacationing with Dorothy's two children at Puys, France, in the August of 1951.

As the story goes, early in the morning of 4 August Dorothy and Agnes were asleep in a bedroom on the second floor of the three-storeyed house where they were staying. They were awoken by 'a most unusual series of sounds coming from the beach', about a quarter of a mile away. The night was fine yet the first sounds seemed like 'the cries of men heard as if above a storm'. It was only after they had been listening for about a quarter of an hour, during which Agnes briefly left the room, that Agnes asked Dorothy whether she had heard anything, at which point the women realised that they had both been hearing the same sounds. The sounds continued, prompting the pair to make independent notes, including a log of the times at which they were hearing them.

As they listened, the sounds seemed to ebb and flow in intensity, seemingly including cries, shouts and gunfire. When they put the light on, they saw that the time was 4.20 a.m. They then went out on to the balcony which looked towards, but had no view of, the sea, whereupon, according to Agnes, the sounds seemed to intensify, and to be a mixture of gunfire, shell-fire, sounds of landing craft and men's shouts. Dorothy's description was similar: 'it came in rolls of sound and the separate sounds of cries, guns and dive-bombing were very distinct. Many times we heard the sound of a shell at the same moment. The roaring became very loud.'

Both women agreed that there was a sudden cessation of all the noises at 4.50 a.m., then an equally sudden resumption at 5.05 (5.07 according to Agnes), rising to such an intensity that they were amazed that no one else in the house seemed to be disturbed, particularly since dawn had broken, accompanied by cockcrows and birdsong. The sounds of dive-bombers became more distinct, then suddenly, at 5.40 a.m., everything stopped again. At about 5.50 more plane noises were heard, then around 6.20, after a dying away of the sounds, Dorothy fell asleep through sheer tiredness. Agnes, who stayed awake, heard cries again around 6.25, but nothing at all after 6.55.

Later that day Agnes and Dorothy enquired whether anyone else had heard the noises during the night, only to find that no one had. Even a woman who was self-confessedly a restless sleeper, and whose light had been on when the noises had been at their height, said she had heard nothing. The two women therefore carefully wrote up their notes and posted them off to the Society of Psychical Research, with a covering letter inquiring whether there had been any similar reports.

At the society, investigators G. W. Lambert and the Hon. Mrs Kathleen Gay took up the case,[9] finding that the timing of the sounds reported by Dorothy and Agnes seemed to match very closely what would have been heard at Puys nine years previously, during the ill-fated Dieppe raid of 19 August 1942. The plan had been for the German coastal batteries along the coast either side of Puys to be taken out by a surprise landing of Canadian troops timed for 4.50 a.m. This was foiled when a small German convoy came across the invaders at 3.47, exchanging fire until after 4.00. Thus hindered, the Canadians' arrival at Dieppe was delayed until 5.07, supported by a shell bombardment from English destroyers at 5.12, and a Hurricane air attack on the German positions at 5.15. The first wave of Canadian ground troops went ashore at 5.20, followed by a second wave at 5.45, and noise in the air renewed at 5.50 with fresh fighter aircraft arriving from England now fiercely engaged by defending German planes.

On interviewing Dorothy and Agnes, researchers Lambert and Gay reported them to be sensible, well-balanced women who acknowledged that they remembered reading in the newspapers about the Dieppe raid at the time it happened, but insisted that they had neither taken any special interest nor researched it before going to Dieppe. They admitted owning a local guidebook which mentioned the raid, but this was found to contain altogether insufficient information to account for their story.

In the event it took seventeen years for there to emerge a serious objection to the sounds being of ghostly origin. This came from a Mr R. A. Eades who in 1968 wrote to the Society for Psychical Research claiming that he and his family had been camping just east of Dieppe at the end of August 1951, and had been woken 'by an indescribable noise which continued for several hours', which they discovered to be a dredger operating in Dieppe harbour. Suspecting that this might have been the true source of the sounds heard by Dorothy and Agnes, Eades made inquiries of the harbour authorities, and learnt that the dredger had indeed been operating from just after midnight to 8.15 a.m. on the morning of 4 August 1951. So despite the case's seemingly good credentials, the true ghostly nature of Dorothy and Agnes's experiences has to be regarded as more than a little suspect.

It is also pertinent that both women had far greater knowledge of World War II matters than they admitted to, as becomes apparent when their true identities are revealed, for which information I am indebted to the researches of Melvin Harris. For forty years the Society for Psychical Research has maintained their anonymity but it can now be disclosed that 'Dorothy' was Mrs Diana Neave, whose husband, Airey (assassinated by an IRA bomb in 1979), played a heroic part in the

Battle of Calais in 1940. In the post-war Nuremberg trials, Airey Neave led the prosecution of several important Nazis for war crimes, including for atrocities committed directly in reprisal for the Dieppe Raid. Diana, who had worked in underground intelligence during the war, helped Airey as a researcher, and would have had easy access to files with every operational detail. 'Agnes' was in fact one of Airey Neave's three sisters, and had served in the WRNS. Could their special knowledge have coloured their reports to the Society for Psychical Research? Or could it be argued that precisely such knowledge made them unlikely to mistake the sound of a harbour dredger for that of military action?

Complicating the matter further, the files of the Society for Psychical Research reveal Diana to have had an unusually intense interest in the psychic, her correspondence with the society extending well beyond this particular case. It may also be significant that the guidebook which the women had with them, referring to the Dieppe raid, also specifically mentioned that people had heard the sounds of the Battle of Culloden many years after the event. Overall, therefore, the case cannot be used as serious support for the idea of ghostly happenings echoing the original time at which they occurred.

We find ourselves on rather surer ground, thanks once again to the Robin Hayden case, regarding the time that the ghost perceives himself or herself to be in. Barbara McKenzie's daughter was the first to note that Robin Hayden's footsteps, rather than being heard on the present-day staircase, came instead from the site of the stairs in his own time. This is in fact one of many instances of ghosts being seen to move in the environment of their own era rather than ours: in the next chapter we will come across further examples of ghosts walking through walls and being seen on no longer existent floor-levels.

It might therefore seem that ghosts are locked in their own age and place, with the timing of their appearances bearing at least some relation to the circumstances of their own past. Unfortunately, however, it is not quite as straightforward as this, for there are other examples which show that certain ghosts seem to have at least an awareness of circumstances of the present day.

For instance, as we noted of the ghostly chanting heard at Beaulieu Abbey, on at least two occasions this occurred on the eve of a burial at

Beaulieu. As described by the Montagu motor museum's Michael Sedgwick:

> It [the ghostly chanting] . . . occurred on the night that someone in the village had died. The second time I heard it was . . . also on the eve of a burial.[10]

It was as if the ghostly monks of centuries ago somehow remained aware of present-day events, and felt obliged to perform their traditional offices in response to them.

But perhaps one of the most fascinating instances of a ghost's apparent awareness of current circumstances – and in particular of the time of day – was described to me by a long-time friend and colleague, television producer David Rolfe. David and his wife Jacqui live in a converted wing of a period mansion not far from Burnham, Buckinghamshire. Around 1986, when their eldest daughter Sophie was sixteen, Jacqui gave birth to a second daughter. In the early months, while Jacqui needed to get up during the night to attend to the new baby, David slept in a separate bedroom, his task being to get up early to take Sophie to school.

David aimed to be up by 7 a.m., but one morning, when it was particularly important for him to be on time, he overslept. Suddenly he was awoken by a rattling of the door knob and the door opening, and half opening his eyes, he found himself confronted by a woman dressed as a Victorian housekeeper, standing only feet from where he lay. She looked totally solid, and her expression seemed to be saying to him: 'You really *ought* to be getting up.'

Instantly conscious that for the first time in his life he was seeing a ghost – with all the disbelief that that arouses – David momentarily shut his eyes, expecting that when he opened them again she would have disappeared. But to his astonishment, this was not the case. As he now tried to focus on her appearance she simply faded into nothingness. He estimates that the whole experience lasted only approximately fifteen seconds, yet in his words it was 'very real'.

If we accept this – and it has been the only known appearance of this ghost – the only inference to be drawn is that whoever the ghostly housekeeper was, she was aware of David's circumstances and felt it her duty to provide a helpful wake-up call. This seems therefore, rather than a haunting in which the ghost is in need of help *from* the living, to be a timely and practical-minded appearance in order to give help *to* the living. Indeed, it suggests there may be a type of ghost we have not yet considered – one not tied to a time and place by some great tragedy, but instead looking after the living occupants of a house rather like a fairy godmother or guardian angel.

It is difficult enough for us to believe that some ghosts are locked in their own time and space while others exhibit every apparent consciousness of the present day, yet harder still to credit is that in very rare instances there are certain ghosts that may show awareness of the future. In fact we have already come across one possible instance of this with regard to the passing caller appearance of the just-deceased Catholic priest Fr Thomas Ford to Fr Walter Cooksey (see pp. 65–6). As may be recalled, unknown to any living person at that time, Fr Cooksey was chosen a few weeks later as Fr Ford's successor at the latter's Bromley parish. Since, up to and including the time of Fr Ford's death, the two priests did not know each other, the only conceivable explanation seems to be that by some means Fr Ford learned on his death who his successor would be and made a special post-mortem appearance to him.

However, seemingly yet more prescient of the future was a well-witnessed ghostly occurrence which took place in New Zealand in 1886, anticipating the worst volcanic disaster in the country's history. On the morning of 31 May 1886 a party of tourists assembled on the waterfront at the Maori village of Te Wairoa for a sightseeing cruise on Lake Tarawera in the thermal Rotorua region of New Zealand's North Island. The area is one of outstanding natural beauty, dominated by tree-clad Mount Tarawera, the Maoris' 'Burnt Peak' (because it was a supposedly extinct volcano), and including a then world-famous wonder, the Pink and White Terraces, a breathtaking seven-acre pink, white and turquoise natural staircase created by hundreds of years of geyser activity. The party included the noted Maori guide Sophia; Mrs R. Sise and her husband and daughter from Dunedin on New Zealand's South Island; a Dr Ralph; Father Kelleher, a Roman Catholic priest from Auckland; a Mr Quick, also from Auckland; three other Maori women, and six Maori rowers.

The first sign of something odd was when, before anyone had even got on board the waiting boat, the level of the lake rose alarmingly, temporarily marooning the party, before subsiding with equal suddenness. This seriously alarmed the Maoris, who proved reluctant to embark, the guide Sophia being heard to mutter, 'I don't think I shall see the Terraces again.' After everyone had finally got on board and the boat was under way, there was a further surprise in store. As described by Mrs Sise:

> After sailing some time we saw in the distance a large boat, look-
> ing glorious in the mist and in the sunlight. It was full of Maoris,
> some standing up, and it was near enough for me to see the sun
> glittering on the paddles. The boat was hailed but returned no an-
> swer. We thought so little of it at the time that Dr Ralph did not
> even turn to look at the canoe, and until our return to Te Wairoa in
> the evening we never gave it another thought. Then to our surprise
> we found the Maoris in great excitement and heard from McCrae
> [a permanent resident] and other Europeans that no such boat had
> ever been on the lake.[11]

Unappreciated at the time by the Europeans – and it subsequently emerged that besides Mrs Sise's party, a second tourist boat on the lake that day had also witnessed the spectacle – what they had seen was a Maori war canoe, complete with two rows of occupants, one line rowing, the other standing wrapped in flax robes and with their hair plumed in special feathers as for death.

But as the Maori witnesses were all too well aware, no *real* canoe of that kind had been out on the lake that day, or within living memory. What they had seen was a ghost, one that the Maoris, nurtured on a legend of a fierce cannibal chief whom their 'High Priest of the War Canoe' had imprisoned deep inside Mount Tarawera, and who it had long been feared might one day escape, unhesitatingly interpreted as an omen of disaster.

Whatever credence we may attach to the Maoris' legend, the inescapable fact is that the 'ghost' war canoe was very well observed, by both the Maoris and the Europeans. Mrs Sise wrote all about it in a letter to her son in Dunedin that evening. And a passenger on the second tourist boat, Josiah Martin, even made a sketch of it from which, together with the eye-witness descriptions, the artist Kennett Watkins created a fine oil painting, now in the Auckland City Art Gallery [pl. 17].

An equally inescapable fact is that a mere ten days later, on the night of 10 June 1886, the supposedly extinct Mount Tarawera suddenly erupted, spewing out fire, lava, mud and rock with enormous violence. The village of Te Wairoa, together with two others, was totally obliterated, and 153 people, including six Europeans, lost their lives. Lake Tarawera was temporarily substantially drained away. And the Pink and White Terraces were destroyed so utterly that even their location can no longer be determined with any precision.

From these facts there is a compelling implication that the appearance of the ghostly war canoe was somehow linked to the volcanic disaster. And if we accept this, then it is difficult to avoid the inference that for some ghosts at least there is knowledge not only of events past and present, but also of events future. While I do not even begin to understand how this can be, it is something that certainly needs to be borne in mind as part of our overall attempt to understand the nature of ghosts.

If the issues surrounding *when* ghosts appear are perplexing enough, what now of those pertaining to *where* they appear? What of the enigma of ghosts and place?

CHAPTER ELEVEN

Ghosts and Place

The association of ghosts with the places they haunt might often seem too obvious to merit special attention.

After all, Clarissa Mills is known to have worked in the very office at Nebraska Wesleyan University where Mrs Buterbaugh saw her ghost. Major William Braddell was a member of the Naval and Military Club, therefore it might seem not too unreasonable for his ghost to appear in the club's Egremont Room. And Robin Hayden lived in his parents' farmhouse at Hook, so it is only to be expected that he would haunt the site of that home.

But of these three familiar examples, only Clarissa Mills died relatively close to where her ghost appeared – in fact in a room just across the hallway from the office where she worked. And so far as can be determined (the American Society for Psychical Research's investigators seem to have been more interested in Mrs Buterbaugh than in Miss Mills), hers was the most peaceful of the three deaths, seemingly of a heart attack after having struggled to the office through a bitter wind.[1] Of the others, Major Braddell was killed a mile or more from the club, while commanding his Kensington anti-aircraft battery during a German air raid. And Robin Hayden shot himself in a field about 150 yards from Hayden's Farm.

Given that each of these individuals would have had a perfectly dignified funeral, followed by burial in a cemetery some distance from the scene of their haunting, why should their ghosts have chosen to manifest where they did? Of course, no one can be sure. But in each case there does appear to be one common and logical factor linking them to the place of their haunting: very strong emotion.

For instance, Clarissa Mills would seem to have been highly dedicated to her work as a musical instructor, her particular speciality having been choral singing. The tall music cabinet into which her ghost was seen reaching, and which stood in the office where she worked, was found to contain choral works – Bach, Pergolesi and Thomas Whitney Surette's *Concord Choral Arrangements* – all dating back to her time. It is not unreasonable to infer that her work was her life, and that in dying suddenly she left behind, there in the office that had been her world, an emotional attachment strong enough for her ghost to be bonded there. It may also be relevant that the object of Mrs Buterbaugh's visit to the office where she saw Clarissa's ghost had been to convey a message concerning choral singing to the professor who was temporarily using that office.

As for Major Braddell, if we consider why his ghost might appear in the Naval and Military Club's Egremont Room, it seems rather more than coincidence that this was precisely where, only a few days before he himself died, his two dining companions, Colonel William Gordon and Major Crozier, were killed while he was away taking a telephone call. Among his fellow officers Braddell had the nickname 'Perky' on account of his normal cheeriness, but on the deaths of his two friends he was reported to have commented: 'What a dreadful business!' Almost inevitably, such a comment must have cloaked much deeper feelings. Were these the emotions that caused his ghost to be latched to the Egremont Room?

The case of Robin Hayden is perhaps the most straightforward of all. His parents' farmhouse, the natural centre of his life, would also have been the focus of his emotions because it were there that he would have fought out the battle in his mind between the intensity of his love for the local publican's daughter, and the near fanatical puritanical opposition he knew he could expect from his parents and their employers, the Burberrys. It is hard to think of a more appropriate expression for that conflict of emotions than the ghostly, heavy-footed pacing up and down that the McKenzie family heard. Clearly his emotions were so powerful that even his suicide failed to resolve them.

Unresolved emotional conflict that becomes focused on a place therefore seems to be a significant factor determining why ghosts haunt where they do. And the same applies to cases where someone has been murdered and the body has been left unburied – hence the classic case of the Athenian ghost encountered by Athenodorus, its Japanese counterpart, and others of the same ilk.

But are all ghosts and ghostly experiences associated with particular places the products of seemingly sentient individuals still emotionally attached to those locations? Or do some at least have no sentient being behind them? Are some mere memory traces somehow etched into the fabric of the environment?

Here we confront the rarer but by no means uncommon instances in which the ghost experience may take the form not merely of a single apparition, but of a whole scene from the past which in the mind of the percipient occludes exactly the same setting from the present day, as if in a timeslip. Something of this kind was reported by Mrs Buterbaugh immediately following her encounter with the Clarissa Mills ghost. As she told Dr Gardner Murphy of the American Society for Psychical Research:

> Up until the time she [Clarissa Mills] faded away I was not aware of anyone else being in the suite of rooms, but just about the time of her fading out I felt as though I still was not alone. To my left was a desk, and I had a feeling there was a man sitting at that desk. I turned around and saw no one, but I still felt his presence. When that feeling of his presence left I have no idea, because it was then, when I looked out of the window behind that desk, that I got frightened . . . when I looked out of that window there wasn't one modern thing out there. The street, (Madison Street) which is less than a half-block away from the building, was not even there and neither was the new Willard House. That was when I realised that these people were not in my time, but that I was back in their time.[2]

Mrs Buterbaugh went on to explain further the view she saw from the window:

* * *

The window was open. Even though it was fairly early in the morning it appeared as though it were a very warm, summer afternoon. It was very still. There were a few scattered trees – about two on my right (east) and about three on my left (west). It seems to me there were more, but these are the only ones I can be definite about. The rest was open field; the new Willard sorority house and also Madison Street were not there. I remember seeing a very vague outline of some sort of building to my right and that is about all. Nothing else but open field.[3]

Dr Gardner Murphy discovered that Mrs Buterbaugh's impression of what she could see out of the window seemed to correspond with an old photograph of the university's earlier surroundings. Another notable feature seeming to indicate a genuine timeslip character to her experience was an extreme quietness, quite out of phase with the real surroundings, in which students were noisily changing classes. As she told Gardner Murphy:

It was not until I was back out in the hall that I again heard the familiar noises . . . The girls that were going into the orientation class as I entered the rooms were still going in and someone was still playing the marimba.[4]

In relation to such experiences the case that is inevitably most commonly called to mind, because it is so well known, is the so-called Trianon Adventure at Versailles, France. Back in August 1901 two English spinsters were walking through the gardens of the Palace of Versailles, just outside Paris, looking for the Petit Trianon, the mini-palace beloved of Marie Antoinette. Becoming lost they came across two men in grey-green coats whom they took to be gardeners, who gave them directions. The spinsters felt a still, eerie quality to the atmosphere.

Coming to a bridge and a kiosk, they encountered a man with a repulsive pockmarked appearance. Then a man with buckled shoes ran up behind them and gave them further directions. As they approached what they took to be the Petit Trianon, the elder of the two spinsters saw a fair-haired, middle-aged woman in an 'old-fashioned' dress sketching on the lawn just below the terrace. Then a young man directed them to the Petit Trianon's front entrance where, joining a wedding party on a guided tour, they found themselves in normal circumstances once more.

On the spinsters' own admission, apart from the briefest exchange – 'Do you think the Petit Trianon is haunted?' 'Yes, I do' – neither of them properly discussed the oddity of their experience for the next three months, and only then did they begin to make notes. On separate occasions both returned to Versailles, finding that some of the surroundings they had formerly seen were now dramatically changed. For instance, there was a long-established rhododendron bush where the woman had been sketching. Researching the costumes of the individuals they had seen, they found that these matched the pre-French Revolution period. What the elder of the pair could remember of the woman sketching seemed to match portraits of Marie Antoinette. They wrote up their story and in 1911 had it published pseudonymously under the title *An Adventure*, claiming that they believed they must somehow have 'entered within an act of the Queen's [i.e. Marie Antoinette's] memory'.

The publication caused quite a sensation, running into several editions, and public interest was further fuelled when it was revealed that the spinsters were elderly Charlotte Moberly, daughter of a bishop of Salisbury and for a quarter of a century principal of St Hugh's College at Oxford, and Derbyshire vicar's daughter Eleanor Jourdain, sixteen years Miss Moberly's junior and her vice-principal at St Hugh's.

Despite the women's seemingly impeccable credentials, doubts were raised about the experience, particularly by the Society for Psychical Research's ever-diligent weeder-out of the spurious, Mrs Eleanor Sidgwick. With characteristic tartness she commented in a review:

> No detailed account of the experiences was apparently written till three months later . . . and it is unusual to be able to rely on one's memory of things seen after even a much shorter interval of time.[5]

Opinions of the Trianon Adventure's validity have fluctuated ever since, among individuals both outside and inside the field of psychical research. In support, other visitors to Versailles have occasionally claimed similar experiences. In early October 1928 Haslemere schoolmistress Clare

M. Burrow and one of her pupils reportedly came across 'an old man . . . in an old green and silver uniform' who shouted at them 'in hoarse and unintelligible French' and who seemed to have 'completely vanished' when they looked back.[6] In September 1938 Mrs Elizabeth Hatton of Oxford saw a peasant man and woman with a trundle cart who likewise 'seemed gradually to vanish' as she watched.[7] In May 1955 a London solicitor and his wife reportedly came across two men and a woman in eighteenth-century costumes who then mysteriously disappeared.

Favouring a much more down-to-earth explanation, in 1965 Frenchman Philippe Jullian argued that the people seen by the Misses Moberly and Jourdain were most likely the Count Robert de Montesquiou and his friends performing a period-costumed tableau vivant – something which apparently they were wont to do around the turn of the century at locations like Versailles.[8] Miss Jourdain's literary executor and former pupil Dame Joan Evans was clearly convinced by this explanation and thereafter refused to allow any new edition of the book. It has also recently been suggested that suppressed lesbian inclinations on the part of Moberly and Jourdain may have prompted them to fantasise an encounter with Marie Antoinette, the latter having been something of a role model for those of such tendencies around the turn of the last century.

It has to be acknowledged that just as the supposed 'Dieppe raid' noises could have been caused by a dredger, so in a large open-air location like Versailles the Misses Moberly and Jourdain could easily have misidentified as ghosts what might in reality have been a perfectly innocent group of people dressed in period costume. Whatever the validity of the Trianon Adventure, to regard it as an experience from which deductions can be drawn would be distinctly unsafe.

When, however, someone reports, in all seriousness, that just feet from them they have seen an army of Roman soldiers step out of the wall of a cellar and march across the floor, no such mistake in identification is possible. They are either seriously hallucinating, seriously lying – or seriously telling the truth.

That is precisely what has been described by several independent witnesses, mostly unknown to each other, of what they have experienced during the span of several decades in one specific location, the catacomb-like cellars below the historic Treasurer's House [pl. 18] within the close of York Minster, England. Some of these witnesses are still alive today, prime among them being Harry Martindale [pl. 19], a six-foot four-inch tall, retired policeman, who strikes all who meet him as the last sort of individual given to flights of fancy.[9]

At around lunchtime on a cold February day in 1953, the then eighteen-year-old Harry was an apprentice plumber, working on installing central heating pipes in the Treasurer's House's cellars. He was alone, in darkness except for the lamp he had brought with him, and was standing on a short ladder, hacking into the wall when, in his own words:

> I heard a trumpet call. My first thought was that someone had got a wireless on loud. Then I realised the sound was coming from the wall. The next moment out popped the top of a soldier's helmet. My immediate reaction was to step backwards, and I fell off the ladder, then scuttled back into the corner of the cellar. As I did so the soldier wearing the helmet came out of the wall. He had the trumpet and walked across to the opposite wall. After him a great big cart-horse came out head-first. Behind came at least twenty men in double file, but I couldn't see anything of them from the knees down, except in one place where part of the floor had been dug away. I was so shocked it felt as though my hair stood on end – everyone I saw looked just like real human beings.[10]

On rushing back upstairs, still in a state of shock, the first person Harry came across was the Treasurer's House's then curator. Seeing the expression on Harry's face, the curator said: 'By the look of you, you've seen the Romans, haven't you?' It was a remark that was of the most enormous relief to Harry, for until then he had been seriously doubting his own sanity. Now he realised he could not have been the only person to have had the experience.

At the curator's request, Harry wrote down a detailed account of all that he could remember of a happening that had lasted, at his best estimate, perhaps ten seconds. Particularly vivid was his memory of the trumpet carried by the first soldier. Somewhat similar to a long posthorn, this was not curved in any way, and looked 'rather battered', as if it had been used over a long time. Harry insists that he heard it blowing throughout the time that the soldiers were passing him, even long after the trumpeter himself had disappeared through the wall.

The soldiers were nothing like the Roman soldiers as portrayed in the films of the 1950s that Harry had seen. In stature they seemed surprisingly small: 'Not much more than five feet' in height. Their helmets were decorated with bedraggled, un-dyed plumes of feathers and their kilts dyed a streaky green. Although they seemed to have little armour, there was at least one round, bulbous shield and their weapons included spears and short dagger-like swords. They walked rather than marched, no more than two abreast, and not in any proper formation, and appeared to be 'extremely tired', dishevelled and unshaven.

After Harry had written down all that he could remember, the curator showed him reports already in his files of others who had previously experienced something very similar. Sadly, the whereabouts of those original reports is no longer known, but an earlier curator allegedly had the same experience in 1946; so too did a visiting American professor in the 1930s. Earlier still, while the Treasurer's House was privately owned by a Mr Frank Green, a young lady attending a fancy-dress party reportedly went down into the cellars, possibly while playing hide-and-seek, and found her way barred by a man dressed as a Roman soldier. Although this 'soldier' did not speak, he placed his spear across the passageway, firmly indicating that she should go no further. Initially supposing him to be another of the partygoers, she went back upstairs to ask who had come dressed in this manner. The host told her very firmly that no known guest was wearing any such costume.

Besides these somewhat imperfectly attested occurrences, at least one other living person claims an experience of the Romans similar to Harry's. This is Mrs Joan Mawson,[11] who, with her first husband Tom Morcum, lived and worked as curator-caretakers at the Treasurer's House in the years shortly after Harry's experience. At this time the house still did not have full central heating, and at weekends, when no maintenance man was on duty, the Morcums had to go down into the cellars to attend to the boilers themselves. Part of the route demanded bending to get through a low arched tunnel of brick [pl. 20], and whenever Joan did this she was usually accompanied by her faithful white bull terrier. However, at around 5 p.m. one winter Sunday in 1957 both she and the terrier were in for a shock. As recalled by Joan:

We got to the top of the steps and then went down a few steps into

the tunnel and she [the bull terrier] refused point blank to go. In
fact she turned on her tail and went howling up the stairs. I couldn't
understand it, because this dog was so true she would follow me
anywhere. I got halfway through [the tunnel] and . . . [at first] I
thought it was people up above, horses up above coming along. I
could hear in the distance this noise of horses. Not running, not
galloping, but you knew it was the sound of hooves coming along.
The next thing I realised there was somebody behind me. I sensed
it, and was petrified – it's no good saying I was anything else. I
curled up huddled against the wall wondering what on earth was
happening.

The next moment Joan found herself overtaken by what, like Harry, she
unhesitatingly identified as a troop of Roman soldiers. Some were within
two feet of her and, just like Harry, she saw them only from the thighs
up, as if they were walking through thick mud: 'Nobody had legs, from
about the knees. You didn't see any feet, horses' or humans'.'
Yet there was nothing transparent or ghostly about the figures:

They were completely solid. There was no pretending it was just a
vision wandering past you. In fact, if I hadn't been so frightened I
think I could have put my hand out and expected to touch a solid
person.

As they passed, the troop went on in a direction that Joan gauged would
lead, at twentieth-century street level, to York Minster. Unlike Harry,
who saw only one horse, Joan saw several, mostly being led by the
men. But the general state of exhaustion was just as he described:

They were so tired-looking! Dishevelled! Their uniforms were so
dirty. There were easily four or five horses going along. And quite
a number of the soldiers with them. And you could see the reins
quite easily. And the tops of them.

In the event, Joan had the same experience on two or three further
occasions, though in each case with slight but intriguing differences.
The second time they all looked very much dirtier than the first:

* * *

The horses were so splashed with mud. And you could see this.
And they looked exhausted, as though horse and riders had had a
long journey somewhere.

On the third occasion the soldiers were mostly on horseback, but leaning
on the horses' necks as if almost asleep on them.

Unlike Harry, Joan did not hear the trumpet during any of these
experiences. But although for many years she did not mention anything
even to her own family (this was partly because of her first husband
Tom's ill-health), when she did it was to learn that her ward, Caroline,
who lived with them in the upstairs part of the house, had frequently
heard from her room what could only have been the same ghostly Roman
trumpet. Yet neither Caroline nor Joan's husband Tom ever saw the
soldiers during the many trips that they had made down into the cellars.

For both Harry and Joan such was the shock of their experiences –
and neither knew of the other for some twenty years – that it was only in
1974, when Harry was reluctantly persuaded to make his story public,
that Joan opened up a little about what had happened to her. Yet besides
the several independent experiences, the sightings also seem to check
out historically.

Thus Harry's statement that the soldiers carried round shields initially
caused some doubt, on the grounds that Roman infantry never had round
shields. Then it was discovered that about the time that the Sixth Legion
was withdrawn from York in the fourth century, they were reinforced
by auxiliaries who did carry round shields.

Similarly, excavations by archaeologist Peter Wenham and others
established that remains of the Roman road known as the Via Decumana,
leading from Roman York's north-eastern gate to its legionary
headquarters, lie just about eighteen inches below the floor level of the
Treasurer's House's cellar. Not only does this road run towards the
Minster, taking the route along which Joan saw the Romans moving,
height-wise also it is at the level at which she and Harry saw their Romans
[pl. 21].

This readily explains why both saw the men and horses 'thigh-deep'
in the floor. In fact, in Harry's case, because he was in a part of the
cellars where, unknown to him at the time, the archaeologists had been

excavating, he was able to see the men's very 'home-made'-looking cross-gartered sandals and the horse's shaggy-looking fetlocks precisely where they had cleared. In a portion where the old Roman road was missing they even 'appeared to be walking on air'.

Slightly complicating this is an intriguing remark by Mrs Mawson that she felt she could see rather more than should physically have been visible within the cellar's narrow confines: 'For such a small tunnel you were amazed what a lot you saw.' She speculated that in part at least 'it must have been through the brickwork as well that you were seeing them'.

But this aside, in essence we find ourselves back to exactly the same observation that was made of Robin Hayden's footsteps – that some ghosts seem to move in space as if the physical environment was unchanged from their own time. They seem frozen in both time and space: in time because they are able only to repeat certain movements that they performed at a crucial moment when alive; in space because those movements happen in the identical place in which they would have occurred when the ghost was a living person – irrespective of changes that might have occurred over many years.

So are such 'whole scene' ghosts – including, as in Mrs Buterbaugh's experience, a whole ghostly landscape, and, as in the York experience, a whole troop of men and horses – simply place-locked recording tracks with all the impersonality of a compact disc? Or, despite the ghosts' seeming multiplicity of human, animal and vegetable content, can one or more sentient beings be detected behind them?

In the York experience, one argument in favour of the former alternative is the fact, as attested by both Harry Martindale and Joan Mawson, that the Romans exhibited absolutely no awareness of their twentieth-century observers – a great relief to both, as they would have found any ghostly reaction to their presence even more frightening.

Contrarily, however, we cannot be altogether sure even of this, for if we take account of the altogether more anecdotal story of the 1920s party-goer, we may remember that the Roman soldier she encountered reportedly deliberately barred her way. The slight but significant differences between Harry Martindale's and Joan Mawson's experiences similarly suggest that these may not have been totally mechanical, in the manner of an inanimate recording.

But rather more positively indicative of something genuinely sentient behind even such ostensibly mechanical 'whole scene' hauntings is provided by another, similarly dramatic case of this type[12] described to me by Canon Dominic Walker, vicar of Brighton parish church, and chairman of the Christian Deliverance Study Group.

In 1979, when Canon Walker was one of those responsible for attending to hauntings and poltergeist phenomena occurring in the Diocese of Southwark, he was called to a young family nearly terrified out of their wits by what had happened to them at their home in Streatham, south London. One night they were awoken by what sounded like burglars. However, when the husband opened the bedroom door, to his disbelief he saw walking along the landing groups of people 'with heads downcast and carrying what looked like brown paper parcels'.[13] They were wearing period clothes, and as he watched, they simply disappeared through the far wall. The family quickly fled the house, and the father went to a phone box in the street to call the police. From here, as he looked back at the house, he was able to see the ghostly figures still walking past the landing window.

A young police cadet with a dog answered the call, and, in what we may now regard as a classic canine reaction to ghosts, the dog refused point-blank to enter the house. But when the cadet did so, to his utter astonishment he saw exactly the same people as had been reported by the family. They were dressed in very old-fashioned-looking clothes, they were carrying bundles, and they appeared to be in mourning. The policeman left the house in a state of considerable shock, and only after Canon Walker had performed a special service of blessing could the family be persuaded to return to normal residence.

On subsequent investigation, two pertinent and arguably closely related facts emerged. First, the family living in the house had lost their new-born baby in a cot-death tragedy only three weeks previously. They had been beset by grief and guilt at a time when people were suspicious of parents who had suffered a cot death, and the night the ghostly mourners appeared was the very first on which their other two children had been moved back into their own bedroom.

Second, as revealed by the local vicar, this case was one of a number of similar strange occurrences in this particular part of his parish, which, he had learned from old records, had been built over a plague pit. There can be little doubt that the brown paper parcels being carried by the people on the landing were the shrouded bodies of children who centuries before had died of the plague. Why the ghosts should have been seen on an upper storey level is a mystery that can only be answered by further information about the house's exact location, which due to loss of the Deliverance Study Group's records of this particular case is not available.

The important feature in this case is that it would seem that the emotions aroused by the death of the Streatham family's baby somehow triggered past scenes of similar human grief over infants' deaths at the same location. As in the case of the Beaulieu monks heard chanting in response to present-day deaths, the implication has to be that a sentient mind or minds from centuries ago was somehow responding to this recent cot death. Accordingly, while the appearance of the haunting may seem to have been a mere mechanical 'memory locked in the woodwork' (and indeed the Deliverance Group has dubbed such hauntings 'place memories' on this assumption), the reality may be the existence of an altogether more sentient and sympathetic intelligence than has previously been supposed.

With the issues raised by such place-tied ghosts still far from resolved, one question spurs us ever on. If ghosts can and do link themselves so closely to places, can they also be more mobile? Could there be circumstances in which they may attach themselves to people, and even to objects?

CHAPTER TWELVE

Ghosts That Attach Themselves to People

Whatever ghosts are, thankfully for the most part they keep to wherever they haunt. Normally, if they occupy a house, they do not follow outside that house's environs those to whom they appear. But there are exceptions, and it is those with which we are concerned in this chapter.

Like the phenomenon of ghosts, the phenomenon called 'possession' is known all around the world and has been observed since Biblical times and no doubt long before. Most cases of this kind do not concern us, as possessing entities are most commonly, in religious parlance, demons, or, in psychiatric parlance, splintered aspects of a person's psyche referred to as 'multiple personalities'. There is rarely any suggestion that the possessing entity is the ghost of a dead person.

One interesting and well-observed exception, albeit from more than a century ago, was a case which took place in Watseka, Illinois, in the United States, focusing on a rather disturbed teenager called Lurancy Vennum.[1] In 1877, when Lurancy was thirteen, she began to go into strange trance-like states, some involving her taking on disagreeable personalities. Her parents feared insanity and in the hope of avoiding committing her to an asylum they put her under the care of a Dr W. Stevens, who experimented with hypnotising her.

Under hypnosis, Lurancy described being surrounded by ghosts, one of whom she named as Mary Roff. This was a local girl who had been similarly subject to bouts of seeming insanity, and who had died twelve years earlier. Still under hypnosis, Lurancy announced that she would allow the ghost of the dead Mary Roff to 'possess' her, and the next day, long after she had been brought out of the hypnotic trance, it became apparent that she was behaving as if she *was* Mary Roff, even demanding to be taken back 'home' to where the Roffs lived. On looking out of the window and seeing Mrs Roff and her surviving daughter Minerva walking along the street, she exclaimed, 'Why, there comes Ma and my sister Nervie!', and moments later was embracing them as if they were her true family.

With considerable reluctance the Vennums eventually agreed to their daughter going to live with the Roffs. On 11 February 1878, as she was passing the house where the Roffs had lived when Mary was alive, she stopped and needed considerable persuasion that the family no longer lived there. On arrival at the Roffs' new home she immediately recognised the piano that the dead Mary had known, and greeted the gathered Roff relatives and acquaintances by name with easy familiarity. For example, seeing Mrs Wagner who, as Mary Lord, had been Mary Roff's Sunday School teacher, she remarked: 'Oh Mary Lord, you've changed the least of anyone.' Seemingly aware that she was in another person's body and that her own lay dead in the ground,[2] she told the family that the 'angels' would allow her to stay until some time in May.

During these ensuing weeks she continued to exhibit every sign of genuinely possessing the dead Mary's memories and personality. She gave a detailed account of how she had once stayed at a water-cure place in Peoria. She correctly identified an old velvet head-dress that she had worn 'when my hair was short', also a collar that she had tatted. She pointed out where a family dog had died, and where on his arm one of the male members of the Roff family had been burnt by a stove pipe during Mary's lifetime. When any of the Vennums called on her she treated them as if they were strangers, though with Mrs Roff's encouragement she paid visits to the family and gradually learned to be friendlier towards them.

On 21 May, she calmly went around saying her farewells to the Roff family and their neighbours, set off for the Vennum home and at some point on the way 'became' Lurancy Vennum once more. Four years later, she married a local farmer, and although occasionally the old 'Mary' might remanifest if she visited the Roffs, she settled down to a conventional life as a wife and mother.

Did the ghost of Mary Roff, who died at about the same age that Lurancy was in 1878, genuinely take over the body of Lurancy Vennum during the fourteen weeks she stayed with the Roffs? Although several leading psychical researchers of the time, including the highly sceptical Australian Richard Hodgson, became convinced of this, the case might seem to us too old to carry conviction were it not buttressed by other more recent examples of ghosts that have attached themselves to people, manifesting sometimes inside, sometimes alongside their bodies.

One example of the latter was described at first hand some thirty years ago by the international concert pianist Michael Howard Romney-Woollard, professionally known as 'Michaeli'. All his life Michaeli had nurtured an ambition to visit the Civil War battlefield of Edgehill in Warwickshire, the historical ghostly associations of which we noted in an earlier chapter. In June 1960 he decided to fulfil his wish and set off for Warwickshire in the company of two friends, one a former army officer. Shortly after stopping for lunch in Banbury, they lost their way, whereupon, in Michaeli's own words:

> having no means of discovering precisely where we were, I asked my friends to stop for a few minutes. Getting out of the car I looked around me, and by some strange instinct, which seemed to come directly from the past, I was able to direct them to the site correctly, which then lay some two miles away from our stopping position. As we went along the countryside, I became conscious of the fact that all the scenery was familiar to me, although I have never visited that part of the country before, and I mentioned this odd fact to my companions, who appeared to take it all with a 'pinch of salt'.[3]

Although this observation is interesting in its own right in relation to the well-known phenomenon of *déjà vu*, more immediately relevant to us is Michaeli's account of what happened next. Arriving at the Edgehill site, which he discovered to be occupied by an army ammunition depot, he and his companions were permitted to view it with an escort of two soldiers:

> As we approached a lane on the site, near to a place where

Cavaliers and Roundheads are buried together, I became very disturbed, for I was aware that hundreds of unseen men were watching me. My agitation must have been quickly noted by my two friends, who asked me why I looked so unwell and frightened, but all that I remember saying was that I wished to return home immediately.

On my return to my house in London that evening, unaccompanied by my companions, I was aware of a most terrifying fact, which was that I had brought back with me one of the dead from the battlefield . . . This unseen but very evident visitor was, I knew, beside me everywhere I went in my house, and remained with me for about a month after. In my mind I would see a man, clad in the period; and I would describe him as a Roundhead, for he wore armour, and had a small moustache, with deep piercing eyes, and carried a sword. His presence in my house caused me such alarm . . . that I soon became highly nervous and unwell, and at night left lights burning in all my rooms till morning came, when I felt less uneasy with the coming of daylight.

Insisting that he was not 'an adherent of Spiritualism', Michaeli claimed the experience as 'the most terrifying' of his life, and one he would be unable to forget 'to the end of my days'.

We might feel inclined to dismiss all this as just an artiste's overactive imagination, were it not for other reported cases of ghosts seeming to latch on to living people, sometimes in ways of which the living person has no conscious awareness.

The man who is arguably the leading expert in this field is Hampshire psychiatrist Dr Kenneth McAll, whose serious inaccuracies in reporting a conventional haunting we highlighted back in Chapter 1, as a result of which it is important to treat his claimed possession cases with similar caution. Even so, as we stressed earlier, McAll's personal integrity is not in question, and it is therefore worth quoting one of the cases from his 1982 book, *Healing the Family Tree*, so that the broad pattern he favours may become apparent.

This particular example,[4] dating from the 1950s, concerns two women from within a single family who without any obvious cause had developed disturbed, irrational behaviour. The first of these was Margaret,[5] in her seventies, who was living with her younger sister Nellie.

Nellie, who brought the case to McAll's attention, related how Margaret would without the slightest provocation suddenly become extraordinarily violent and aggressive towards her and everything around her, smashing objects without cause, then afterwards becoming profusely apologetic and quite unable to account for her behaviour.

Nellie and Margaret's mother Helen, who had died four years earlier at the age of ninety-six, had been prone to the same sort of disturbing behaviour. And their niece Rhonda, daughter of their youngest sister Ailsa and married with three young sons, had also begun to exhibit similar tendencies, even though she was only in her early thirties. One evening Rhonda's husband had arrived back from work to find their home nearly wrecked, with badly damaged furniture, broken windows, general chaos, and his wife quite unable to account for what had gone wrong. He was so alarmed by this and related incidents that he threatened to leave Rhonda, taking the children with him, a move which prompted Rhonda to seek independent psychiatric help.

It was a curious reaction from Margaret that led McAll to suspect that a ghostly ancestor rather than rogue genes might be responsible for the disturbed behaviour among these successive generations of women. At his suggestion, Nellie had tried using a simple exorcist-type invocation the next time Margaret became violent. Margaret immediately grew even more aggressive, savagely slapping her sister across the face, and screaming, 'It's Great-Aunt Agnes! It's Great-Aunt Agnes!' Mystified as to who this Great-Aunt Agnes might be, McAll set about trying to trace the family's ancestry, finding that there was indeed an Agnes, born in 1814, who had been the grandmother of Margaret and Nellie's mother Helen.

Furthermore the family tree [see fig. 3 overleaf] also revealed a most curious pattern. As McAll explained:

For the past six generations the eldest female in the family had shown signs of similarly disturbed behaviour. This trait had begun in about 1750 when a murder had been committed in the family. The eldest daughter, Elizabeth, became an alcoholic and destroyed much family property before she drank herself to death at the age of forty. Subsequently each eldest daughter in the family had had violent temper tantrums . . .[6]

The Family Tree of Margaret and Rhonda

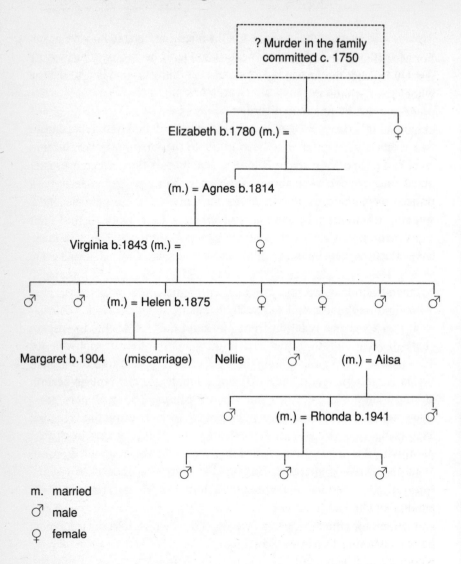

Fig. 3 **Family tree of Hampshire psychiatrist Dr Kenneth McAll's patients Rhonda and Margaret**, showing the line of descendants following a family murder committed c. 1750. According to McAll, the eldest female in each subsequent generation developed during adulthood uncharacteristic and seemingly inexplicable tendencies to unprovoked destructiveness and violence, culminating in McAll's patients Margaret and her niece Rhonda. When McAll held a service of requiem for the unknown ancestor responsible, Margaret and Rhonda's violent behaviour promptly ceased. To protect patient-doctor confidentiality, some names have been changed.

From family tree reproduced in Dr Kenneth McAll's book Healing the Family Tree, *London, Sheldon Press, 1982.*

* * *

For McAll's theory of ghostly influence to be proved valid, the crucial test lay in what might happen if he held a simple service to lay to rest whoever or whatever had been haunting Rhonda, Margaret and their predecessors. When with Nellie, two clergymen and three medical personnel he quietly held such a service the disturbed behaviour in the two women very notably ceased, even though neither of them knew what had been done on their behalf. It seems that just as a conventional ghost may appear to successive occupants of a haunted house, so a possessing ghost may disturb different generations of a family until something is done to lay him or her to rest.

According to McAll, among the classic indications that a ghost may have attached themselves to a living person is that person feeling himself

taken over by a force that is indescribable save as a 'foul smell', a 'weight on the back', a 'black cloud', or a 'directing voice'. During such periods, his words are not his own and his actions are not of his own volition.[7]

While, as already mentioned, some of the detail in McAll's cases must be treated with caution, the broad basis of what he argues is strikingly supported by a similar case reported recently by London's Guy's and St Thomas's Hospital psychiatrists Anthony S. Hale and Narsimha R. Pinninti in the prestigious *British Journal of Psychiatry*.

In this instance the living person on the receiving end of the ghostly interference was a twenty-two-year-old remand prisoner of Sikh parentage who had lived in Britain with his family since the age of six, and whom, for convenience, we will call Sanjay. The offence for which he was awaiting trial was the stealing of a taxi, along with its driver, whom he had technically kidnapped. But this was in fact merely the culmination of a whole string of petty pilferings, truancies, shopliftings and similar that had peppered his life since the age of eleven.

The oddity was that Sanjay was not from the kind of deprived or disturbed background that might have been expected to breed such offences. His parents were financially comfortable professionals who gave him a generous allowance. He had no need for the items he stole, and as assessed by the two psychiatrists, he was:

*   *   *

an intelligent, well-educated and insightful young man, western-
ised in his appearance and outlook.[8]

So what could have happened to trigger his disturbed behaviour? As the
psychiatrists learned from Sanjay himself, members of his family, the
family doctor and others, when he was eleven an aunt who was jealous
of his parents' success had spitefully fed him and his brother sweet rice
that carried a curse with it.

Mumbo-Jumbo though this might sound to the sceptically minded,
for Sanjay's brother the effect of it was reportedly 'years of physical
weakness and impotence'. For Sanjay it was much worse. He was
reputedly rendered powerless by possession by the ghost of a particular
old woman who had died several years before and was buried in a
cemetery some distance away. Strikingly reminiscent of the ghost-
possession symptoms described by Dr McAll, for Sanjay the coming of
this old woman was preceded by a fog which he

> would see drifting towards him, settling initially on his chest mak-
> ing him breathless, then entering his body through nose and mouth,
> making him retch and wheeze as he resisted, and taking control of
> his whole body, including his voice . . . While possessed, lasting
> from half an hour to several days . . . [he] was aware of his sur-
> roundings through all senses, though often blunted as though
> through a haze. He lost motor control, but retained awareness of
> emotions, remembering fear, anger and guilt. He would 'struggle'
> mentally to prevent his body's actions, usually unsuccessfully. He
> experienced command hallucinations, and occasionally the ghost
> commented on his actions to unheard others. Even when not pos-
> sessed, he thought the spirit could listen to his thoughts, punish-
> ing him if he told people about her.[9]

Among the demands that the ghostly old woman had made on Sanjay
were that he should commit the kidnapping and car theft offences. Some
of these were out of sheer malice, others so that he could travel to the
cemetery where she was buried to look at her grave. She also commanded
him, less successfully, to jump from a railway bridge in front of a train

as a punishment for trying to resist her. Although Sanjay acknowledged that he was aware of what was happening to him while he was under the woman's control, and pleaded guilty to the criminal offences, he specifically gave being 'under the control of a ghost' as his defence when committed for trial.

Having reluctantly come to believe that their son might genuinely be possessed, Sanjay's parents had some while earlier tried sending him to India to be exorcised there by a Hindu priest. But as in the case of Dr McAll's Margaret, this move simply seemed to increase the ghost's anger. Moslem and Christian attempts at exorcism similarly failed.

Predictably, Sanjay's warders in the prison where he was on remand simply dismissed him as a wilful malingerer, while Hale and Pinninti came, on their own admission, within a whisker of diagnosing him as a paranoid schizophrenic. Some unexpected developments, however, led the psychiatrists to change their minds and to regard Sanjay's old woman ghost as more real than they could have dared suppose. To their astonishment the prison chaplain one day telephoned them in a state of considerable agitation to say that he had just witnessed the old woman possess Sanjay. Hale and Pinninti relate how the chaplain saw:

> a descending cloud and an impression of a face alarmingly like a description of the dead woman [i.e. the ghost] given to us by the patient, of which the chaplain denied prior knowledge.

Furthermore, 'frightened cellmates' of Sanjay's reported witnessing similar happenings. Although via Professor Hale I have requested a fuller statement from this as yet unidentified prison chaplain, it has so far been unforthcoming, seemingly out of concern to protect Sanjay's true identity. Meanwhile, and anti-climactically, it would appear that Sanjay has responded encouragingly to treatment with the anti-psychotic drug clopenthixol.

In addition to the above cases, 'ghost-busting' Welsh parson the Revd Aelwyn Roberts of Llandegai, near Bangor, has recently described a case encountered by him of a ghost not only latching on to a living person – in this instance, the ghost's grieving widow – but continuing to haunt her even when she moved house. Unfortunately, as in all the Revd Roberts's cases, we have to suffer his indiscriminate changing of names and locations and his non-disclosure of true dates, but even so the case is instructive.

The individuals concerned were a young north Wales family, husband Brian, his wife Bethan and their two young sons.[10] Shortly before getting married Brian had inherited his father's smallholding and carrier business, the latter simply an old Bedford van for transporting other farmers' animals to market. Struggling to make ends meet, Brian all but abandoned this occasional transporting for altogether more regular work at a local factory – until one Saturday morning when Bethan found a note to say that he had left early in the Bedford to go to Builth Wells. On the spur of the moment, and in return for some welcome ready cash, he had agreed to transport some cows for a local farmer.

Brian returned at 7 p.m., shaking and white-faced, and confessed to Bethan that because of the winding-down of the carrier business he had let the Bedford's tax and insurance lapse. He had thought it worth risking on just this one occasion – until on his way back he was stopped by the police, who warned him that they would most likely prosecute, and that he could be ruinously fined as much as £300. Predictably, Bethan told him in no uncertain terms just what a fool he had been, and stormed off to the bedroom, slamming the door behind her. To her horror, a few minutes later she heard a gunshot nearby. Immediately rushing out, she found Brian's body lying by the stile that led to the paddock. His shotgun lay beside him and he was clearly already dead.

At the inquest Bethan freely admitted that they had had a blazing row just before the tragedy, and suicide might have seemed the obvious verdict. However, the police found the shotgun old and defective, liable to go off at the slightest touch; also that he had been accompanied by a very frisky sheepdog, who could have accidentally tripped him in some way. Furthermore, Brian seemed to have killed himself on the top rung of the stile, which the coroner considered most unusual and out of character in all his long experience of suicides. Erring therefore on the side of caution, he recorded a verdict of accidental death.

Initially this helped ease Bethan's feelings of guilt, but matters took an unexpected turn when Brian began to haunt. Although Bethan could never see him, about two or three times a week, just as she was going to bed she would hear a rap, rap on the chest of drawers, just the sort of sound that Brian used to make when nervously drumming his fingers.

This was followed by an equally familiar half-whistle, one that had always been a sign of Brian feeling guilty about something. On these occasions Bethan instinctively felt that Brian was actually with her in the room, sitting on her bed. But they gave her no comfort, instead causing her to fall into deep depression. On her parents' advice she sold the smallholding and moved with the boys to a cottage that her parents had noticed for sale near where they lived.

At first it seemed an ideal move, not least because the profit from the sale of the smallholding left the family financially better off than they had ever been when Brian was alive. But after three months Bethan began to experience Brian haunting her in the new cottage just as he had in the old farmhouse. It seemed to her as if he disapproved of the move, and although her doctor prescribed anti-depressants, these did nothing to alleviate either her feelings or Brian's rappings and whistles. In desperation she called upon the Revd Roberts, who in his turn brought in his faithful consultant sensitive, the bard Elwyn Roberts.

Elwyn Roberts hypnotised Bethan and his own sensitivity to ghosts seemed to put her in direct touch with the dead Brian. During this communication, of which the Revd Roberts could hear only Bethan's words, Brian apparently imparted that he really had committed suicide, but that it had been a spur-of-the-moment act of weakness which he deeply regretted for its selfishness and for the strains he had put on her and the boys. He wanted her to know that he loved her and was desperately sorry for what he had done. This was what he had been trying to convey to her all along, even moving house with her in order to do so, although until Elwyn Roberts's intervention all that had got through were the rappings and whistlings.

Whatever we may make of Elwyn Roberts's mediumistic intervention, according to the Revd Roberts the outcome of the contact made that night was that the haunting promptly ceased.

If we accept a case of this kind as valid, inevitably it and the others we have investigated raise considerable speculation as to how many ghosts have latched themselves on to living people in this manner. To get any reliable quantitative information is virtually impossible, not least because if people are reticent even about their house being haunted, they are inevitably going to be even more so about *personal* haunting, with all its implications of mental illness.

We noted how close psychiatrists Hale and Pinninti came to diagnosing Sanjay a paranoid schizophrenic. And Canon Pearce-Higgins once estimated that more than one in four cases of mental illness may be due to what he called 'possession by discarnate spirits' (in our terms, ghosts).[11] Even today, therefore, given our continuing ignorance about the origins of many forms of mental illness, no one can be sure how common possession by ghosts may be.

Whatever the answer, and despite the cautious scepticism with which some of the above cases need to be treated, there has to be a strong inference that not only places, but individual people *can* be haunted, particularly by people who have some close family relation to them.

And if this is the case, what about movable, inanimate objects? Are there haunted objects? And, indeed, can seemingly inanimate objects be ghosts themselves?

CHAPTER THIRTEEN

Ghost Objects and Animals

For anyone with a sense of history, to hold in one's hand even the most mundane of old artefacts – a Roman coin, a Palestinian oil lamp or a prehistoric flint scraper – can conjure up vivid mental images of those who once made and handled that same object many centuries ago. Something of this potency must lie behind the popular vogue for stories of haunted and cursed objects that bring trouble and even death to those who would deny their magical power.

Are such stories just the stuff of fiction? Or are there genuinely old objects that continue to carry the ghostly presence and power of someone long dead? Certainly there are claims of such objects, but as with all ghost material our first priority is to weed out what we can of the spurious.

Take for instance the famous (or infamous) Busby Stoop chair. In the village of Sandhutton, just west of Thirsk in north Yorkshire, there stands the Busby Stoop pub, where until sixteen years ago the landlord kept under lock and key an old comb-back oak chair said to have been that in which a coin-forger called Busby had his last earthly drink before being hanged for murder in 1702. According to legend, as Busby was led out to the nearby scaffold he spitefully laid a curse of sudden death on anyone who might sit in the chair after him, a curse so potent that it has lasted to the present day.

Back in the mid-1970s this legend was apparently treated with all seriousness by the pub landlord of the time, the late Anthony Earnshaw. As he told visiting journalist Paul Bannister:

* * *

Soon after I became licensee there was a big, athletic army ser-geant-major in here, drinking with some other soldiers. They had all read the story . . . and the sergeant-major insisted on bringing the chair out of its corner and sitting in it for the evening. Two weeks later one of the soldiers came in. The sergeant-major, a big, healthy chap who never had a day's illness in his life, had dropped dead three days after he was here.

Last year they were building some new houses about a mile away. Some bricklayers came in at lunchtime. One of them, a young lad of seventeen, took up a dare to sit in the chair. Two hours later, he fell from some scaffolding and was killed. His father came in after the funeral and pleaded with me to destroy the chair. I was afraid to do it. But I was so shaken, I put the chair in the cellar.

Four months ago a very good friend of mine came in with an-other man. They asked to see the chair. I took them down to the cellar but one of the girls called down to me a moment later. I was wanted on the telephone in the bar. When I went back to the cellar, my friend was white-faced and shaken. He said the other man had sat in the chair and as he did so he had felt a sense of evil. That was a Friday night. The following Tuesday morning the man who sat in the chair dropped dead in Ripon market-place. He was forty-two years old and in good health. That was when I put Busby's chair under lock and key.

Even that wasn't enough. Another friend, Harry, a member of my Masonic lodge, heard about the chair and wanted to see it. He persuaded me to show it to him, but only after he promised not to sit in it. Well, I showed it to him, and we were about to leave the coach house when I was called to the kitchen. One of the barmaids had cut her hand. I rushed off, not thinking. When I came back, Harry was laughing. He told me he had broken his promise and sat in the chair. He was found dead less than forty-eight hours later.[1]

To hear such a blood-chilling and factual-sounding tale direct from a down-to-earth Yorkshire pub landlord might seem convincing enough. Author Paul Bannister, to whom landlord Earnshaw told the story, has said that he even looked up the deaths described by Earnshaw in the local records, and found that they checked out. But to discover causes of death from death registers is by no means easy, and it is unclear whether Bannister went to this trouble, particularly bearing in mind that not one of the alleged fatalities is properly identified. It is also unclear how much Earnshaw, who died in 1994, had his tongue in his cheek when he told his tale to Bannister.

For it needed but one phone call by me to the Busby Stoop's present landlord, who has been licensee for the last eight years, to establish that whatever the truth of the deaths described by Earnshaw, no Busby chair was known at the pub, or anywhere else in the village, before the end of the Second World War. This much the landlord has learned both from elderly villagers and from a visiting Canadian who had been stationed at the nearby airfield during the war. Rather than the chair having been in the pub since 1702, it would seem that both it and its legend were introduced by a man called Tom Collins, the pub's first landlord after the war, who very likely invented the story of the curse as a ploy to attract a bit of extra trade. Today Busby's chair hangs harmlessly on the wall of the Thirsk museum, a house that was the birthplace of Thomas Lord, founder of Lord's Cricket Ground.

If the credentials of this purportedly haunted object are now somewhat in tatters, altogether better attested – albeit arguably the most incredible case in this book – is a story deriving from the highly respected scholar of Celtic studies Dr Anne Ross, one of the leading experts on Britain's early Celtic inhabitants.

In this instance the central objects were two small stone heads [see fig. 4 overleaf] that were dug up from the garden of a house in Rede Avenue, Hexham, west of Newcastle-upon-Tyne, some time in 1971.[2] Although the family who found them had no idea of their origins or how old they were, they began almost immediately to experience strange happenings. The heads would be found to have moved, seemingly by themselves; there were strange noises; and a frightening black shape began to be seen, seemingly neither human nor animal.

When the next-door neighbour, Mrs Ellen Dodd, was called in by one of the family's children, who complained that something nasty was touching him, she was confronted by, in her words, a 'half-human, half-sheep-like' shape which rushed out of the room. On another occasion

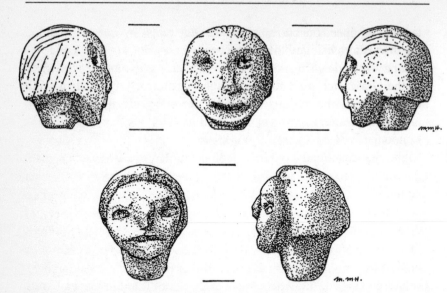

Fig. 4 **The two stone heads from Hexham**, thought to be of Celtic origin, seemingly haunted by a half-man, half-wolf creature who followed them in Southampton.

As reproduced in Anne Ross's article
in Archaeologia Aeliana, *5th Series, Vol. 1.*

the front door of the house inexplicably burst open. Eventually able to stand no more, the family moved out, and the heads were sent to a Newcastle-upon-Tyne museum. Provisionally identifying them as of a cultic type associated with Britain's early Celtic inhabitants, the museum forwarded them to Dr Ross as the recognised expert in this field.

Anne Ross was at that time living with her archaeologist husband and their children in Southampton, and although she had previously been sent many other such heads, which tend to turn up in odd locations all over the country, she acknowledges that there was something about this particular pair that made her go intensely cold, even upon opening the parcel.[3]

The very first night that the heads were in the house she woke up in the early hours, again feeling extremely cold, and acutely aware that something was with her in the upstairs bedroom. Looking towards the door, which was illuminated by a light always left on overnight in the hallway, she saw a six-foot-high black form that appeared to be half-man, half-wolf. With remarkable courage she followed and from the landing glimpsed the creature leap over the banister, land with a plop in the downstairs hallway, then disappear into the back of the house. She was now joined by her still bleary-eyed husband, and they made a search of the house, only to find no trace of the creature. The next morning they carefully said nothing to the children in order not to alarm them.

Four days later, upon Anne and her husband's return from a trip to London, they found their fifteen-year-old daughter nearly hysterical with fright. She described having been confronted by the same creature that Anne had seen. As she opened the front door the wolf-man was crouched on the stairs. He then leapt over the banisters, again plopping loudly as he landed, and disappeared into the music room, though when the daughter gingerly opened the door to this, she found it empty. During the next few days all members of the family became painfully aware of the intruder as doors began to open and shut inexplicably, the plopping sound was heard in the hallway while the family were having a meal, and there were various crashing sounds. The source of the trouble seemed obvious: the stone heads. It was accordingly decided that they had to go.

But where? Even more than twenty years after the event a discreet veil has been drawn over exactly what happened to them, for three attempts to bury them provoked fresh disturbances. In a letter to me Anne Ross has stated candidly: 'The whole experience was so traumatic that I have done a very deliberate "Freudian" forgetting, and never refer to it or think about it if I can possibly help it.'[4] She is convinced that the heads 'possessed a strange and disturbing evil power'[5] linked with the ghostly wolf-man, and although because of their very crude fashioning in stone she cannot be totally sure they were of pagan Celtic origin, the prevalence of the head cult among the Celts and the high concentration of Celtic remains around the Hexham area make this very likely.

For us, the important feature of this case is that despite the heads having been physically transported from Hexham to Southampton, a distance of over three hundred miles, the ghostly wolf-man remained attached to them. Unlike the majority of our conventional ghosts therefore, it was not locked to a place, but to an object, or in this case objects.

However difficult it might be to believe such a story, it has in fact an interesting partial parallel deriving from much the same part of England, this time focusing on two Saxon stone crosses belonging to the church of St Andrew at Aycliffe, a few miles north of Darlington. One of these is carved with the image of St Peter being crucified upside down, the other with pagan symbols, and for many centuries they stood in the grounds of the church.

In the 1870s the crosses were brought inside to protect them against erosion and vandalism, and without anyone suspecting a connection, both the parish community and the church itself imperceptibly acquired an unsettling reputation. The village became noted for an abnormally high number of unhappy relationships. As experienced around 1976 by the Revd Granville Gibson, then filling in between incumbents, the church seemed to be haunted. People reported feeling an alien presence near the font at the back of the church. While the organist was practising, and the church was thought to be empty, the main door would close with an alarming crash. There was an indefinable yet very real sense of oppression.

It was accordingly decided to hold a special service in the church to 'lay' whatever might be responsible. The Revd Peter Brett, now a residentiary Canon at Canterbury Cathedral was called upon to perform the ceremony, and as described by Canon Michael Perry, the Durham diocese's special adviser on exorcisms at that time:

> All went smoothly until the 'pagan' cross was approached. Here tremendous resistance was sensed, and it was only with great difficulty (experienced by all present) that the rite was completed.
>
> The following Sunday members of the congregation expressed surprise at the way in which the whole church seemed lighter, warmer, different, cleaner than hitherto. No one knew of the exorcism except the priest concerned [i.e. the Revd Granville Gibson], the diocesan adviser [Michael Perry], and those whom he had invited to the exorcism . . . Pastoral relationships and Christian work in the parish have since improved considerably.[6]

If the above story might indicate that the haunting of objects, as distinct from places or persons, is mainly or entirely pagan, this is countered by a case involving a box of papers that reposes in the library of the Queen's College, Oxford. It was deposited there by a Victorian clergyman who for reasons best known to himself gave himself the *nom de plume* Cuthbert Shields. Although Shields had no known connection with the college, on his death around the year 1900 he bequeathed to it the box of papers, with instructions that it was not to be opened for fifty years. When the college dutifully obeyed this instruction in the 1950s, they found inside simply an uninteresting set of letters and religious tracts.

That same night the librarian of the time happened to leave the box lying on his desk, whereupon, in what seems rather more than a coincidence, a fellow of the college, Dr P. E. Russell, letting himself into the library late at night, reportedly saw the figure of a clergyman in old-fashioned clothes at the desk looking through the papers.

Unfortunately Dr Russell, now Professor Russell and long retired, says he can no longer remember this incident.[7] But what would seem to be the same figure was quite definitely seen in the mid-1970s by the then assistant librarian at the college, Mrs Penson. As recalled by the present keeper of the archives, Dr J. M. Kaye, in a letter to ghost expert J. A. Brooks:

Going into the library one evening I found . . . Mrs Penson in a great state of alarm, she asked me who the person was who entered the library just before I did. I said there was no such person, which was the case: the library door is visible for a long way before one reaches it. Mrs Penson said, however, that an elderly man in a black coat had entered just before me, and had walked up the library. She had left her desk, from which there is a very limited view of the library floor, but when she got to a position from which she could see more, there was nobody in sight.

She was so alarmed that I and an undergraduate who entered while we were talking volunteered to search the whole library, upper, lower, and even the basement stacks. This we did, and found nobody there. It would not have been possible, in the time available between Mrs Penson leaving her desk and my entering, for a person to have reached the steps, at the far end of the ground floor, which give access to the upper or basement library, and there is nowhere in the building a person can hide. I only took the matter seriously because Mrs Penson (who died a few years ago) was far from being an imaginative person, or prone to 'see things'.[8]

* * *

Typifying the misinformation all too frequently found in books on ghosts, J. A. Brooks has stated in his *Britain's Haunted Heritage* that 'Cuthbert Shields has been seen on many occasions'. However, from my personal inquiries of Dr Kaye, this would seem to be untrue, for Mrs Penson's and Professor Russell's sightings appear to have been the only ones recorded. Even so, Mrs Penson's attestation seems further confirmation that an object, as distinct from a place, may have its own personal ghost.

If ghosts can, for want of any better way of understanding the link, be 'in' a thing, either animate or inanimate, they seem also to be able to be 'of' a thing, that is, to take any form, again both animate and inanimate. Thus, whatever the nature of the wolf-man seen by Dr Ross,[9] there is certainly no shortage of other experiences of ghost animals.

For instance, stretching right back to antiquity ghost birds have been seen as harbingers of doom. In the Middle Ages many believed in Caladrius, a prophetic bird which appeared to those who were sick. The Oxenham family of Devon were for generations haunted by a white bird whose appearance heralded a death in the family, while white swans traditionally signal the death of a bishop of Salisbury.

With regard to animals, Edmund Lenthal Swift, Keeper of the Crown Jewels at the Tower of London from 1814, reported[10] how in 1816 a sentry on guard outside the Tower's Jewel House looked up around midnight to see what appeared to be an enormous bear at the door of the regalia room. Although he lunged at the bear, his weapon simply passed through it, and as the animal's paws reached towards him he collapsed in a faint, to be carried away unconscious by his fellow-guardsmen. The interesting feature here is that back in the thirteenth century the long-lived King Henry III, who succeeded to the English throne at the age of nine, had a menagerie built at the Tower in which he kept two bears. The first was presented to him in 1246 by the Mayor of Northampton. The second, a spectacularly large polar bear, was sent to him from Norway in 1252. This latter, normally kept tethered by a muzzle attached to an iron chain, was regularly transferred to a long strong rope and allowed into the River Thames to catch fish for itself. Was one or other of these the ghost bear seen by the guardsman?

Today, unsurprisingly because of their popularity as domestic pets, dogs and cats are commonly reported as ghosts, and several are included

180

Collective ghosts . . .

(Above) **Ghostly Maori war canoe**, filled with human occupants, as seen by Europeans and Maoris on Lake Tarawera, New Zealand, the morning of 31 May 1886, from a contemporary painting by Kennett Watkins. The apparition seems to have warned of the eruption of the volcano Mt Tarawera ten days later, killing 152 people. Despite Watkins' artistic licence, the canoe looked solid to all witnesses.

(Right) **The Treasurer's House, York**, in the cellars of which there have been several sightings of a whole troop of Roman soldiers (see over).

Where Romans came through the wall . . .

(Above) **Harry Martindale** photographed in the cellar of the Treasurer's House, York, c. 1974, when the story of his experience became public. In February 1953 he was installing central heating in this cellar when he witnessed a very solid-looking troop of Roman soldiers, together with a horse, come through the wall on the right, and trudge across to disappear into the opposite side. He fled into the corner in which he is seen standing (see plan opposite).

(Right) **One of the tunnels beneath the Treasurer's House**, with Harry Martindale in the background. It was in a tunnel immediately adjoining this that Mrs Joan Mawson had a similar experience to Harry's, except that she saw more horses. She insists she saw more of both the soldiers and the horses than could have been physically possible within the tunnel's actual confines.

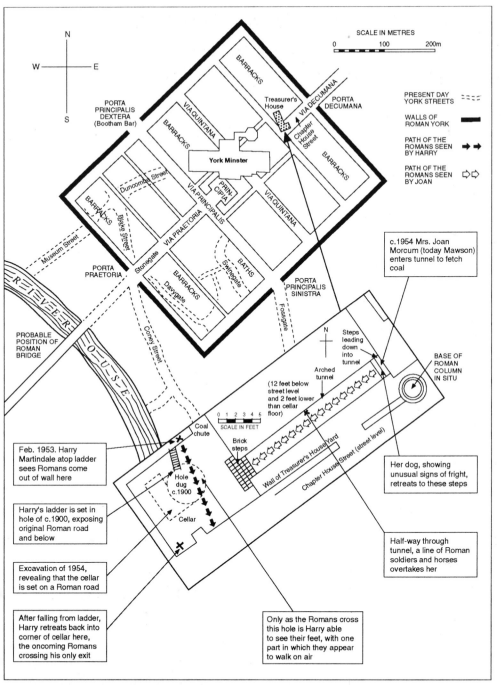

Plan of Roman York (Eboracum), with locations of present-day Treasurer's House and York Minster superimposed, also (inset) **Plan of Treasurer's House tunnel and cellar** in the 1950s, showing where Harry Martindale and Mrs Joan Mawson independently witnessed the Roman soldier ghosts. Although the old Roman street plan is partly conjectural, one puzzle is that while Joan Mawson's Romans were convincingly following the line of the Via Decumana, Harry's moved almost at right-angles to this. They could possibly have been coming from the Barracks, except that they seemed to be returning from a patrol, rather than beginning one.

Illusion and reality . . .

(Right) Illusion: Theatrical poster of 1827 advertising a magic lantern show featuring illusions of the famous ghost ship the *Flying Dutchman*. In the early hours of the morning of 11 July 1881 what seemed to be this ship, in 'a red light . . . all aglow' was reported by thirteen crewmen of H.M.S. *Inconstant* on which the future King George V was travelling between Melbourne and Sydney. According to one theory, the 'ghost' was created by a secretly deployed magic lantern.

(Below) Reality: Sceptical-minded Canon Dominic Walker. Vicar of Brighton parish church, and chairman of the Anglican Church's arm for dealing with seemingly paranormal disturbances. Canon Walker attributes many reported ghosts to 'psychological projections'. However, he was astonished when one very 'real'-looking ghost – of a one-legged woman suicide – appeared to him and others for several minutes during a service he was conducting to lay her soul to rest.

THE
FLYING DUTCHMAN.

FOR THE BENEFIT OF
MR. KLANERT.

KING'S THEATRE, RICHMOND, MONDAY, OCTOBER 1, 1827,
Will be produced (for the FIRST TIME) the extraordinary and unique SPECTACLE, with entire **New Scenery,**
Tricks, Changes, and **Transformations,** called THE

FLYING DUTCHMAN
OR, THE
Phantom Ship!

The SCENERY painted expressly for the Occasion by Mr. MOON.

Captain Vanderdecken (the Flying Dutchman) Mr. KLANERT,
Captain Peppercoal Mr. HAUGHTON, Varnish Mr. BRISTOW,
 Peter Von Brunnell Mr. WYATT,
Tom Willis (a Sailor) Mr. BOND, Myneh_eer Von Trigger Mr. WEBB,
Smutta (Slave of Peppercoal) Mr. EDWARDS, Rockhalda (Hag of the Ocean) Mr. BARRY, Tom Bowling Mr. SMITH,
Jack Rattling Mr. W. MOON, Officer of Marines Mr. FORDE, Sailors, Marines, Spirits, &c. &c.
Lieutenant Mowdrey (in the English Service) Mr. CATHCART,
Listelle (Ward of Peppercoal) Miss FRY,
And Lucy Mrs. KLANERT.
Programme of the Scenery and Action :—

ROCKHALDA'S CAVERN AND MAGIC FIRE;
INCANTATION—DANCE of SPIRITS—VANDERDECKEN RISES out of the SEA.
TURRET CHAMBER with the MAGIC PICTURE.
DUET, LISTELLE and LUCY. They are struck with Fear and Amazement, by a sudden STORM and ANIMATION of the PICTURE!

DECK of a SHIP,
With the GUNS, MASTS, CORDAGE, SHROUDS, &c. &c.
Vanderdecken, in disguise and apparently drowning, is hauled, by a Rope, from the Sea into the Ship. In the course of the Scene, he is discovered
as the Dæmon Captain: the Sailors endeavour to seize him; he eludes them all, and a general Consternation ensues; when they are struck with
Astonishment by the Appearance of the

PHANTOM SHIP!
The HAUNTED CHAMBER *with the* ENCHANTED CHEST *and* PICTURE.
Varnish and Mowdrey disguised as a Boat and his Leader,—Von Brummell as Vanderdecken.
EXTERIOR OF PEPPERCOAL'S HOUSE WITH VIEW OF THE SEA.
Vanderdecken is discovered listening to the Song of Listelle: he retires. Mowdrey enters. Listelle descends from the Veranda. Vanderdecken,
unperceived, touches her Hand: she is paralized and swoons. Mowdrey endeavours to restore her; but Vanderdecken throws his Mantle over her
and they disappear. A dreadful Storm arises. Vanderdecken and Listelle are seen on the Ocean, and the horrible
PHANTOM SHIP again appears!—A Rocky Pass and Entrance to the Cave.
Vanderdecken enters with Listelle in his Arms: he forces her down the Secret entrance of the Cavern. Mowdrey approaches and follows them.
CHAMBER IN THE CASTLE.
Interior of the DEVIL's CAVE with Altar, Magic Book, and Fire!
Vanderdecken, being overcome by Mowdrey and the Charm broken, the last Scene discovers
A distant View of the Ocean with a terrific Storm.
VANDERDECKEN rises in a Flame of RED FIRE!
And the View is terminated by the Vision of the
PHANTOM SHIP!
Ready to receive her Victim.
End of the Play, " CALEB QUOTEM'S FIRE SIDE," *by* Mr. WYATT,
A DANCE, by Miss MERITT,
And " A LITTLE," *in the Character of* BAGATELLE, *by* Mr. KLANERT.
To conclude with the admired and popular FARCE of

DEAF AS A POST.

Captain Templeton Mr. CATHCART, Old Walton Mr. HAUGHTON, Crupper Mr. BRISTOW,
Gallop Mr. EDWARDS, Richard Mr. FORDE, Thomas Mr. W. MOON,
Tristram Sappy Mr. WYATT,
Sophia Mrs. FAWCETT, Amy Templeton Miss FRY, Mrs. Plumpley Mrs. MURRAY,
And Sally Maggs Mrs. KLANERT.
☞ Tickets and Places to be had at the Box Office of the Theatre; Tickets also to be had at the Libraries, Richmond; and of P. NORBURY, Bec—

among the ghost experiences collected by Celia Green and Charles McCreery of the Institute of Psychophysical Research at Oxford. Although the informants are anonymous, the following example is typical:

> The first [experience] was when I was upstairs in the bathroom and I saw a small brown cat walking across the floor. It was so real it never struck me that there was anything abnormal. Thinking that my little tabby cat Pussy Pockets had followed me from downstairs I bent down to pick her up. As I did so I noticed a curious thing, her right hind leg seemed to have faded rather from sight, although she still stood upright as if on four legs. By the time my hands had reached her level and I brought them together to gather her up, I realised that I was only grasping thin air. There was no cat there at all.[11]

Ghosts have also been reported in even more remarkable inanimate forms. We noted in an earlier chapter the Maori war canoe that signalled the tragedy about to befall the villages on the shores of Lake Tarawera, but inevitably the best-known ghost ship is the *Flying Dutchman*, which is supposed to haunt the waters of the southern hemisphere.

Like the Maori war canoe and the ghost birds, superstition has it that the *Flying Dutchman* is a harbinger of doom, and undeniably it does seem to have acted in that way in respect of its best-attested sighting, associated with the young George V. In 1880 the then fifteen-year-old Prince George and his elder brother Prince Albert Victor were aboard HMS *Bacchante*, accompanied by a flotilla of ships, on a round-the-world voyage. While they were calling in at various ports in Australia, the two princes temporarily transferred, with their tutor, Revd Dalton, to another ship of the flotilla, *Inconstant*, for the short leg of the voyage between Melbourne and Sydney.

In the early hours of the morning of 11 July 1881, while the ships were virtually becalmed by lack of wind, an extraordinary event took place which the two princes recorded in the detailed diary they kept of all their experiences:

> At 4 a.m. the *Flying Dutchman* crossed our bows. A strange red light as of a phantom ship all aglow, in the midst of which light the

masts, spars and sails of a brig 200 yards distant stood out in strong relief as she came up on the port bow. The look-out man on the forecastle reported her as close on the port bow, where also the officer of the watch from the bridge clearly saw her, as did also the quarterdeck midshipman, who was sent forward at once to the forecastle; but on arriving there was no vestige nor any sign of any material ship to be seen either near or right away on the horizon, the night being clear and the sea calm. Thirteen persons altogether saw her . . .[12]

Although this passage is often quoted as a personal experience of the young Prince George himself, more careful scrutiny suggests that the sightings were those of others as described to him and his brother later that day, the princes themselves having probably been asleep in their cabin at the time. Even so, from the thirteen eyewitnesses we have little reason to doubt that some form of phantom vessel was seen that morning.

Furthermore, in accord with contemporary superstition, the witnessing of the *Dutchman* was followed by a real-life tragedy. As the princes' diary continued:

At 10.45 a.m. the ordinary seaman who had this morning reported the *Flying Dutchman* fell from the foretopmast crosstrees on to the topgallant forecastle and was smashed to atoms. At 4.15 p.m. . . . he was buried in the sea. He was a smart royal yardman, and one of the most promising young hands in the ship, and everyone feels quite sad at his loss. At the next port we came to the Admiral also was smitten down.[13]

However, before we accept as true the experience's ghostly nature, we should consider the princes' particular noting of the 'strange red light, as of a phantom ship all aglow'. As has been remarked by the UK's foremost expert on magic lanterns, Doug Lear, it is more than possible that someone on one of the companion ships of the flotilla, or even on *Inconstant* itself, could have been projecting from a porthole on to the dawn mist or a suitable foresail a lantern slide of a sailing ship. In support of this theory, the princes' diary specifically noted:

* * *

The *Tourmaline* and *Cleopatra*, who were sailing on our starboard bow, flashed to ask whether we had seen the strange red light.[14]

It is all too rarely appreciated today that as early as the late eighteenth century practitioners of the magic lantern were showing some surprisingly sophisticated animated spectacles. Further fuelling suspicion are the calmness of the weather conditions (aiding a magic lantern's deployment), the semi-darkness of the hour at which the ghost ship appeared, and the fact that slides specifically of a phantom *Flying Dutchman* had been part of lantern show entertainers' boxes of tricks since the 1820s. Doug Lear has from as early as 1827 a poster for the King's Theatre, Richmond, advertising a magic lantern show of the *Flying Dutchman* as the top attraction, this specifically including illusions of the ship and its captain being seen in 'a Flame of Red Fire' [pl. 22].

But if the *Flying Dutchman* ghost really was a joke, it clearly lost any humour with the death of the young seaman. And whether of the *Flying Dutchman* or some other ghost ship, apparitions have continued to be experienced. In 1923, for example, Fourth Officer N. K. Stone, serving on the P & O vessel SS *Barrabool* between Australia and London, reported:

On 26 January 1923 we left Capetown . . . my watch on the bridge commenced at midnight; I was assisting the Second Officer . . . on his watch. About 0.15 a.m. we noticed a strange 'light' on the port bow; I may add here that it was a very dark night, overcast, with no moon. We looked at this through binoculars and the ship's telescope, and made out what appeared to be the hull of a sailing ship, luminous, with two distinct masts carrying bare yards, also luminous; no sails were visible, but there was a luminous haze between the masts. There were no navigation lights, and she appeared to be coming closer to us and at the same speed as ourselves. When first sighted she was about two or three miles away, and when within about half a mile of us she suddenly disappeared. There were four witnesses of this spectacle, the Second Officer, a cadet, the helmsman, and myself. I shall never forget the Second Officer's startled expression: 'My God, Stone, it's a ghost ship.'[15]

* * *

Also on record is the Second Officer's independent account of the same experience, provided ten years after the event for ghost researcher Sir Ernest Bennett:

> My impressions . . . differ in [only] one or two minor respects from Mr Stone's narrative. On the night of the incident in question, on turning out for my 12 to 4 a.m. watch, I distinctly saw the silvery appearance of a full-rigged sailing ship. Stone and I both levelled our glasses and were astonished to note that no sails were set, or in other words that the yards were bare. The only conclusion was that the vessel was a derelict, and abandoned, when to our increased amazement, she simply vanished.[16]

Much more recently a retired Devonian couple Frankie and Jeff Clarkson, sailing in the South Atlantic on a round-the-world voyage, had a similar experience. As related to journalist Daniel Farson, they were six miles out of Cape Town, and Jeff Clarkson was below decks when Frankie spotted a square-rigged sailing vessel coming towards them. In her own words it was:

> a lovely sight with white sails against the dark evening sky . . . except that she was sailing against the wind. As I called to Jeff to come on deck the ship turned with a single movement and came a mile nearer.[17]

Then Frankie saw the solitary figure of a man and felt that something disastrous would happen if her husband saw it too. Simultaneously the ship veered and vanished, and by the time Jeff had joined his wife there was nothing to be seen.

It is important to note the differences as well as the similarities in these three accounts. They are sufficient to make it apparent that even if all three are equally reliable, they can hardly be of the same ship.

As well as sailing ships, it seems possible even for cars to create ghosts, for as described by a Mrs E. A. Hughes of Welshpool:

> In October 1976 my husband was driving with me through France.

We were making our way from Lyon to Versailles using minor roads. The sun was setting but we had not yet put our lights on. There were the traditional poplar trees every few yards along the sides of the road. Suddenly a car of the old bull-nosed Austin type began to cross the road very slowly in front of us. It seemed to be about a foot above the actual road level. My husband braked. The Austin glided noiselessly on. Then a car with its headlights on came towards us; the headlights shone brightly through the windows and under the wheels of the crossing car. There was no sign of anyone driving. The car with the headlights passed by. The other one disappeared across the road. We stopped and each said to the other, 'Did you see that?' . . . There was no road crossing ours, which had no hump in it to account for the odd space between the phantom car and the road surface: and on either side of our road, beyond the poplar trees, there were only ploughed fields stretching to the horizon . . . My husband died in December 1986, so this is now my memory alone. But we both certainly saw it and had no means of suggesting it to one another before we spoke. Neither he nor I ever saw a ghost before or since that time.[18]

What we are to make of all this is anyone's guess. The apparent fact that ghost objects, of sometimes substantial scale, as well as ghost people (wearing ghost clothes), ghost limbs and ghost animals can all be experienced raises more questions than answers. The impression has to be, as has tended to be suggested all along, that the existence of the ghosts is largely in the mind – yet each ghost has sufficient reality that two or more minds can experience him, her or it simultaneously.

If, despite so much continuing mystery, we have charted at least something of the extraordinarily wide parameters of what ghosts may be, and their relationship to present-day time and space, one further question looms. That is, why should some person or creature who has died, or something that has long ceased to exist, continue to manifest, in a ghostly, substance-less way, to someone still living? Bluntly, if ghosts really do exist, *why* do they do so?

Part III

In Search of Why Ghosts Exist

'In haunted houses . . . we find normally sad unhappy souls who have
got lost on the way to paradise. They need our compassion and
prayers and not to be cursed and consigned to outer darkness.'

Canon John Pearce-Higgins

CHAPTER FOURTEEN

Circumstances in Which Ghosts Can Become Activated

As noted earlier in this book, there are several distinct varieties of ghosts, including ones we have not included as 'true' ghosts.

For instance, we chose to exclude poltergeists, because they seem to originate in a living person, rather than anyone dead. We also excluded those whom we dubbed 'passing callers', because at their death they appear anywhere in the world to someone they know, then never disturb again. More recently we have come across ghostly appearances of a helpful or warning nature, such as the Victorian housekeeper's wake-up call to David Rolfe, an encounter hard to regard as a haunt in the fullest sense.

But so far as mainstream ghosts are concerned – that is, those who spasmodically manifest in the same location over perhaps several generations – what exactly is it that causes them to haunt? Why do they persist in troubling the living, while others do not? These questions have for at least the last two and a half thousand years repeatedly vexed those trying to come to some serious understanding of what ghosts may be, as in the case of the ancient Greek philosopher Plato. Back in the fourth century BC, in his *Phaedo*, Plato has one of his characters refer to ghosts as:

> souls not fully cleansed and freed from the visible material world, but still retaining some part in it, and therefore visible.

Five centuries later the Greek satirist Lucian set into his *Philopseudes* the dialogue:

* * *

Perhaps . . . what Tychiades means is . . . that the only souls who wander about [i.e. behave as ghosts] are those of men who met with a violent death – anyone, for example, who hanged himself, or was beheaded or impaled, or departed his life in any other such way – but that the souls of the dead who died a natural death do not wander. If that is his theory, it cannot be lightly dismissed.

Indeed, when we look at more modern ghost cases in which we are familiar with the circumstances of the individual seemingly responsible for the haunting, there is much to support Tychiades' view. Almost invariably a true ghost seems to be associated with someone who either in life or in the circumstances of his or her death suffered some deep trauma or tragedy.

The late Bishop Mervyn Stockwood, in his autobiography *Chanctonbury Ring*, recalled how after one of the vicars in his diocese died of a heart attack in his early forties, the vicar's successor 'complained of odd happenings – noises, footsteps, crying' at the vicarage. On the strength of what the 'sensitive' Tom Corbett had told him about the ghost at his own official residence Stockwood took an unnamed male sensitive, most likely the same Tom Corbett, to check the vicarage out. Stockwood was confidently told that the 'odd happenings' were indeed the dead vicar's ghost,

> deeply troubled because, although he [the vicar] had given the impression of being a faithful parish priest, he had in fact been involved in all sorts of tragic practices.[1]

Although at first Bishop Stockwood could not believe this of the vicar in question – 'it was out of keeping with everything I knew about him' – careful investigation revealed the 'tragic practices' to be all too true. It would have been helpful to know rather more about this case, but in understandable deference to any further distress that might be suffered by members of the deceased vicar's family, Bishop Stockwood has gently but firmly declined to give any further details.

Altogether more common, of course, is the ghost who has been the victim of some murder or unjust execution – and who has not been given what he would have regarded as the proper burial rites. We may recall how the Athenian ghost confronted by the philosopher Athenodorus seemed to have been a man who died in such circumstances,[2] as was the Japanese ghost described by A. B. Mitford (see pp. 72–3); likewise the ghost at Cork concerning whom merchant Sir James Houblon wrote a letter to diarist Samuel Pepys.[3]

But while in the above cases the exact details are hazy because of the time that has elapsed, there are more recent examples of a similar nature which are better attested. One such is the already mentioned 'Man in Grey' ghost reputed to haunt London's famous Theatre Royal, Drury Lane. According to the theatre historian W. Macqueen Pope, who claimed to have seen the Man in Grey himself 'on numerous occasions'[4] during the 1940s and 1950s, all witnesses give the same account of what he looks like:

> a man of medium height, dressed in a long grey riding cloak of the early 18th century, wearing a powdered wig of the period and a three-cornered hat; the cloak covers most of him, but he has a sword which can be seen under it, as it swings at his side, and he has high riding boots. Sometimes he carries the hat in his hand. He has been approached near enough for his features to be visible and they are those of a handsome man with a squarish chin.[5]

The most fascinating feature is the route that the Man in Grey invariably takes when he walks [see fig. 5 overleaf]. As described by Macqueen Pope in an interview with Peter Underwood in 1955, the ghost is:

> first seen occupying the first seat of the fourth row of the upper circle, and then moves across the theatre along the gangway at the back until he finally disappears at the far end into the wall near the royal box.[6]

Around 1848[7] a gruesome discovery was reportedly made by workmen carrying out renovation work in the Theatre Royal's same upper circle. According to Macqueen Pope:

> workmen employed on the Russell Street side of the upper circle

191

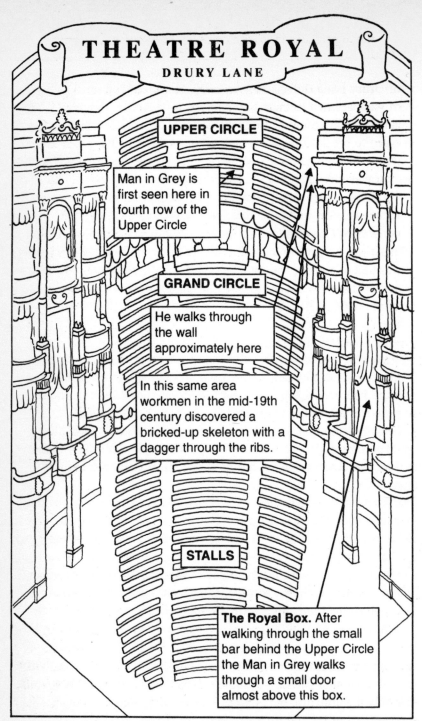

THEATRE ROYAL
DRURY LANE

UPPER CIRCLE

Man in Grey is first seen here in fourth row of the Upper Circle

GRAND CIRCLE

He walks through the wall approximately here

In this same area workmen in the mid-19th century discovered a bricked-up skeleton with a dagger through the ribs.

STALLS

The Royal Box. After walking through the small bar behind the Upper Circle the Man in Grey walks through a small door almost above this box.

Fig. 5 **Seating plan of the Theatre Royal, Drury Lane,** showing the locations where the 'Man in Grey' ghost has been sighted, in relation to where the skeleton was found during the middle of the last century. Although accounts agree that the 'Man in Grey' is seen in the fourth row of the Upper Circle, there are variations regarding exactly which seat.

From seating plan supplied by courtesy of Mark Hayward, General Manager, Theatre Royal, Drury Lane of Drury Lane (left-hand side facing stage) came upon a portion of what seemed to them the main wall, which rang hollow. They called the attention of the foreman in charge to this, and he decided to break through and see what was wrong. It was far more wrong than he had imagined. For when the workmen had hewed their way through the wall, they found themselves suddenly bursting into a small room, which had been bricked up. In that room was a skeleton, and in that skeleton's ribs was a dagger. The dagger was of Cromwellian design, but that proved nothing. An inquest was held, an open verdict returned; and the skeleton, which was that of a male, was interred in the little graveyard on the corner of Russell Street and Drury Lane, believed to be the graveyard mentioned by Dickens in *Bleak House*.[8]

The unavoidable inference is that the Man in Grey seems to have been indicating by the very route of his walk where his body lay. But if this is so, why should he continue to haunt the theatre a century or more after he had been given a decent burial nearby? Was this burial, for some as yet undetermined reason, not to his liking?

Ghostly hauntings seem persistently linked to dead people who, it could be argued, did not receive the burial rites they would have regarded as their due. Another such example derives from the writer of children's stories Noel Streatfeild.

Born in 1895 the daughter of the Revd William Streatfeild, a country parson later to become Bishop of Lewes, the young Noel grew up in a rather isolated vicarage at St Leonards-on-Sea, Sussex, where she, her brother and three sisters all regularly saw the ghost of a little girl wearing a crinoline and the sort of long, frilled pantelletes worn by women and children in the first half of the nineteenth century. They also sometimes saw a ghostly adult woman with the little girl.

Although both Noel's father and mother brushed aside any talk of these ghosts as incompatible with their Anglican beliefs, visitors would see them too, as did the incoming vicar and his wife when the Streatfeilds moved to another parish. For some reason the new incumbent's family saw only the little girl, but gradually they in their turn accepted her as if she was part of the furniture.

But the real shock – and revelation – came when the new vicar decided to modernise the vicarage. The improvements included taking out a very heavy, old-fashioned staircase, and in order to dismantle this the workmen had to take up its treads. As they prised up the second from the bottom, to their astonishment they found two skeletons, one of a woman, the other of a child. And when these were given proper burial the hauntings promptly ceased.

Unfortunately, we simply do not know enough about the skeletons' owners to be able adequately to relate them to their associated ghosts, let alone to be able to deduce why they should have haunted. However, although the woman and child seem to have been victims of murder, they appear to have ceased haunting on being given a proper burial – unlike the Theatre Royal's Man in Grey, who to the best of our knowledge, seems only to begin from that time.

Clearly we need more examples, particularly ones in which we can be virtually certain of a ghost's identity. In this regard, two cases of twentieth-century suicides are particularly instructive.

The first of these is the familiar case of the eighteen-year-old farmer's son Robin Hayden of Hook, who shot himself while torn between loyalty to his puritanical family and love for the local publican's daughter. Robin's body had received an ostensibly proper funeral in the local cemetery, recorded in detail by the local paper, the *Hants and Berks Gazette*, which narrated how the Revd C. H. C. Baker had 'officiated in the church and at the graveside; how 'the blinds of nearly every house were drawn down'; how 'a vast number of friends and relatives were at the church and at the graveside'; how 'there was a large number of magnificent floral tributes'. We are even told that the coffin was of polished elm with brass handles, and are given the wording of its inscription.

This prompts us to ask why, if Robin was laid to rest with such ceremony, he haunted the site of his parents' farmhouse fifty years after his death, even after the building itself had been pulled down. Was it just because he had committed suicide? Or was it because, specifically as a suicide, he had disqualified himself in the Anglican Church's eyes from receiving the full rites for the burial of the dead?

In this latter regard a possibly crucial clue comes from the *Hants and Berks Gazette* report, which mentions that Robin's coffin was taken from the church 'after the first part of the burial service had been read'.

Furthermore, when we turn to the Order for the Burial of the Dead in the Anglican *Book of Common Prayer*, which the Revd Baker would have used for the funeral, we find the chilling rubric:

Here it is to be noted that the Office ensuing is not to be used for any that die unbaptised, or excommunicate, or have laid violent hands upon themselves.

Most telling of all, however, is what happened when, at the McKenzie family's behest, the Revd Ben Hutchinson visited their house specifically for the purpose of 'commending the soul of Robin to rest'. As the family can attest, to their very considerable relief the haunting ceased. Which raises the question: what did the Revd Hutchinson's service provide for Robin Hayden's repose which the Revd Baker's original burial service did not? Could the burial service's cold-hearted discrimination against Robin because of his suicide have prompted his subsequent manifestation as a ghost? And if so, does this bring us at least a little closer to understanding how hauntings happen?

If we find this rather too much to accept on the basis of just one case, another, again involving someone who took their own life, exhibits similar features. On the evening of Friday 11 September 1953, fifty-year-old Francis George Crute, who was the organist at St John's Church, Montpellier Road, Torquay, and taught music at the local grammar school, was found dead in the scullery of his Torquay home. Although he left no note, he had failed to turn up at the school earlier that day and was found gassed, leading a coroner's inquest to conclude that he had committed suicide.[9]

Six months later there was a change of vicars at St John's, and the new incumbent, thirty-seven-year-old Revd Anthony Rouse, soon began implementing several improvement and modernisation schemes, one of these being the temporary removal of the church's organ for a complete overhaul. Curiously there had been talk of occasional ghostly phenomena associated with this organ for many years, the church having had a very talented organist in the Victorian era, Henry Ditton-Newman, who had died tragically young and whose ghost had occasionally been seen by previous vicars, along with phenomena such as the organ seeming to play by itself.

But upon the refurbished organ being returned it began to be associated with rather more insidious and disturbing phenomena. In 1958 the then organist Frederick Fea wrote to the Bishop of Exeter saying that he and others repeatedly felt a presence near them when playing the organ.

> I have never seen the ghost, but there is a feeling of somebody watching, and one gets that very strongly at certain times. For two years running I have noticed it on the same Fridays and the same Sundays. It makes one feel paralysed and you just cannot think or play normally. I have felt that I just could not get through a hymn because of the feeling of strain. In fact I have always finished the hymn, but more by will-power than anything else. The feeling also seems to paralyse the choir. They find it very difficult to sing and the results are not what one would wish.[10]

The Revd Rouse was also having disturbing problems, in his case focused on the top floor of his vicarage. These took the form of unaccountable feelings of despondency and frustration, at times so overwhelming that they made him giddy. But when he sought medical help his doctor could find no physical cause for what was ailing him.

When Rouse learned of Fea's similar experiences, he consulted a medium, a Mrs Leith-Walker at the College of Psychic Studies in London. She told him that the cause of the difficulties was a man who had earned his living by playing an instrument with his hands and who has gassed himself. He had been an organist at the church but had not received the funeral that he felt should have been his due, given all that he had tried to do for the church's musical standards. In order to lay this organist's ghost she recommended that someone should go to his grave, sprinkle on it some holy water, and say some prayers.

It was Mrs Leith-Walker's specific mention of an organist who had gassed himself that made Rouse realise for the first time that rather than the long-dead Henry Ditton-Newman it had to be Francis Crute who was the cause of the debilitating malaise. Crute had killed himself on a Friday, one of the days on which Fea particularly noted the invisible presence at the organ. And on first taking up his post in Torquay, Crute had also lived temporarily on the vicarage's top floor, where Rouse most acutely encountered the feelings of despondency.

When Rouse looked up the details of Crute's funeral he learned that the coffin containing the organist's body had not even been allowed into the church. Instead it had been left in the hearse outside. Clearly the officiating vicar had interpreted overly harshly the rubric about suicides in the Anglican *Book of Common Prayer*, allowing it to override all that Crute had given of his time and talents to the church and its music.

But the most crucial indication of why Crute was haunting lay in what happened when, in accord with Mrs Leith-Walker's recommendations, a propitiatory rite was conducted at the organist's grave. After consulting with his local bishop, on New Year's Day 1959 Rouse visited Torquay cemetery in the company of Malcolm Russell, a countertenor at Exeter Cathedral for whom Crute had been a profound musical inspiration. Together they sprinkled holy water, recited a psalm, and prayed that Crute should be granted eternal rest. Exactly as in the case of Robin Hayden, all the ghostly phenomena ceased from the moment that the rite was carried out.[11]. As we will explore more closely in a later chapter, trite though this act of praying for a dead person may seem, it is a type of prayer that really does seem to achieve results, inevitably indicating something of what the ghost needed all along.

While still on the subject of why ghosts become activated, a clearly related question is why they appear to whom they do when they do. As we have already noted, there are some people such as sensitives and the occasional genuine medium, to whom ghosts are always more readily apparent than they are to the rest of us. But as we have also found, there are occasions when ordinary people without any prior belief in ghosts or pretensions to being psychic can and do have genuine ghost experiences. Why should this be? Is it somehow connected with the circumstances of the living, as well as of the dead person doing the haunting?

One case that we have come across which has given some indication of this is the Streatham plague victims haunting, in which the seeming trigger for the appearance of the ghosts was the cot death of a young baby. But while it was this baby's death that prompted the haunting, the ghosts were seen not only by that baby's parents (whose emotions could arguably have tuned into those who had buried children at this same site centuries before), but also by the young policeman called to the scene, for whom no such empathy is likely. So while some circumstance pertaining to a particular modern-day person can spark off a haunting, the ghost may still have sufficient objective reality to be perceived by others.

Another case illustrative of this same point is one described to psychical researcher Andrew MacKenzie in 1972 by the Revd Alan Taylor, then vicar of Marton, Gainsborough, Lincolnshire.

> Shortly after my arrival here [at Marton] I became aware of a curious circumstance at the Parish Communion. On some Sundays, while administering the elements, I was aware of another person in the sanctuary apart from myself and the two altar servers. Although I never saw him in an objective sense I formed a clear impression of an elderly man with a bald head and a mane of white hair flowing over his ears. He appeared to be wearing a dark green cassock. I have never seen one this colour though very old black cassocks sometimes have a greenish tinge. I presumed that it was the presence of some previous incumbent . . . I was talking [about this] about a year ago to an old lady who was born in the parish and was for many years the organist . . . She said the description I gave fitted exactly the old man who was a choirman here at the turn of the century. It seems that when the church was restored and rebuilt in 1891 . . . as the colour scheme was green and red the choir were supplied with dark green cassocks. These were replaced with black just before 1914.[12]

The pertinent point here, as noted by the Revd Taylor, is that his awareness of the ghost seemed

> in some way connected with one of my servers, a boy of about thirteen, as it seemed to be more definite when he was serving, although he is always in church. I have noticed it less often in the last year or so although the boy I mentioned still serves regularly and is now fifteen.

Although it was Taylor who was perceiving the ghost, the trigger was seemingly the pubescent altar server, and the ghostly old choirman's somewhat unhealthy-sounding interest in him, something which notably waned as the boy grew older.

Seemingly a natural sensitive, Taylor told MacKenzie how four or five times a year when conducting funerals he seemed to 'pick up some emotion or image' which was not his own. He felt that location and human emotions were highly important factors in relation to ghosts:

> I think . . . that the state of the emotions is vastly more important than the state of the mind . . . My own experience leads me to suspect that what transmits is emotional rather than mental and the mind clothes the feeling with the image.[13]

This ties in neatly with our earlier remarks on the apparent link between hauntings and strong emotions, and suggests that in addition to the circumstances already described in which a ghost may be particularly liable to haunt, there are also certain people who, because of unusual circumstances and/or their own strong emotions, may actually attract ghosts.

Whatever, the question that now arises is: if there really are troubled personalities behind at least some ghosts, how should they be treated? Should they be forthrightly sent away, in the manner of the traditional exorcist? Should they be systematically tracked down with scientific instruments in the quest to find proof of their existence? Or is there another, rather more effective and altogether more sympathetic, way of treating them?

Exorcists and Ghost-Hunters: Some Reactions to Ghosts That Can Be Less Than Helpful

When an ordinary family finds that their home is haunted, their first reaction may well be one of fear. This is by no means universal. Some, as in the case of my wife and I at Abercrombie House, can be surprised at being altogether less frightened by the experience than they might have expected – though we had the considerable advantage of being together, and in a house in which we were staying for only one night.

Even so, fear is a common and perfectly understandable reaction. But it is also unhelpful. Although I know of not one seriously attested case of a ghost physically harming a living person,[1] there are occasional reports of individuals almost literally dying of fright as a result of seeing a ghost, among these the sentry who encountered the ghost bear at the Tower of London,[2] who is reported to have died just two days afterwards. In essence, to be frightened of a ghost – however unavoidable – is almost bound to be counter-productive, being as unrewarding to the living person confronting the ghost as it must be unhelpful to the ghost in whatever he or she may hope to achieve.

Even when no fear is involved, an equally common and understandable reaction is an anxiety to get rid of the ghost just as soon as possible. Particularly when the haunting happens in a family house this usually prompts the notion of calling for an exorcist. Indeed, it was to cater for precisely such appeals for help that in the early 1960s the Anglican Bishop of Exeter, Bishop Mortimer, formed what was then called the Exeter Exorcism Commission. From this ultimately developed the Christian Deliverance Study Group, which today provides for a clerical specialist in each diocese specifically to help with cases in which priests and members of the public are suffering supernatural difficulties.

The group has developed both expertise and a formidable armoury (indeed Canon Michael Perry has specifically described them as 'weapons') of exorcistic rites. The mildest of those prescribed for use in haunted houses is a simple blessing. The officiating cleric visits each room, defines its function, blesses it and any living occupants, and prays that 'all powers of evil may be put to flight'.[3] A somewhat stronger rite carries the dread adjuration:

Be gone from this place, every evil haunting and phantasm
Depart for ever, every unclean spirit,
Be banished, every delusion and deceit of Satan,
Be put to flight, every evil power . . .
In the Name of God, Father, Son and Holy Spirit, we order you,
    every evil spirit, to leave this place, harming no one, and to go
    to the place appointed to you.[4]

Only a relatively small proportion of public calls for exorcisms, however, concern ghosts. The greatest demand comes from people who have become caught up with the occult powers of evil, often after dabbling with black magic, ouija boards and the like. Some truly horrifying cases underline how badly things can go wrong when people try to conduct their own exorcisms.

Recent examples include a man in Barnsley who in 1975 killed his wife after an all-night exorcism. This had been conducted by bungling lay experimenters who failed to rid him of the demon of murder.[5] In London in 1980 two Pentecostal Christian men punched and kicked a mentally unstable woman to death trying to rid her of the demon of 'Judas Iscariot'.[6] And in Australia in 1993 a husband asphyxiated his wife in near-identical circumstances.[7]

Even in the case of calls for an exorcist in which ghostly phenomena do seem to be involved, a high proportion of these relate to poltergeist activity, which as we have already noted seem largely to be associated with living young people, rather than anyone dead. It is well recognised by the clergy who attend and investigate such calls that exorcism is almost invariably inappropriate in poltergeist cases. As remarked by the late Canon John Pearce-Higgins:

From my experience I would say that if called in to 'exorcise' [poltergeist cases] the clergy do more harm than good. The Church represents moral authority – the establishment – par excellence. Since so many of these poltergeist cases appear to be a protest against authority . . . if the clergy come and perform some solemn rite to exorcise a 'spirit' (who in any case isn't there!), they only increase the 'super-ego' pressure against which the poltergeist phenomena are a subconscious protest, and the records almost invariably show that after such a religious performance the phenomena tend to redouble their energies.[8]

Even in those cases involving 'true' ghosts, it is all too rarely realised that the holding of a full-blooded exorcism is regarded by those operating the exorcism service as a last rather than a first resort.

Graphically illustrating the widespread ignorance on this subject, not only among lay people, but even on the part of some very senior Anglican bishops, are remarks by the late Bishop Mervyn Stockwood concerning the woman ghost whom he twice experienced in his bedroom at his official residence in south London. As described in his autobiography, after first 'planning to make a careful study of her and, if possible, to take photographs', he then changed his mind because of fear of the ghost on the part of his Arab cook:

Munir, an Arab from Jerusalem, had just joined my household. Although I never mentioned the apparition to him he became convinced there was a ghost in the house. I treated the matter lightly, but as the weeks went by I realised he would not remain unless I 'did something'. As it is easier to obtain the services of a new ghost than those of a new cook, 'do something' I did.[9]

Explaining what that 'something' was, he stated candidly:

Unfortunately, I had to exorcise her.

* * *

Now one can only hope that Bishop Stockwood did not mean those words quite as chillingly as they sound. For his apparent meaning is that having reluctantly forgone the keeping of this interesting ghost to study like some trapped butterfly, his only, and 'unfortunate' recourse was to get rid of her. This raises two key questions. The first is: for whom was this decision unfortunate, for Bishop Stockwood, or for the ghost? Are we right to suspect that the bishop was thinking rather more of his own leisure interest than the ghost's long-term welfare?

The second and far more serious question is: where on earth, in exorcising the ghost, did Bishop Stockwood think that he, or his appointed exorcist, was sending her? He would surely not have used the word 'unfortunate' if he thought this might be to heaven. So if not to heaven, where else? The unavoidable impression is that this was a matter he hardly troubled himself over.

Nor was Bishop Stockwood alone in this somewhat cavalier attitude. As noted by the bishop's own diocesan exorcist, Canon Pearce-Higgins, an 'astonishing' flaw in the Bishop of Exeter's Report on Exorcism, from which the Anglican Church's exorcism service sprang, was:

> inadequate recognition . . . that the majority of [ghost] cases in this country involve only earthbound discarnate human spirits [i.e. what we have chosen to term 'true' ghosts] and therefore require a requiem rather than an exorcism.[10]

It would seem that still deep within rather too many a psyche, both Anglican and those of other persuasions, is the assumption that exorcism is the automatic recipe for ghosts because ghosts by their very nature must be evil. Peter Underwood readily demonstrates this in his autobiography when he cites the case of a nun-like white figure persistently seen by the Reverend Mother and others at the House of Compassion at Thames Ditton, Surrey:

> Attempts to exorcise the phantom lady . . . in the affected room were unsuccessful, and this failure, it was suspected, showed that the ghost was not of an evil nature: indeed its manifestations have never been in the least frightening.[11]

* * *

Although Underwood does not disguise the fact that he dislikes exorcisms because they destroy the very evidence which he has spent so much of his life pursuing, the disquieting feature of his remarks is their implicit assumption that a ghost must almost automatically be 'of an evil nature' unless the failure of an exorcism denotes otherwise. Notable also is how he characteristically insists on referring to this ghost as an 'it' even though her femininity seems to have been agreed by all, including himself.[12]

Fortunately the Christian Deliverance Study Group today follows the rather more enlightened thinking of Canon Pearce-Higgins, and in what we would define as 'true' ghost cases they start with a requiem, or laying to rest, rather than an exorcism. In the next chapter we will look more closely at this commendably sympathetic and positively rewarding approach.

But before we do so we should consider one other major reaction to ghosts that is arguably every bit as unhelpful as that of the overzealous exorcist: that of the overenthusiastic ghost-hunter.

Prompted no doubt by media fascination with the paranormal, ghost-hunting is a growing sport. For years the rather exclusive Ghost Club, under Peter Underwood, was virtually the only UK-based group to indulge in collective stake-outs of allegedly haunted houses. Their quest was to seek out ghosts wherever they had been reported, and to return with some form of irrefutable proof that ghosts exist.

In 1994, stung by criticisms of his style of leadership, Peter Underwood resigned from the club to found what he has called the Ghost Club Society. This operates in much the same way as the continuing original Ghost Club, and has thereby effectively doubled the UK's ghost-hunting operations. Additionally, several more localised ghost-hunting groups have mushroomed in recent years, among these the Grimsby-based Ghostbusters UK, who wear 'Ghostbuster' T-shirts, and travel to reputedly haunted sites in their 'Ghostmobile', crammed with ghost-detecting equipment. There is also a Burnley Paranormal Research Association in Burnley, Lancashire, a similar group in Kent and no doubt others. The United States has among several like-minded organisations the Ghost Research Society, which was founded in Chicago and is currently led by former fast-food outlet manager Dale Kaczmarek. Like the British groups the society conducts stakeouts of haunted sites, and has its own journal, *The Ghost Tracker's Newsletter*.

So what does a ghost-hunting group do when it arrives at a site at which a ghost is reputed to be active? Although different groups inevitably vary in how they operate, Peter Underwood has usefully summarised the procedures adopted on those stakeouts that he has helped organise:

> The programme will largely depend on the reported manifestations, but usually we meet the owner who will describe in full the disturbances or manifestations and we will then tour the whole house under the guidance of the owner who will point out any relevant areas. The owner then leaves us for the night. At the request of the owner we may agree to parts of the property (perhaps sleeping quarters or 'unhaunted' areas) being considered out of bounds and these areas will be sealed and clearly indicated.
>
> A Base Room will then be selected from where the whole of the investigation will be supervised. Various apparatus will be distributed in strategic places (for example where manifestations have been reported) and also 'trigger' objects (articles that might attract the attention of the haunting entity). Movable objects may be ringed with chalk so that any subsequent movement is registered. A rota of regular patrols and checking of instruments and quiet periods and possible seances will also be drawn up and meticulously carried out with immediate and detailed reports being compiled of instrument readings and *anything*, however trivial, that may be of relevance to the case in hand.[13]

Underwood's casual mention of 'various apparatus' and 'instruments' is in fact a masterpiece of understatement, for elsewhere in his writings we learn the full extent of what he recommends as the sort of equipment that no self-respecting ghost-hunter should be without:

> a bag, box or case for the easy transportation of the . . . equipment . . . a notebook (together of course with pens, pencils, a pencil sharpener and eraser) . . . a few sheets of plain paper for sketches, plans, etc . . . sticks of chalk and artists' willow charcoal . . . for marking walls and furniture . . . a reel of black synthetic thread . . .

to stretch across stairways, corridors, passages and doorways . . .
thin fuse wire . . . which, when broken, will break an electric cir-
cuit and alert the watchers . . . a camera or cameras (ideally three,
one for colour film, one for black and white and one for infra-red,
also a cine camera, and of course a plentiful supply of all their
respective films) . . . tape measures, both a simple dressmaker's
yard measure and an architect's 33-ft leather-cased winding tape . . .
a spring balance . . . a strain gauge . . . a small hammer; a screw-
driver or two; a bradawl; some pliers; some wire clippers and a
plumb-line . . . transparent envelopes and containers for question-
able and dubious substances . . . talcum powder, flour or sugar to
sprinkle for footprints or fingerprints . . . luminous card and paper . . . a pair of stout scissors, a pen-knife and several magnifying
glasses . . . a reliable torch with batteries . . . a dependable watch
(preferably with luminous dial, and synchronised with that of all
other watch-owners present) . . . thermometers (a good supply of
the simple and inexpensive ones, suitable for indoor or outdoor
use) . . . portable and static sound recorders . . . frequency change
detectors; instruments for measuring atmosphere pressure, vibration, wind force and humidity . . . a large scale map of the area . . .
a compass . . . one or two mirrors placed in strategic positions.[14]

Also recommended are a few baubles that might be of special interest to
the particular ghost being hunted, such as toys for a child ghost, or a
crucifix for a religious one, forcibly reminding one of the worthless
trinkets that Columbus took along as gifts for his 'Indians'.

Peter Underwood gives some ostensibly very sound reasons for the
use of all the technical gadgetry, pointing out that the value of any
ghost investigation:

is limited if at the end the only evidence is the verbal report of the
individual investigator. Whatever information such a report contained, there would be no means of checking its validity without
corroborative evidence. All or part of the investigator's report could
be coloured by his own imagination or hallucination resulting from
the mental atmosphere built up by the actual circumstances of the
enquiry. Sleeping alone in a room where paranormal phenomena

are claimed to exist could create a feeling of expectancy which caused the investigator to be more than normally prone to tricks of his own imagination, particularly if he was in any way apprehensive. An investigator might be quite certain in his own mind that whatever he experienced was a reality, but he still could not deny the possibility of psychological self-deception if his report were challenged.[15]

But what happens when such apparatus is deployed? In his *The Ghost Hunters* Underwood describes admiringly a copybook carrying-out of his recommendations (and more) by a former honorary secretary of the Society for Psychical Research, John Cutten.

In 1967 the society received a report of a seeming haunting that was happening on Monday nights at four-weekly intervals at a century-old house in Primrose Hill, north-west London. Different occupants of a particular bedroom had been disturbed around 3 a.m. by what seemed to be a presence in the room. On the most alarming of these occasions one of the occupants had been pulled out of his bed by the presence and saw standing in the middle of the room the ghost of an elderly man, short, very broad-built, and with an unusually small head.

According to the pattern, the likeliest time for this ghost to reappear would be the night of Monday 20 March. John Cutten volunteered to spend the night in the haunted room, and arrived at the house that evening with a large suitcase carefully packed with a set of apparatus very much along the lines recommended by Underwood.

At 12.25 a.m. Cutten shut himself alone in the haunted room. He then sealed the door, its keyhole and the window in a way that would make it very obvious if these were opened by normal means, and rigged up a line of cotton at a height of four feet all round the room, set so that if it was touched it would fire off an infra-red camera. He linked this same camera to a thermostat so that it would also fire if there was a drop of more than three degrees in the room temperature.

Cutten then set up his ordinary camera, which was equipped with an electronic flash, so that he could manually operate this from his bed, using a cable-release under the pillow. Both cameras were pre-focused to the middle of the room, since this was where the ghost had been reported. Close by he also set his tape-recorder, pre-set so that it would begin recording with just the touch of one button. At 1.40 a.m. he settled down to sleep, intending to wake (without alarm), at 2.30 a.m. In the event he overslept by twenty-five minutes, but was still in time for the ghost's expected appearance at 3 a.m.

However, the hour passed without the slightest manifestation of anything ghostly, and when he got up to check his equipment, all was in order. At 3.07 a.m. he got back into bed, slept until 4.47 a.m., again checked his equipment, then slept through to 7.30 a.m., his normal wake-up time.[16] So the result of all this effort was precisely nothing.

On the positive side it has to be said that had the residents at the Primrose Hill house, perhaps for some form of sensationalism, tried to fake a ghostly appearance for Cutten's benefit, then his careful methodology should have picked this up. Indeed, if a hoax *had* been intended, it might be that the would-be pranksters abandoned their attempt once they realised what they were up against.

On the negative side, however, had there genuinely been a ghostly old man at the house, are we to suppose that this individual would have been encouraged or discouraged by all the equipment Cutten had prepared for him? It is revealing at this point to turn from John Cutten to what has happened on the hundreds of occasions when groups of ghost-hunters have sat out the night in an allegedly haunted house, their cameras and tape-recorders at the ready, all in the hope of bagging the sights and sounds of a ghost.

The fact is that despite the undeniable impressiveness of the ghost-hunters' equipment and methodologies (and ghost-hunting groups do contain some very level-headed and objective individuals), to the best of my knowledge there is not a single instance of a ghost-hunting group having even one truly unequivocal face-to-face encounter with a ghost – irrespective of whether they are subsequently able to produce visual and sound recordings of this. While Peter Underwood mentions occasions on which the odd member has seen a fleeting dark shape, or some of those present have heard the rustle of a dress (which may subsequently turn out even to have been tape-recorded), one looks in vain in his books for any really convincing group experience. The Ghost Club's current general secretary/treasurer, Commander Bill Bellars, has commented pertinently:

* * *

there is some evidence to suggest that 'they' [i.e. ghosts] may resent the appearance of investigators: the ghost-hunter's particular 'Murphy's Law' has it that 'when a ghost-hunter enters through the front door, the ghosts hurriedly leave through a back window!'[17]

One perfectly legitimate way of interpreting this is of course the natural reaction of the avowed sceptic towards the existence of ghosts: that since ghosts do not exist, ghost-hunters' repeated failures either to have collective ghost experiences or to be able to produce any truly convincing visual or audio evidence are only to be expected.

But if we accept that ghosts genuinely do exist, then the only available explanation seems, in all seriousness, to be that suggested by Commander Bellars: that ghosts are somehow aware of the intentions of those who would hunt them, and react adversely to this.

Bill Bellars' idea is in fact by no means new. Nearly two thousand years ago the Greek geographer Pausanias wrote in his *Atticis* of the apparent replays of the Battle of Marathon that were still being experienced in his time:

> To go on purpose to see the sight [i.e. the ghostly battle] never brought good to any man. But to him who chances to light on it unwittingly and by accident the ghosts are not angry.

When Peter Underwood wanted to arrange for the Ghost Club to stake out the reputedly haunted mansion Newark Park in the Cotswolds, an almost identical sentiment was expressed to him by the house's owner, Texan-born Bob Parsons.

> I can promise nothing of ghosts – when people wish to hear them, they do not, I have found.[18]

While we can only guess at why ghosts decline to appear to those who make special efforts to track them down, among those preoccupied with the mystery of ghosts there seem to be two totally polarised approaches.

On the one hand there are the would-be exorcists: those who react towards ghosts with much the same hysteria that others reserve for spiders and snakes. For them ghosts are loathsome and unwelcome intruders that need to be banished into outer darkness as quickly and expeditiously as possible, with no questions asked. We can hardly expect any ghost to feel cooperative towards them.

Then there are the would-be hunters: those who see ghosts as tantalisingly elusive game beckoning to be tracked down and captured with all resourcefulness. Lured by the possibility of being the first to get an authenticated, totally non-ambiguous video-tape of a suitably period-costumed ghost walking and talking, for them cameras, tape-recorders and all the rest of the gadgetry are almost the exact equivalents of big-game hunters' rifles. So should we be surprised that ghosts avoid them?

The glaring deficiency common to both approaches is a staggering inability even to begin to think of ghosts as actual people, let alone people with real problems. However much we delve among the accounts of ghosts as related by Underwood and others, we are hard put to find any real human interest in, and sympathy for, why any one particular ghost might be a ghost, and what his or her purpose might be in manifesting to the living. Time after time ghosts are coldly referred to as 'it'. This is all the more astonishing in the light of what we have come to realise in these pages: that if we have learned anything of ghosts, it is that they are emotion, indeed, raw human emotion at its most intense, and that at least something of a real, sentient consciousness lies behind them.

So is there a third, more sympathetic approach, one directly between the Scylla of the overzealous exorcist and the Charybdis of the overenthusiastic ghost-hunter? As we are about to see, indeed there is . . .

CHAPTER SIXTEEN

Helping Ghosts to Go the Right Way

When, on the night that my wife and I experienced the 'breathing' ghost at Abercrombie House, I silently prayed for whoever was with us to be granted eternal rest, I have to admit to a well-over fifty per cent self-interest in the prayer's efficacy. It is not easy dozing off to sleep when there is someone invisible, whom you strongly suspect to be dead, seemingly standing right next to you trying to attract your attention with insistent-sounding breathing.

In composing the prayer I have also to admit to having had very little comprehension of, or faith in, what I was trying to do. All that came to mind was having read years before in Andrew MacKenzie's book *Hauntings and Apparitions* the account by classics lecturer's wife Mrs Lawson of her experiences of the nun-like ghost at Abbey House, Cambridge.

Matters came to a head when the nun repeatedly came to Mrs Lawson while she was ill in bed:

seeming to grudge me any comfortable long sleep and standing for so long at the foot of my bed and latterly sighing – the only sound I heard from it.[1]

Mrs Lawson went on:

at last one night I said quite slowly and distinctly, 'In the name of the Holy Trinity, poor soul, rest in peace.' It went away to the curtain and I have never seen or heard it since. That same night it appeared to my husband who was sleeping in the bedroom up-stairs . . . stared at him and disappeared. He has not seen it since.

As in our Abercrombie House experience, the truly extraordinary feature is that there should have been such an immediate and effective response to such a simple prayer, one that in my own case was not even said out loud. Despite more than twenty years as a practising Roman Catholic, my old agnosticism still has the greatest difficulty in coming to terms with the idea that something so simple could instantly stop a ghost haunting, let alone release him or her to some form of eternity.

Yet once one begins to appreciate something of the heated doctrinal divisions that even the most basic act of praying for a dead person arouse between Christian denominations, and indeed between those of other religions, it becomes apparent that there is absolutely nothing simple about it. When we look back in history, virtually every culture, right across the world, has practised some form of praying for the dead, from the ancient Egyptians, to the classical Romans, to African Negroes, to Australian aborigines, to the very developed forms of 'ancestor worship' still practised by the Chinese and Japanese.

With specific regard to the Japanese, we may recall from the case of the murdered 'blind shampooer' ghost quoted by A. B. Mitford (see pp. 72–3) how after the householder of the haunted house found the shampooer's skull he:

> called in a priest and buried the skull in a temple, causing prayers to be offered up for the repose of the murdered man's soul. Thus the ghost was laid, and appeared no more.[2]

Such praying for the repose of the dead, whether ghosts or otherwise, continues to be treated very seriously by many present-day Japanese, as is evident from their continuing efforts all round the Pacific region to gather up the bones of their relatives killed during World War II, and to accord them the rites they consider proper. After the bones have been gathered, they

* * *

are laid before a makeshift shrine consisting of the Japanese flag, some candles, incense and (as with all Shinto ceremony) *sake*. The men remove their hats and stand, eyes closed, in a neat line to pray for the souls of their fallen ancestors . . . The bones are then collected in white jute sacks and taken to the local police head-quarters where they are arranged in rows behind a table bearing more offerings of incense and *sake*. Prayers are again offered, and the collectors bow, one by one, towards the row of skulls before locking the door . . .[3]

In the more familiar context of the world of the Biblical Old Testament, although the law of Moses strictly forbade trying to communicate with the dead, it certainly did not prohibit praying for them. That Jews of the second century BC prayed for their dead is quite evident from a Biblical passage describing how the Jewish leader Judas Maccabeus took a collection for sacrifices to be offered for the souls of some of his dead soldiers who had been discovered to have lapsed into paganism. The sacrifice was to help free the men from their earthly sins and thereby ultimately enjoy eternal life. As the passage remarks:

For if he [Judas Maccabeus] had not expected the fallen to rise again it would have been superfluous and foolish to pray for the dead . . . This was why he had this atonement sacrifice offered for the dead, so that they might be released from their sin.[4]

After the coming of Jesus, praying for the dead on the part of the earliest Christians is widely attested by pictures and inscriptions in the catacombs of Rome. On one tombstone now in Rome's Lateran Museum, a Christian husband declares that he has had this inscribed for his beloved wife Lucifera 'in order that all brethren who read it may pray for her, that she may reach God'. Early Christian fathers such as Cyprian, St Cyril of Jerusalem, St John Chrysostom and St Augustine explicitly stated their approval of praying for the dead, which was supported by both the Orthodox Church in the East and the Roman in the West, and which continues in both to this day.

The difficulty arises when we appreciate that underlying the whole practice, both Christian and non-Christian, is the premise that at least some people who have died live on in a state that can be improved by the prayers of those who are still living. Within a Christian context this implies that besides the theoretically immutable eternities of Heaven and Hell there must be, for those dead people who can be helped by prayers, a somewhere or something more intermediate: in other words a 'Purgatory'.

This was the doctrine that in the Middle Ages spawned the overblown industry in which many thousands of monks spent their days chanting prayers for the souls of those who had died rich enough to pay for them to do so. Inevitably it was a natural target for abolition by the Protestant Reformation, Article 22 of the Church of England's constitutional Thirty-Nine Articles declaring the Protestant position in no uncertain terms:

> The Romish Doctrine concerning Purgatory . . . is a fond thing vainly invented, and grounded upon no warranty of Scripture, but rather repugnant to the Word of God.

But it is one thing to declare, on the basis of erudite theological arguments, that at death the soul goes immediately either to Heaven or Hell, and that Purgatory does not and cannot exist. It is quite another, when confronted by responsible individuals seriously attesting to ghostly hauntings, to argue that there can be anything other than *some* form of intermediate state – particularly when it becomes apparent that the simple act of offering prayers for ghosts can and does put an end to their haunting.

Significantly, while the pre-Reformation Middle Ages, with all its praying for the dead, has left behind very few reports of ghosts, very much the reverse seems to have been the case during the earliest decades after the Reformation. Although in his treatise *Of ghostes and spirites walking by nyght* the Swiss Protestant Lewes Lavater steadfastly refused to believe in a Purgatory, nevertheless he found himself obliged to admit, in a passage which sounds as if ghosts were distinctly more communicative in the late sixteenth century than our own time:

> Many times in the night season, there have been certain spirits heard softly going, or spitting, or groaning, who being asked what

they were, have made answer that they were the souls of this or that man, and that they now endure extreme torments. If by chance any man did ask of them by what means they ought to be delivered out of these tortures, they have answered that in case a certain number of Masses were sung for them, or pilgrimages vowed to some saints, or some or suchlike deeds done for their sake ... then surely they should be delivered. Afterwards appearing in great light and glory, they have said that they were delivered, and have therefore rendered great thanks to their good benefactors, and have in like manner promised that they will make intercession to God and Our Lady for them.[5]

Although this passage inevitably sounds quaint from the perspective of the scientific-minded twentieth century, nevertheless it now behoves us to reflect upon how many cases we have already come across in which a ghost's hauntings have been stopped by sympathetic prayers for the repose of his or her soul. There was Mrs Athol Horne Stewart at Abercrombie House; the Japanese blind shampooer; Mrs Lawson's nun at Abbey House; Eddie Burks's gentle dealing with Thomas Howard; the Bristol cinema projectionist; Robin Hayden at Hook; and organist Francis Crute at Torquay.

It is particularly notable in the three last-mentioned examples that it was Protestant clergy, for whom the dead are theoretically beyond any possible mediation by the living, who said prayers for the repose of the souls of the dead persons whom they believed the ghosts to represent. As we discovered in the last chapter, the Anglican Church's Christian Deliverance Study Group has quietly but positively adopted the policy of holding requiems rather than exorcisms for them.

Perhaps the most remarkable example of 'laying to rest' that we shall study in this book is a case handled by the current clerical chairman of the Christian Deliverance Study Group, Canon Dominic Walker [pl. 23], whom we encountered earlier in connection with the Streatham 'plague pit' haunting. It may be recalled that Canon Walker on this occasion did not actually see the ghosts. Indeed, in more than twenty years of visiting households claiming problems with paranormal phenomena, he has never seen the ghost or ghosts in question – but for one spectacular exception.[6]

Around 1979, when he was rector of St Mary's, Newington, Dominic Walker was helping with visits throughout the Diocese of Southwark when he was called to the aid of a young family living in a modest semi-detached house in Carshalton, Surrey, on the outermost fringes of Greater London. The family, whom we will call the Parkers, consisted of the husband, his artistically inclined wife, their two daughters aged nine and eleven, and some chihuahua dogs, and they had not long moved into the house before Mrs Parker began to have serious concerns for her own sanity.

The reason for this was that on several occasions while she was on her own in the upstairs part of the house she saw the ghost of a middle-aged woman with one leg. The woman would initially seem to be quite solid, but would then vanish in front of her. On two of the occasions Mrs Parker was in the main bedroom. On the third she was in the bathroom and saw the ghost in the mirror, as if she was standing behind her, but when she turned round in fright there was no one there.

Initially Mrs Parker said nothing to any of her family until one day one of her daughters, who had just been on her own in the main bedroom, came rushing downstairs crying: 'Mummy, Mummy, there's a woman upstairs with only one leg!' From this, and from the fact that her chihuahua dogs showed quite uncharacteristic reluctance to venture into the upper part of the house, Mrs Parker realised with almost equal measures of gratitude and alarm that she had not been hallucinating, and that there must be at least some reality to the woman whom she had seen. Using her artistic talents, she made a careful sketch of what she could remember of the woman's appearance and began showing this to her nearest neighbours.

Unhesitatingly the older of these identified the woman as Anne Allen, who some thirty years before had lived in the upstairs part of what was now the Parkers' house, at a time when this had been divided into flats. Anne had had to go into hospital, and in the course of her treatment it became necessary to amputate her leg. As if this was not traumatic enough, on her return to the flat she found an eviction order waiting for her. Overcome by depression, she took her own life, an act which she committed in the same part of the house that was now occupied by the Parkers' main bedroom.

Aware that the house's previous occupant had stayed there only nine months, Mrs Parker now became curious to find out why she had moved so quickly. On being contacted this woman told her that she too had seen the ghost on a number of occasions, and like Mrs Parker had so seriously doubted her own sanity that she had actually asked to be admitted to the local psychiatric hospital. Fortunately the hospital had refused her, assuring her that she really was sane. After that, her only recourse had been to sell the house at the earliest opportunity.

The Parkers now realised that their home was haunted, and they sought the help of the Church, as a result of which Dominic Walker was asked to take charge of the case. Having heard what the Parkers had to tell him, he decided – in full accord with the revised thinking described earlier – that, rather than any expulsive exorcism, what was needed was a sympathetic requiem for the repose of Anne Allen's soul.

The main bedroom was the obvious location for the ceremony, and accordingly Dominic Walker set up an impromptu altar on the Parkers' dressing table. Then, with the family gathered around him, he began the prescribed opening prayers. Moments later, to his utter astonishment, he became aware of a woman with one leg standing beside him.

I only had a glance . . . and realised that it was the same woman whose picture (drawing) I had been shown [i.e. Anne Allen]. She was not smiling, aged about sixty and in ordinary clothes – something like a cardigan and skirt. My immediate thought was that either I had become too involved in the case and this was my psychological projection or that I was being set up by a tabloid newspaper and it was trickery. I continued with the requiem and said nothing to the family about my sighting. After the service they told me she had appeared when we began to pray for her and during the Eucharistic Prayer she smiled and disappeared. In fact, I didn't tell the family that I had also seen her because I think at that stage I hadn't had time to think through what had happened and needed to consider the possibility of some hysterical reaction/ projection . . . After the requiem the family said she appeared during the Bidding Prayers and disappeared during the words of consecration. Certainly when I turned around again to give the family Communion she wasn't there, but she must have been there for several minutes.[7]

* * *

Canon Walker admitted to me frankly that his impression at the time, on realising that he was probably seeing a ghost, was one almost of disappointment. Exactly as in some of the sightings we noted earlier, to him Anne Allen looked in every way solid and ordinary. But to hear this story told so matter-of-factly by a thoughtful and highly respected churchman – one still only in his mid-forties and ready to dismiss many ghost experiences as mere psychological projections – is worth more than any number of ghost photographs or recordings of purportedly ghostly sounds.

For it is clear that this sighting by Canon Walker was no fleeting 'I thought I saw a dark shape' type of experience. As in the case of those who witnessed the Roman army at York, he was either seriously hallucinating – or he genuinely saw Anne Allen's ghost standing right next to him. And in the strongest support of the latter option, this same ghost had not only been earlier experienced by at least three independent witnesses, but was also seen on this very same occasion by all four members of the Parker family.

Yet again we find ourselves confronted with a haunting associated with an identifiable, real-life person who committed suicide, and who therefore presumably received the Anglican Church's abbreviated funeral rites. And yet again the act of praying for the repose of the ghost's soul demonstrably *worked*. We are assured that having disturbed at least two generations of occupants of the Carshalton house, after Canon Walker's requiem service Anne Allen's ghost appeared no more.

As we have argued in previous instances, the unavoidable inference from this is that Anne Allen's ghost contained something very sentient of the once real-life person. Not only did she responsively appear when prayers were begun on her behalf, she disappeared immediately following the appeal for her soul to receive eternal rest. Furthermore, there was one additional and deeply touching factor in this case. As avowed by Canon Walker, she was seen positively to *smile* upon her release. If there remain any doubts that ghosts are not real people, desperately needing compassion and prayers from those in the land of the living, the attestation of that smile should dispel them all. For anyone frightened that they have a ghost in their home that they cannot get rid of, the Anne Allen case should give them all the encouragement they need to believe that ghosts can and should be helped to go on their way – but the *right* way.

One further case, of a different yet clearly closely related kind, deserves mention at this point. In March 1988, after having read one of my books, a Mr R. J. Comber, a nurse then living in the village of Charlton Mackrell, Somerset, asked if he could share with me an experience that hitherto, because he had felt so disturbed by it and thought no one would believe him, he had told only to his wife and his parish priest. In his own words, now reproduced with his full permission:

In December 1963 my first son, a baby of a few weeks, died tragically of pneumococcal meningitis during that terrible winter. I was very young and immature at the time, with no way of coming to terms with it, or handling death in any suitable way. To my great shame now – though I knew so little at the time – I did not give my son a proper Christian funeral, but merely arranged through the undertakers for his body to be laid to rest in the absence of his family. It is an appalling thing to admit, and against everything I now believe in, but at the time it seemed the most 'sensible' thing to do.

Fifteen years later (the summer of 1978) I was at home at this same typewriter one evening preparing some very uninteresting marketing reports for a sales company I was working for. I had had one glass of lager and was very relaxed, half listening to a mass for four voices by William Byrd on my stereo in the background. It had briefly struck me for no particular reason that I could think of that one of the boy singers must have been at the age that my son would have been at the time.

Suddenly all the hairs of my head stood up. I distinctly heard a child crying two feet from my right shoulder. I turned but there was no one there. I heard a boy's voice saying over and over again, 'Father, please put me to rest. Father, please put me to rest.'

I instantly knew that it was my son, even though he had died as a baby. I was dreadfully afraid and had to see my parish priest who gave precise instructions for the commending of his soul which he ordered me to do myself. There was no repetition of this incident, yet some weeks later when I was seated in my armchair watching TV I saw at the top corner of the room what I can only describe as a diamond-shaped object brilliant with all the colours of the rain-bow, saying over and over again, 'My bonds are free!' with an expression of transcendent joy.[8]

Here then was a case of a dead son seemingly waiting for the right moment to 'haunt' his father, and who although clearly not a place-bound ghost, needed to be properly laid to rest.

If we accept such cases as pivotal to our understanding of what ghosts are, why they are, and what they need from the living, then much else falls into place. It now seems possible to say with considerable confidence that although ghosts are often people who have been murdered or have committed suicide, their problem seems to be not so much due to this as to their not having subsequently received the funeral rites that they would have considered appropriate.

In the case of a murder victim this may be because the body had been hidden away in some inappropriate location, as in the stories of Athenodorus's Athens ghost, the Japanese shampooer, and Sir James Houblon's Cork victim. In the case of a suicide victim, clerical disapproval of their action may mean that their funeral service was truncated in an unsympathetic way, even though they received a proper burial. As we have noted, an abbreviated funeral service was until recently mandatory in the case of Anglican suicides, and may well have been directly responsible for the ghostly activities of Robin Hayden, Francis Crute, Anne Allen and the Bristol cinema projectionist, all of which ceased when a service of laying to rest was performed.

The same principle may also explain why, as attested by Lewes Lavater, there was such a plethora of hauntings immediately following the Reformation. It may also shed light on why to this day, certainly in England, a remarkably high proportion of hauntings happen to be by monks and nuns; individuals who, by their very occupation, are likely to date back to the time of the Reformation.[9] The reason would seem to be that when England's monasteries were forcibly closed and their large clerical populations dispossessed, many would not have been buried with the traditional rites that they regarded as their due. Effectively they would be in much the same position as those who in more recent times committed suicide and who for different reasons were not given *their* full burial rites.

There is a strong temptation at this point to consider where, upon a ghost being released by the prayer of someone living, the soul of the person concerned might go to. For sensitives such as Eddie Burks there is no mystery to this. The souls of those who have been released are met by deceased loved ones and welcomed 'into the Light' in essentially the manner described by those who have had near-death experiences. As Eddie Burks described the closing moments of his encounter with the ghost of Thomas Howard at Coutts Bank:

I then sensed, half saw, his [Thomas Howard's] daughter approaching. I knew he had a great love for her. As I said this he immediately responded:

'You lift my heart, for she was dear to me.'

I saw her more clearly as she approached him. She was dressed in Elizabethan costume, but entirely in white, and she radiated light. She took both his hands. He was awestruck by her beauty. They turned walking towards the Light, she holding his left hand in her right hand. He then looked back for a moment to thank us for helping him . . .

For many, with their credibility threshold already tested by what we have come across so far, this may be too much to take. But whatever, what we have discovered is that, traversing all boundaries of religion, the common key which seems to reach and release all ghosts is that of prayer by the living on their behalf – prayer that as we have seen can be of the simplest and most impromptu kind. As Canon Pearce-Higgins once beautifully expressed it:

In haunted houses . . . we find normally sad unhappy souls who have got lost on the way to paradise. They need our compassion and prayers and not to be cursed and consigned to outer darkness.[10]

Suddenly, rather than ghosts seeming to offer the most tantalisingly intangible evidence for their own existence, we find that in reality they lie at the cutting edge of proof of the existence of life after death, and of our potential understanding of what life itself may be all about . . .

CHAPTER SEVENTEEN

The Case That Would Not Fit . . .

Throughout the researching and writing of this book, one individual whose work with ghosts I kept in a kind of mental limbo was Eddie Burks, to whom we referred in an earlier chapter in connection with the Coutts Bank hauntings. Part of the reason for this was that Eddie's sensing of ghosts tends to consist mainly of feelings, emotions and pictorial imagery, not the sort of hard facts of names and dates that a historian instinctively looks for. Another reason was that while I was working on this book, Eddie was writing his own, together with journalist Gillian Cribbs, for the same publisher, Headline, to be published several months ahead of mine. It would have been quite wrong for my book overly to duplicate material from this.

A further reason was that I felt the need to test Eddie in order to be rather more sure of the validity of what he said he was sensing. To this end I wanted to find an active haunting that had not yet been publicised in any way, and that Eddie could therefore not possibly know about by normal means. This would enable me to cross-check his sensing against what I had already been told by those who had reported the haunting.

To find such a case is not easy, and in the event it came my way purely by chance, as happened when my wife and I experienced the Abercrombie House ghost. A retired Bristol senior police officer, whom we regularly meet while dog-walking, knowing that I was working on a book on ghosts happened to mention that a local professional family of his acquaintance had been having a long-term haunting problem. The husband had recently left home and the continuing ghostly phenomena were adding a further burden to the wife's distress. Was it a case I might be interested in?

On 24 January 1995 I visited the house that was the scene of this haunting, an ultra-modern dwelling in a pleasant village a few miles outside Bristol, with outstanding views towards the River Severn. For the better appreciation of these views the house's spacious lounge is set on the first-floor level, with the kitchen and bedrooms below, and it was there that I interviewed the wife, to whom for understandable reasons of privacy we will refer as Mrs Armstrong.[1]

The mother of two sons, Mark and James, now in their mid-twenties, Mrs Armstrong is neat, attractive and to all appearances well balanced. Although she suffers from back problems which have been diagnosed as multiple sclerosis and which cause her sometimes to walk with a stick, she was fully mobile when I met her, and did not mention the problems to me during the initial interview. Her home is well ordered, and the partial notes which she made of the phenomena as they were happening have enabled a much more detailed account than is often possible. As we will discover, this is all the more valuable in the light of the unusually baffling nature of the phenomena themselves.

In June 1990, just after she and her husband had purchased the house but before they had even moved in, Mrs Armstrong dreamed three times in a week of a figure in white standing in the corner of the lounge just to the left of the main window looking towards the Severn. It was difficult to put a sex to the figure, but she thought it was female. In the third of the dreams the figure seemed to glide diagonally across the room to the opposite corner and drop through the floor. Directly below is a cupboard housing all the fuse boxes and controls for the mains electricity supply.

However neither Mrs Armstrong nor any other member of the family had the slightest suspicion that the new house might be haunted until shortly after they moved in. The first experience came while Mrs Armstrong and her husband were on the ground floor. Although they knew they were the only people in the house at the time, both clearly heard footsteps overhead, as if someone was moving around upstairs in the lounge. Investigation revealed that there was no one there, and as they realised, one immediately peculiar feature of the footsteps was that they did not cause any rattling of the kitchen utensils hanging in the kitchen, even though normal overhead footsteps did.[2]

Next, while sitting alone in the lounge Mrs Armstrong saw out of the corner of her eye the very same white figure of her dreams. It was standing in the corner of the south-western side of the lounge, exactly as it had appeared in the dream, and it was even just visible as a reflection in the television screen, which was off at the time. Then it seemed to move and vanish. Although Mrs Armstrong said nothing of this experience to either of her sons, shortly afterwards Mark reported hearing someone behind him while he was sitting on the lounge sofa. He likewise briefly glimpsed a white shape before this again vanished.

In the succeeding weeks more footsteps were heard, on one occasion by Mark and Mr Armstrong together, on another by James alone. They were so heavy that they seemed to be a man's, and they seemed to go along behind the sofa that faces the main window. James in his turn saw the fleeting shape.

Matters took on a particular intensity, however, in September 1992. On the 21st the lights were found switched on in the attic room, which was rarely used. The next day, at 3.45 in the afternoon, while James was in his downstairs bedroom, both he and Mrs Armstrong heard the ghostly footsteps very heavily overhead. On this occasion they felt the sounds to be so disturbing that they temporarily left the house to sit in the car, but when they eventually went back inside the footsteps were even louder – as if a very large person was moving with difficulty, or carrying something heavy. On this occasion Mrs Armstrong again caught the briefest glimpse of the figure in white against the lounge's exposed brickwork.

Now seriously scared, she and James drove into Bristol to collect Mr Armstrong from his office. When they all returned together they found that the lounge cupboard doors had been flung wide open, a leather cushion was on the floor, and their hi-fi console had been turned upside down. Among subsequent activity there occurred more footsteps, the scattering of papers, and the rising and dimming of the house lights.

On 29 September 1992 Mr Armstrong had his own experience of what seemed to be a different ghost, preceded by a dream involving coloured shapes floating around in the lounge. He woke at 3 a.m. to see one of these shapes walk through the door of the bedroom where he and his wife were sleeping. In what he is convinced was full consciousness he saw a tall, gaunt-looking male figure move to the foot of the bed and stand looking down. The figure then disappeared upwards through the ceiling light – and thereby back into the lounge that seemed to be so much the focus of all the ghostly activity. At 6 a.m. all in the house clearly heard the sound of breaking glass and a dog barking, both as if they were happening indoors. But upon investigation there was no damage, and the barking had certainly not come from Beth, the family Labrador, who had all along shown her own fear of the ghostly presence.

Although not churchgoers themselves the Armstrongs now sought clerical help, as a result of which there arrived at their home two local clergy, the Revd Peter Haddock from Wells Cathedral and the Revd Vaughan Pollard from Nailsea, together with a healer called Richard Sheridan. They brought with them a portable altar, but seem to have held only a ceremony of blessing which failed to get rid of the problem. Even while the ceremony was going on Mrs Armstrong distinctly heard a movement behind the sofa, when no one visible was there. She also experienced an intense coldness, similarly felt by the Revd Pollard.

In fact, not only did the heavy footsteps continue, there also began serious disturbances to electrical appliances, in the manner of the poltergeist activity noted earlier. The dishwasher, freezer and microwave all failed in quick succession. In the case of the freezer this turned itself into an oven and back again in the space of twenty-four hours, a happening the manufacturers declared impossible. There was a mysterious turning back of the clock on the immersion heater. Particularly alarmingly, in July 1993 there was a complete 'crash' of all the electrical power. Armies of technicians were called out and eventually traced the trouble to a very unusual failure to mains apparatus set deep into concrete. This was notably below the very same cupboard into which the white figure had seemed to disappear in Mrs Armstrong's third dream.

Continuing into early 1995, at various times the hi-fi equipment switched on of its own accord and went to deafeningly full volume. On these occasions the remote control would never work and the stereo would have to be switched off manually. The footsteps and fleeting white shapes persisted, the sounds sometimes being heard even while someone was in the lounge, most usually along a track behind the main sofa.

On learning all these details, and aware that the house dated from no earlier than 1976, my first approach was to try to find out more of the history of the site on which it had been built, in case the haunting related to an earlier dwelling, in the manner of the Robin Hayden case. A neighbour of the Armstrongs who had been born in the village proved very helpful, but from her I learned very positively that the site had simply been the garden of a long-established nearby house. The only edifice of any possible significance had been a two-tier wooden astronomical observatory built in the 1920s by a member of the Fry family (of chocolate fame) who happened to be an astronomy enthusiast. But this observatory had been dismantled except for a remaining spiral staircase, and there seemed nothing in the manner of Mr Fry's passing, even though it had been at an early age, to suggest that he might be responsible for the hauntings.

A second possibility, particularly in view of the disturbances to the electrical equipment, was to regard the case as a poltergeist one, perhaps generated by one or other of the Armstrongs' two sons. But neither seemed to fit the mould of the disturbed adolescent so typical of those cases positively associated with poltergeist activity. And as just one example, the very first footsteps had been heard by Mr and Mrs Armstrong when neither of the sons were in the house.

A third possibility was sparked by Mrs Armstrong's mention that the wife and daughter of the architect from whom they had purchased the house had been heavily into dabbling with ouija boards. As I was aware, this activity is said to stir up entities who might come from anywhere, latch themselves onto a location and remain long after those who attracted them have moved elsewhere. But to postulate that this was the cause had to be the wildest guess.

Accordingly, faced with a haunting in which nothing seemed to fit, and in which the ghostly footsteps and other phenomena were continuing even after the local churchmen's attempt to lay them to rest, the case seemed a natural one in which to involve Eddie Burks. And rather than specially bring him down from Lincoln, with all the pressure to perform that that would entail, I felt it best to wait until he happened to be coming to Bristol anyway, for one of the visits he periodically makes to the Bristol Cancer Help Centre. That opportunity came in the third week of March 1995. On the evening of 20 March I collected him from the cancer centre and after a meal at my home drove him the few miles to the Armstrongs' house. I told him that I was quite deliberately saying absolutely nothing about any of the phenomena that the Armstrongs had been experiencing, and he expressed not the slightest objection, assuring me that he was happy to volunteer whatever he sensed.

It proved an intriguing exercise, far more productive of immediate communication than I had dared anticipate. Even while we were driving down the road in which the house stands, he told me he felt that someone not in the land of the living was trying to attract his attention. In order for him to stay 'in tune', he asked for any introduction to be as brief as possible, and accordingly within moments we were in Mrs Armstrong's lounge where at his own request an upright chair was placed for his use just in front of the fireplace. During the course of the next forty-five minutes he would sometimes sit in this, and sometimes walk around, while I took longhand notes of what he said he was sensing.

First he stood speaking slowly and deliberately, but assuming a somewhat twisted posture, as if in pain:

Agitation . . . An old person, by the feel of it, possibly arthritis. A very definite limp with the walk.

Then he began slowly pacing up and down behind the sofa, along the very route on which the Armstrong family had so repeatedly heard the heavy footsteps:

I want to place my arm on the furniture, just to steady myself. A curved back. Old. Uncertain on the feet. I am not picking up the personality yet. For some reason I feel the presence most strongly up and down this side of the room. This person paced up and down a lot.

He paused:

I want to draw this person closer. I'm not quite sure whether it's a man or a woman at the moment. The stature is less than mine. I think an arthritic spine. Very sharp pain at the base of my spine. I need to go through the death experience of this person.

230

*　*　*

At this point he unhurriedly emptied his pockets of their contents and placed them on the table. He seemed to sway:

My goodness! Very unsteady. Very unsteady on the feet. Losing sense of balance. Why is this person being a little elusive? I think whoever this was collapsed in the end. I am feeling the strength going out of my legs. Pain rising through my trunk. The word 'neglect' comes through very strongly. A sense of grievance. Oh! A lot of agitation to her now, at least I think it's a her. I am puzzled that I can't get the gender yet. I think it's a woman, but I'm uncertain, which is unusual. Must be a reason for that.

Mrs Armstrong, who was watching intently, would later remark how this forcibly reminded her of her own uncertainties regarding the gender of their ghost or ghosts. Eddie went on:

There's . . . a strong sense that her aggravation is brought on by neglect. This person feels they were not looked after properly. Oh!

Eddie was now holding his arm and breathing very heavily:

The sensations I am getting are very unpleasant. A crippling of the spine. An incorrect movement sends pains through my ribcage and right up to the head. Whether this was at the end I'm not sure. It may have been. This feeling of neglect has been carried into the present. Even now, they are feeling, 'Why will they not take notice? How much longer have I got to put up with this?'

As if in a stage whisper he told us:

I have got to calm this person down. At the moment there is too much emotion, and not enough verbal communication. They are inclined to be spiteful. They are now saying, 'I am glad someone understands what I have been going through.' They are almost pleased at having someone to share this discomfort.

*　*　*

231

Still puzzling over the ghost's gender, he struggled for a mental image that was clearly eluding him:

> There's a reluctance to help on the part of this person. Tentatively – a woman, but with a very dominant masculine character? I think quite a deep voice. Very demanding . . . Stature quite a bit smaller than mine. Unable to walk upright. Had to steady herself when she walked. Always needed something to put her hand on. She despised a walking stick: 'Sign of weakness,' she says immediately. 'Sign of weakness.'

At this point Mrs Armstrong found herself thinking of her own periodic dependency on a walking stick, and wondering whether Eddie was somehow tuning in to her multiple sclerosis plight, of which even I at the time knew nothing.

Eddie now seemed to be feeling the ghostly woman's death:

> I think [she] collapsed finally over there . . .

To Mrs Armstrong's astonishment, he indicated the very spot in the room at which, in her dream, she had seen the ghost drop through the floor to the cupboard below, the cupboard where, in 1993, the house's electrical supply had so mysteriously failed. Eddie went on:

> Legs collapsing underneath, up into the spine. Death pains. That was the end. The emotion is so strong about neglect. I can't get her to let go of that and give me some idea of what was behind it. She says, 'They had a good time. They didn't care about me.' I don't know who they are at the moment. Family? I'm not even sure of that at the moment. She's very reluctant to give anything away.

He described how he was sensing that the woman seemed to be a very difficult character whose determination to be self-sufficient had failed during her declining years. Yet she was not miserly or possessive. Then, after all his difficulties trying to get through to her, suddenly he felt the beginnings of a breakthrough:

* * *

232

She's softening now. For the first time a lighter feeling is coming in. The crippling body characteristics are being released. She's beginning to stand more upright. She's sensing that some change is afoot. But of course she is having to express a release of these feelings before her body can let go of its deformations. Her discomfort is being taken from me, thank goodness. She's releasing now some of the memories of the earlier part of her life. She had a strong physique. An impression of about five feet five inches. A handsome woman in her younger days. Blonde hair. Light straw colour. I'm getting the feeling of her being very proud of her hair.

With some clearer impressions at last coming through, Eddie now tried to get a feeling for when the woman lived, and here some images of forms of transport that flooded into his mind provided a clue:

She knows about motor cars because they are figuring in her memory at the moment. She didn't like them very much – noisy and unreliable. Edwardian times? . . . I think she lived through the Great War. She was indicating a moment ago that the youngsters are always wanting to go out in the car. She says, 'I couldn't go anyway. My back wouldn't let me. But that didn't stop them.' I think these youngsters were her nephew and niece, or two nephews and nieces. She gave them house room. I think they needed this but it was also to give her company . . . I believe the house was left to her by her father. Her back trouble had its origins much earlier in life, possibly even congenital, and it was a factor in her not getting married. Some of her attitude later in life was lack of fulfilment. It soured her. Yes, this makes sense of her attitude later in life. She fought against this weakness. She hates weakness. Hence her determination not to use a stick. She would have liked to get out of the house more, but it became more difficult as she grew older.

With more and more impressions now flooding into his mind, Eddie felt sufficiently confident that he had won the ghost's trust to begin thinking of manoeuvring towards the goal of freeing the house from the haunting. Again in a stage whisper he told us:

* * *

I have got to try and get her away now. She is being more cooperative now, as you will have gathered.

For Eddie, it was crucial in this release process that the ghost should be
met by one of her deceased relatives, rather in the manner that those
who have suffered near-death experiences and those in the last moments
before dying have reported. But if she had not married, and had borne
no children, who would this be? Eddie told us:

I have picked up about her father, but nothing about her mother.
Her mother died while she, the child, was very young, possibly
even in childbirth. Perhaps not unconnected with the child's damaged spine, though I wouldn't be sure of that. She never really
knew her mother. Her father figures a lot in her affections. She is
bringing up other memories of being taken to the seaside, not far
from here. She went with her father, a great excitement and thrill
to her. She was in her early teens . . . I'm trying to see the vehicle
they were in – a horse-drawn vehicle of some sort. I'm getting
glimpses of her on the beach – overdressed, as they were in late
Victorian and Edwardian times. A very happy memory for her. I
think her father is likely to come for her . . .

Moments later Eddie saw that the receiving relative was indeed to be
her father.

Her father has come on the scene and he is driving . . . a horse-
drawn vehicle with four wheels – a bit like a hackney carriage, but
less heavily built . . . No, I haven't got it quite right – it's a surrey,
as in the song 'Surrey with the fringe on top'. Maybe it's the vehicle they went in to the seaside. She climbs up and they embrace . . .
He's driving her off into the Light. I think he is taking her to a
seashore somewhere. He is going to introduce her to her mother.
She is looking much younger now. She's free and looking very
joyful . . .

For some while Eddie had been sitting in the upright chair, quietly and matter-of-factly describing what he was sensing. Only now, satisfied that he had released the ghost, did he come out of his semi-trance and turn his full attention to Mrs Armstrong and myself. Although the whole encounter had taken little more than three-quarters of an hour, he assured us that the ghost had been released, and the phenomena that had been besetting the house for several years should be at an end.

What was Mrs Armstrong's reaction, in the light of the phenomena that she and her family had experienced? Somewhat dazed from having it all happen in front of her with so little introduction she remarked how Eddie Burks's initial puzzlement at the ghost's gender strikingly matched her own. She had also been fascinated by the way Eddie had paced with uneven gait along the very same route on which she and the other members of the family had heard most of the footsteps. This was indeed extraordinary, bearing in mind that Eddie had had not the slightest prior awareness that these footsteps formed a prime feature of the case. Equally impressive to Mrs Armstrong was the way that Eddie, who had never been in the room before, pointed out as the place where the ghost had died the very spot where she had seen the ghost of her dream go down through the floor, and where the dramatic electrical failure had occurred in 1993.

For me, however, there were several serious difficulties. Mr Armstrong had described seeing a tall man, not a spinally crippled woman of five feet five inches. And having become used to ghosts that followed the layouts and levels of houses of their own time, I was troubled by the knowledge that there had definitely not been any earlier house on the same site. It was most unlikely, therefore, that the ghostly woman, whoever she was, could have died in the spot that Eddie indicated.

Eddie Burks's reaction to this was to suggest that the old woman must indeed come from elsewhere. Perhaps she had been attracted to the Armstrongs' house by a similar layout to her own, or some other factor. But what could have brought her here? At this point I perhaps too helpfully mentioned that the house's occupants prior to the Armstrongs had dabbled with ouija boards. Eddie immediately seized upon this as being by far the most likely explanation. Playing with ouija boards could stir up all sorts of unwelcome phenomena, which might also account for the male ghost which Eddie seemed to have been unable to sense. Asked by Mrs Armstrong's son Mark, who had joined us, if the ghost could have caused the disturbances to the electrical equipment, Eddie readily confirmed that highly agitated ghosts, as this one seemed to have been, quite commonly targeted items of an electrical nature.

Mrs Armstrong then volunteered the information that the previous occupants' marriage had broken up in this house. The same thing had also now happened to her own marriage. Her husband was suffering from depression. She herself, during the comparatively short time that she and the family had been in the house, had suffered serious back problems that seemed uncomfortably close to those that Eddie attributed to the ghost. Could all this be due to the influence of the ghost?

Eddie Burks confirmed that it could. Indeed, he thought it more than probable. But now that he had released the woman there was every reason for confidence not only that the house would have no more ghostly disturbances, but also that Mrs Armstrong and the rest of the family would be released from the ghost's malign and negative influence.

And thus, as at the time of writing, the case stands. Although Mrs Armstrong believes that the male ghost might yet recur, to guard against this possibility Eddie performed a simple, visualisation-type rite of cleansing. He also gave her his phone number so that she can contact him in the case of any fresh difficulty which, as he has assured her, can sometimes even be dealt with over the telephone.

At the moment, therefore, the jury is still out in the Eddie Burks case. If the footsteps that have plagued the Armstrongs for the last five years have genuinely ceased, then his insights into what was causing them and his methods of laying ghosts to rest may be regarded as heavily endorsed. If not, then the work of the Christian Deliverance Study Group has to be seen as considerably the better proven. Only time will tell . . .

If You Meet a Ghost, Be Kind . . .

Whatever the eventual truth about the Armstrong family's ghostly visitants, our search has come a long way since that warm Australian night when my wife and I so unexpectedly encountered the ghost of Abercrombie House. Whereas formerly I held no particularly firm views on the existence of ghosts, and in general felt the subject far too ephemeral and elusive to be worthy of serious study, now I feel able to venture some surprisingly positive conclusions.

First, and with the full support of my wife, I can attest from first-hand experience just how real an encounter with an apparent ghost can be. From this, and from what others have related in the course of this book, there can be absolutely no doubt that non-psychic and thoroughly self-questioning people from all walks of life can and do have experiences they find difficult to interpret as other than ghosts. Some of these may of course be explained away as hallucinations. Others may be what Canon Dominic Walker labels 'psychological projections'. Yet others may have become so distorted by faulty memory and by over-enthusiastic story-telling that any truth behind them has been all but lost. Yet even when all these possibilities are taken into consideration, there remain too many cases too well attested by too many independent witnesses for them not to involve something very real and very mysterious.

Our second firm conclusion, therefore, is that ghosts do indeed exist. Furthermore, very evident from all that we have seen is that they take not one, but several forms. We have, for instance, noted the variety commonly dubbed poltergeists, and how these seem to derive from some ability emanating from living people to move objects at a distance. Because these do not seem to pertain to anyone who has died, we have chosen not to count them as true ghosts, although it is worth keeping in mind that some of the apparent true ghost cases that we have seen have involved poltergeist-type phenomena.

Likewise, we have noted a complete genre of ghostly appearances by persons just deceased to friends or loved ones at around the time of their deaths – the type of ghost we have dubbed 'passing callers'. These we have similarly chosen not to count as true ghosts, firstly because they seem to make their appearance solely around the time of death, and secondly because this appearance may be anywhere in the world where the person to whom they wish to appear happens to be. If to haunt is an essential characteristic of the true ghost, then 'passing callers' do not exhibit this. They seem free and unconstrained, rather than being confined to any one particular location.

These varieties aside, true ghosts we would define as sensory manifestations that can take the form of either apparitions, or sets of sounds, or smells, or feelings, or physical disturbances to inanimate objects, or various combinations of these, all seemingly to pertain to people who have died.[1] Typically, they seem frozen in space, because, with rare exceptions, they stay confined to the same locations and move on old, no longer extant floor levels. They also seem frozen in time, because they are seen wearing the same clothes and appurtenances that they would have worn in life. They may even be accompanied by animals and by vehicles they once used. Given that we have come across reliable modern-day reports of ghosts dressed as if in the Roman period, they would seem to be able to manifest, albeit intermittently, over a time-distance of well over a thousand years.

This leads to the crucial question of what they are. If they showed absolutely no responsiveness to the living, then it would be reasonable to infer that they are just empty video-recordings, or similar, somehow impressed into their surroundings in the same manner that a piano concerto is imprinted onto a compact disc, but with nothing sentient really being there.

It is very possible that some ghostly manifestations are of this variety, for example the Roman army seen in the cellar of the Treasurer's House at York, the Streatham plague pit ghosts, and perhaps the Maori war canoe of Lake Tarawera. Caution is needed, however, in interpreting even these as non-sentient, for the timing of the Streatham plague pit ghosts so soon after the living family's cot death tragedy, also the premonitory nature of the war canoe, both suggest the activity of at least some form of consciousness.

Altogether more revelatory, however, are the now-familiar ghost cases such as Robin Hayden at Hook, Anne Allen at Carshalton, the Nun at Abbey House, Cambridge, Francis Crute at Torquay and (as our best guess at identity) Mrs Athol Horne Stewart at Abercrombie House, New South Wales. As we have seen, in each of these cases the ghosts demonstrably responded, or were made to respond, to an action made on their behalf by the living.

Particularly important here is the nature of that action. If this had been a zapping of the ghost with X-rays or neutrons, or something similarly mechanical, then any reaction that the ghost made, even of a negative variety, might reasonably be construed to have been similarly mechanical, just like the magnetic erasing of videotape. But in the cases referred to, all well attested and with more than one witness, the ghosts responded to nothing more than the formula of words. To prayers. To sentiments expressed on their behalf. That demands something sentient, something capable of understanding the words and the sentiments behind them. In other words, a human mind, a mind continuing on beyond death.

Although this book can have no more important or far-reaching conclusion than this, opening as it does a whole new angle on the life-after-death debate, one further observation, deriving directly from my own personal Abercrombie House experience, potentially enables a yet deeper understanding of the nature of ghosts.

This concerns the all too rudimentary prayer that I composed to try to release the ghost, and the crucial fact that I said it totally silently. Although this was addressed, not to the ghost, but to a Higher Authority, I have the strongest impression, not least from the immediacy of the response, that the ghost heard it too.

If I am right in this, then the deduction to be drawn is that ghosts can and do read thoughts, and this may help explain many things. It can account, for instance, for why it is so rare for a ghost ever to be heard speaking. If a ghost reads thoughts, then he or she may reasonably expect to communicate the same way, and be frustrated when the signals fail to get through. Whatever anyone might make of Eddie Burks's claimed sensitivities, quite evident from my own personal observation of his dealing with the Armstrong family case is that to all appearances he communicated with the ghost at just such a telepathic level, thereupon, in his 'stage whisper' mode, audibly translating the gist of this for the benefit of Mrs Armstrong and myself.

If ghosts can indeed read thoughts this would, of course, also explain why ghost-hunters have such a poor success record, and why, as Ghost Club general secretary Bill Bellars has expressed it, 'when a ghost-hunter enters through the front door, the ghosts hurriedly leave through a back window'. There is no need to imagine them doing this literally, but with telepathy in play it is surely not unreasonable that they would seek out only potentially sensitive, receptive individuals, and would decline to manifest, or to 'perform' in any way, for groups of people intent only on capturing them technologically.

For ghosts to operate on some level of thought would also tie in with the manner in which they seem not uncommonly to manifest to living recipients' unconscious minds, as via dreams. As may be recalled, Anthony Crosland made his 'passing caller' appearance to Roy Jenkins via a dream, and Mrs Armstrong dreamed three clearly ghost-related dreams even before she and her family had moved in to their haunted house. Prevalent in the folklore of peoples all over the world is the idea that the dead can and do communicate via dreams, as in anthropologist Geoffrey Gorer's remarks on West African Negroes that according to their traditional beliefs:

> In dreams the soul is free and able to commune with the spirits and the dead who are invisible, though not impalpable, by day.[2]

At this point, as a possible way of understanding how a true ghost may manifest to a living mind, whether via a dream or by some other form of input, it may be worth citing a fascinating instance of how a *false* ghost can be injected into the unconscious mind via hypnosis, as demonstrated by the author Colin Wilson for the purposes of a television programme back in the 1970s.

As is well known to hypnotists, a so-called hypnotic suggestion can be implanted into a hypnotised person whereby, even long after having been brought out of the hypnosis, the person can be made to 'see' an illusion, such as an individual who is not really there, on the giving of a pre-arranged cue. Most usually the cue is a code-word, though in this instance it was the sight of Colin Wilson himself, who says of the experiment in his book *Mysteries*:

A volunteer – a housewife who was known to be a good hypnotic subject – was placed under hypnosis by a doctor. She was told that when she awakened she would be taken to another place where I would approach her (followed by a television camera). As I spoke to her she would 'see' the sinister figure of a seventeenth-century clergyman standing nearby; the man's appearance was described in detail. She was awakened and taken to the Bristol Docks, where I was waiting. As I walked towards her she smiled at me, then her eyes strayed across the water to an abandoned wharf. Her smile vanished, and she asked me with amazement,

'Where did he go?'

'Who?'

'That man.' She pointed to the dock and described an unpleasant, sallow-looking man dressed in old-fashioned clothes, who had been standing on the wharf then vanished. Even when the hypnotist explained that she had been responding to a suggestion made under hypnosis she was obviously only half convinced. Several times during the rest of the afternoon she tried to persuade us to admit that it had been a joke and she had seen a real man. She said there was nothing 'ghostly' about him; he looked quite solid and normal.[3]

The point here is that if a living person, in this instance a hypnotist, can inject such a convincing, yet totally false-image, ghost into another living person's mind, can someone who is dead, i.e. a ghost, do the same with a *true* image of themselves, as they had existed in life? Might this even explain why in several of the cases we have seen that the ghost's face is poorly defined? Could this be because when we try to 'image' ourselves, the one feature we are likely to be poorest at is our face, because unless we are Narcissus, it is the part we see least?

Tenuous though the idea might sound, the tantalising feature is its potential explanatory value, particularly from the point of view of that old chestnut that so perplexed people for thousands of years – why ghosts are seen wearing clothes and other appurtenances from their own time. According to the 'mind-injection' hypothesis, how we see a ghost is arguably not how he or she now actually is, but how they have conjured themselves to us in order to be meaningful in the land of the living.

A phenomenon of very much the same order, along with the possibility of the same explanation, is to be found in near-death experiences, during which those who have clinically died, and who recover, sometimes report having met up with deceased relatives and loved ones who again are never naked. One particular near-death experience illustrating this was that of an American Roman Catholic priest, Father Louis Tucker, who 'died' from ptomaine poisoning at Baton Rouge, Louisiana in 1909.

As described by Father Louis, after the, among near-death experiences, almost commonplace experience of moving down a tunnel he:

> . . . emerged into a place where people were being met by friends. It was quiet and full of light, and Father [i.e. his human father] was waiting for me. He looked exactly as he had in the last few years of life, and wore the last suit of clothes he had owned.[4]

Conscious of the seeming absurdity of this suit of clothes, Father Tucker explained:

> I knew that the clothes Father wore were assumed because they were familiar to me, so that I might feel no strangeness in seeing him, and that to some lesser extent, his appearance was assumed also.

Father Tucker's experience even included precisely the same telepathic reading of thoughts that we have postulated in the case of ghosts. He found himself in his temporary 'in-death' state reading his father's thoughts, and his father reading his in the very same manner that we have noted of Eddie Burks – who, as we may remember, had a near-death experience at the age of five – in his dealing with ghosts. Again in Father Tucker's own words:

242

*   *   *

I knew all these things by contagion, because he did . . . I discovered that we were not talking, but thinking. I knew dozens of things that we did not mention because he knew them. He thought a question, I an answer, without speaking; the process was practically instantaneous.

Also suggestive of ghosts of all types operating at this same level of the unconscious mind is a fascinating analogy from the medical literature on ghost limbs, in this instance involving a sixteen-year-old American girl who had to have both her legs amputated after a car accident. Although the girl specifically requested her surgeon to bury her severed legs rather than to incinerate them, for some unknown reason the latter ignored this request whereupon, in precisely the manner described back in Chapter 7, the girl suffered extremely severe burning pains in the 'ghost' limbs. Referred to a psychiatrist, the girl was hypnotised and given the key suggestion that her legs were still with her in the spiritual sense, even though not physically. As noted in the medical journal *Archives of Surgery*, the result was:

> She reported increased feelings of well-being and seemed to believe that, symbolically, her legs had been restored to her.[5]

In Dr Rupert Sheldrake's opinion this was 'one of the few cases of a complete cure [of ghost limb pains] that I have come across in the medical literature'. Again involving the unconscious mind, or whatever else it is that hypnosis reaches, it is difficult to interpret it as anything other than the 'ghost limbs' equivalent of the laying to rest that we have found to be so efficacious for true ghosts.

Now if we are anything like right in some of the above deductions, and in particular regarding the efficacy that we have attributed to even the most simple rite of laying a ghost to rest, then much else follows. As we have seen, the very fact that this 'laying to rest' rite seems to work is valuable enough from the point of view of our understanding of what ghosts are, and why they are. But – again if we are right – for the ghost the rite's value has to be literally infinite: all the difference between being chained in time and space and being free of such constraints.

In this light, what cannot be emphasised enough is the sheer barbarity of regarding ghosts as entertaining conversation-wagging accessories that no historic pile should be without – the all too widespread ethos that lies behind so many cities' 'ghost walks' and behind many of the current wave of popular ghost books. Prevailing popular attitudes towards ghosts may be likened to that common not so long ago towards caged animals and birds: that as long as they amuse the spectator, any feelings on the part of the animal are a matter of complete indifference.

Equally as unhelpful as the 'zoo animal' attitude towards ghosts is that of fear and superstition: the understandable result of generations of children being taken on 'terror' rides on amusement park ghost trains and entertained with horror-saturated ghost stories and ghost movies. Although seriously attested instances of a ghost harming anyone are virtually non-existent, in adulthood the fear of ghosts that has been injected in childhood tends to become transmuted into a 'brush it under the carpet' attitude that can be as frustrating as it is unreasonable.

Thus, all too frequently in the course of the research for this book the broaching of the very subject of an alleged haunting prompted a near hysteric obstructiveness, as if refusal to talk about it could make it either go away, or appear never to have happened. A classic example of this was Coutts Bank's first reaction to the alleged haunting by Thomas Howard. In order to provide a properly authoritative account of the various ghostly sightings that had prompted the calling in of Eddie Burks, I wrote to Coutts' management very politely requesting copies of any first-hand descriptions by the switchboard operators who had first witnessed the ghost. To facilitate this I freely volunteered to submit anything and everything I might write on the case for the Bank's approval and/or veto as necessary. The response was an adamant refusal to pass on any information whatsoever, culminating, after protests from me, in an abrupt 'Let sleeping ghosts lie'.

The only person within the company who proved willing to be helpful was archivist Barbara Peters, now retired, who very kindly answered my queries concerning the earlier history of the Strand location before Coutts purchased the site.

Shortly before this book went to press there was in fact some softening by Coutts. Their press officer Joan Dickers candidly explained to me

that their earlier policy of blanket non-cooperation had been necessi-
tated by the flood of often less than savoury media interest generated by
journalist Gillian Cribbs' opening news story about the haunting. This
seriously interfered with the Bank's normal business, and with this I
sympathise. Even so, first-hand descriptions by the switchboard operators
of their alleged sightings of 'Thomas Howard' remain outside the public
domain.

Authorities in London's City University proved even more unco-
operative in respect of my inquiries concerning reported sightings by
night porters of the ghost of a professor (whose identity is known to
me), who hanged himself in his office in 1976.

Thankfully not all ghost cases have been beset by such difficulties,
or the writing of this book would have been nearly impossible. Indeed,
on the credit side, I never ceased to be surprised how many ordinary,
self-confessedly non-psychic people, once I mentioned to them that I
was working on a book on ghosts, volunteered stories that they had
sometimes never before told any outsider. The need for such openness
cannot be emphasised enough. Only by the freeing of information about
the circumstances surrounding a haunting: its exact date and time; every
detail remembered by the living witnesses, the historical background to
the location, etc., can we improve our understanding of what ghosts are
and why they are. As mentioned earlier, ideally I would have liked for
every case in this book to have been described without recourse to a
single pseudonym. In the event, in certain circumstances this has proved
impractical, in particular, as in the case of the Armstrongs, where the
family currently wish to sell their house, and where Eddie Burks's
apparent clearing of the ghostly intruders is too recent for anyone to be
one hundred per cent sure of its effectiveness. But full factual openness
should always be the ideal.

In this same regard, what cannot be emphasised enough is the need
for the most fundamental shift in public attitudes towards ghosts. No
family who finds that their home is haunted should feel afflicted with a
problem on a par with rats or the death-watch beetle. No ghosts should
be subjects of amusement and entertainment, as they are currently often
treated by the popular media and by those who promote city 'ghost
walks'. Nor should they be pursued with camera and tape-recorder in
the manner of the ghost-hunters.

Instead, if this book has one conclusion over-riding all others, it is that ghosts are people, people who have died yet who still live on, tied to their old earthly existence in an unsatisfactory manner. They need to be treated with all the sympathy and help we would accord to a living person who was in trouble.

For why they need such help seems quite commonly to be because in their own time the living did not give them the 'laying to rest' they considered appropriate – in the case of Anglican suicides because of the already mentioned truncation of the normal funeral service. One important lesson here, thankfully already being heeded in present-day funerals, is that those who have broken codes by taking their own lives need to be sent off with, if anything, even more ritual solace rather than less.

However, if this was not given at the time and a ghost was therefore brought into being, the further and even more important lesson is that this can be remedied by even the simplest prayer appropriate to whatever religious beliefs the dead person may have had in life. The results, as we have seen in so many instances in this book, can be the swiftest and most dramatic that anyone could wish for, and should be the assurance, for anyone who feels themselves afflicted by a haunting, that an effective antidote is at hand. Even my own impromptu rite at Abercrombie House seems to have held, for the Morgan family have certainly not told me otherwise.

Overall the message has to be one expressed a few years ago by the American ghost expert Hans Holzer:

Be kind to ghosts, if you happen to run into one or one happens to run into you. There, but for the Grace of God, goes you or some-one you know.[6]

If Holzer's advice is followed, there is every reason to believe that ghosts will be grateful. Although for the moment I continue to reserve judgement on the validity of Eddie Burks's special relationship with ghosts, I would certainly *like* to believe in the reality of the communication which Eddie claims he received from the ghost of Thomas Howard, fourth Duke of Norfolk, the evening after he and members of the Norfolk family held a memorial service for the repose of the Duke's soul:

246

* * *

You pleased me greatly with the honour you did me yesterday. Put aside any doubts which you may have entertained concerning the true value of the ceremony, for it has truly relieved me of the vestiges of my sadness and now I feel free to step forwards into the greater Light. I owe you all a debt which I can repay only in the coinage of love whose quality is raised by my greater awareness of the presence of our God. Therefore accept my love, and when you can and when you will, reflect upon me and send me a token of your love. You may think that a gulf of time does separate us, but it is a moment only, and to me you are my brothers and sisters forever united and bound in the love of God. Remember me in your prayers as I will remember you until the blessed day when we meet in joy. Thank you, and I bid you farewell.

It seems a fitting note on which to end.

POSTSCRIPT

My opportunity to 'test' the ghost-sensitive Eddie Burks concerning the ghostly phenomena experienced by the Armstrong family came at the very closing stages of this book; indeed, within hours of when the manuscript was due at my publishers. This meant that there was insufficient interval to check whether or not Eddie's claimed 'release' of the Armstrongs' heavy-footed woman ghost had genuinely been effective. I therefore asked my publishers to allow this postscript at the proof stage of the book, by way of a 'stop press'.

It may be recalled that it was on 20 March 1995 that Eddie visited the Armstongs' house for the first and only time, as described in Chapter 17. On leaving he declared that, although he could not be sure he had cleared all the house's ghosts (the family believed there to be at least two), he was confident that he had 'released' the woman ghost responsible for the heavy footsteps.

It is now mid-June and, on contacting the Armstrong family, I have learned that the heavy footsteps – for them, by far the most disturbing of all the phenomena – have indeed never once been heard since Eddie's visit. There continue very occasional minor phenomena, such as interference with the lights, which suggest the possible lingering of a more minor ghost. But, so far as the Armstrongs are concerned, the improvement had been '100 per cent'. It would seem, therefore, that Eddie's methods can be as efficacious as those of churchmen conducting belated requiems.

By way of a further postscript, I have recently learned of a case in England closely resembling the experiences of my wife and I at Abercrombie House in respect of the 'ghostly' phenomena coming and going with the switching off and on of the electric light. The following derives from a report sent in June 1988 to the Society for Psychical Research by a long-standing friend, Dr Michael Clift, regarding happenings he experienced while staying at Bearwood College, Sindlesham, near Wokingham, in 1983:

On Wednesday 27 July of that year I was visiting an old friend, Lieutenant Commander Michael Hayes, who was history master there and lived in the Tower Flat. The house, a splendid example of Victorian Gothic, was built around 1873 for the [then] owner of *The Times* . . . but has been a school since the 1920s. On several previous occasions I had stayed there overnight, always in the same dormitory on the top floor . . . I had never felt any unease, and had always slept well. On this completely windless summer night it was different. As I was dozing off, I was roused by a lot of noise like that of furniture being moved nearby. I thought at first it was caused by cleaners on the floor below, then by my friend moving about in his flat, then by a lorry discharging planks on the gravel below the dormitory window. None of these survived investigation. I got up three or four times and it was only on the last occasion that I realised *the noise came on when the light was out and faded away when I switched it on* [italics mine]. There was a clear relation between the two and it was then I felt so fearful that I went downstairs and slept until dawn in my car.

There is some suggestion that the cause of this particular haunting may have been the drowning of a ten-year-old boy at the house in 1883, but this remains as yet undetermined. Dr Clift also learned that a cleaner, Mrs Handiside, had independently experienced a ghost in the Tower Flat, though at the time Lieutenant Commander Hayes had declined to believe her.

Such examples make clear that although, as already acknowledged, the subject of ghosts was taken up by me only reluctantly, now that I have done so the bit is firmly between the teeth, and there remain more than a few tantalising loose ends with opportunities for further developments in which you, the reader, may be able to play a part.

For instance, I would have liked to learn a lot more about Anne Allen, the woman suicide from Carshalton, Surrey, whose 'release' by Canon Dominic Walker was described on pp. 217–20. Anne Allen was her real name, and she is said to have died sometime around 1949. Frustratingly, however, Canon Walker no longer has a record of the address where she appeared, nor the current whereabouts of the family disturbed by her (except that 'Mrs Parker' is known to have died). Perhaps you were a neighbour of Anne Allen when she lived in Carshalton? Or are a surviving member of the 'Parker' family who, with Canon Walker, saw her ghost at the requiem he conducted on her behalf?

Similarly, it would be helpful to know the address of the Streatham house that suffered the 'plague pit' haunting described on p. 158. Although the local vicar knew that this had been built over a plague pit, record has been lost both of his identity and the particular Streatham parish under his charge. Were you a member of the family who suffered the haunting? Or the young policeman who attended the family's call for help that night?

There may also be other cases that have been touched on in this book for which you may be able to provide fuller or more accurate details. You may be the prison chaplain who witnessed the ghost who possessed 'Sanjay'. If you are Australian, you perhaps know something of the last days of Mrs Athol Horne Stewart, and why she might haunt Abercrombie House. If you are a Londoner, you may perhaps have come across some contemporary account of the discovery of the body found walled-up in the Upper Circle of the Theatre Royal, Drury Lane (this would help pinpoint its date). You may be able to suggest why Thomas Howard should haunt the site of Coutts Bank. Wherever you live, anywhere in the world, perhaps you can parallel ghost cases described in this book from your own direct experience? Any genuinely authoritative, first-hand information of this kind will be welcomed, and can be forwarded to me:

Ian Wilson
c/o Headline Book Publishing
338 Euston Road
London NW1 3BH

* * *

All serious material will be acknowledged and (as has been my policy throughout this present book) would not be used in any way without the sender's prior permission. Who knows what further trails *In Search Of Ghosts* may yet lead to?

Notes & References

INTRODUCTION

1. Quoted in Andrew MacKenzie, *Hauntings and Apparitions*, London, Granada, 1983, p. 214.
2. Booklet by Rex Morgan, *Abercrombie House*, incorporating 'The Stewarts and Abercrombie House' and 'The Ghosts of Abercrombie', Manly, Runciman Press, 1984.
3. Fax to the author dated 2 December 1994, and in the author's possession.

CHAPTER 1

1. J. B. Phillips, *The Ring of Truth*, London, Hodder & Stoughton, 1967.
2. See Manfred Cassirer, 'The Ghost of C. S. Lewis', *Journal of the Society for Psychical Research*, 55 (January 1988), pp. 33–5.
3. Dennis Bardens, *Mysterious Worlds*, London, W. H. Allen, 1970, pp. 126–8.
4. Kenneth McAll, *Healing the Haunted*, London, Darley Anderson, 1989.
5. Ibid., p. 2.
6. Retired science lecturer and writer, Rodney Hoare.
7. From notes sent to the author by Miss Joan Hughes, 1 June 1994.
8. 'Crisis apparition' is psychical researchers' jargon for a ghost that

appears around the time of the living individual's death to individuals he or she has known in life – see Chapter 4.

9. Rosemary Ellen Guiley, *Encyclopaedia of Ghosts and Spirits*, New York, Facts on File Inc., 1992.

10. Peter Underwood, *Haunted London*, London, Harrap, 1973, pp. 135–6.

11. Melvin Harris, *Investigating the Unexplained*, New York, Prometheus, 1986.

12. Arthur Myers, *A Ghosthunter's Guide*, Chicago, Contemporary Books, 1992, pp. 271–6.

13. Ibid., p. 273.

14. Letter of A. Arnold Wettstein to the author, dated 5 October 1984.

15. Arthur Ellison, *The Reality of the Paranormal*, London, Harrap, 1988, p. 19.

16. Ibid., pp. 19–20.

17. Quoted in Peter Underwood, *The Ghost Hunters*, London, Robert Hale, 1985, pp. 160–1.

18. Ellison, op. cit., p. 20.

19. Letter to the author, dated 23 November 1994.

20. Peter Underwood, *No Common Task*, London, Harrap, 1983, pp. 131–2.

21. Canon John Pearce-Higgins, 'Poltergeists, Hauntings and Possession', in John Pearce-Higgins and G. Stanley Whitby, *Life, Death and Psychical Research*, London, Rider, 1973.

22. Michael Perry (ed.), *Deliverance: Psychic Disturbance and Occult Involvement*, London, SPCK, 1987, p. 16.

CHAPTER 2

1. It should be pointed out that Underwood no longer belongs to the Ghost Club. Because of disagreements at a committee meeting, he left the club and has formed the Ghost Club Society.

2. Peter Underwood, *Ghosts and How to See Them*, London, Anaya, 1993, p. 72.

3. For Underwood's fullest and most up-to-date accounts, see his *Nights in Haunted Houses*, London, Headline, 1994, p. 187ff.

4. Underwood, *Haunted London*, op. cit., p. 157.

5. Underwood, *Nights in Haunted Houses*, op. cit., p. 188.
6. This is reproduced in Underwood's *No Common Task*, op. cit.
7. From a letter of the Revd Hardy to Brian Tremain, 27 July 1967, preserved in the National Maritime Museum archives.
8. Underwood, *Ghosts and How to See Them*, op. cit., p. 63.
9. Hans Holzer, *Great American Ghost Stories*, New York, Barnes & Noble, 1993 edition, p. 260.
10. Michael Hargraves, 'Little Pictures', booklet produced to accompany a Getty Museum exhibition, 7 December 1993–6 March 1994, J. Paul Getty Museum, Los Angeles, 1993.
11. Underwood, *The Ghost Hunters*, op. cit., p. 47.
12. Information principally derived from personal correspondence with Miss Peggy Spencer Palmer, sister of Charles and Arthur, March/April 1985.
13. Underwood, *Ghosts and How to See Them*, op. cit., p. 63 (caption).
14. Indre Shira, *Country Life*, 26 December 1936.
15. G. N. M. Tyrrell, *Apparitions*, London, Duckworth, 1953.
16. Underwood, *Nights in Haunted Houses*, op. cit., p. 163.

CHAPTER 3
1. Perry (ed.) op. cit., p. 12. In the original quotation the Christian Deliverance Study Group appears under its former name, the Christian Exorcism Study Group. I have updated this for the purpose of simplicity.
2. Giraldus Cambrensis, *The Itinerary through Wales*, London, Everyman, 1935, p. 86.
3. Quoted in J. Gaither Pratt, *Parapsychology*, London, W. H. Allen, 1964, p. 88.
4. Ibid., pp. 88–9.
5. Ibid., p. 94.
6. Ibid., pp. 89–90.
7. Ibid., p. 113.
8. As quoted in W. G. Roll and J. G. Pratt, 'The Miami Disturbances', *Journal of the American Society for Psychical Research*, Vol. 65, 1971, p. 419. The punctuation has been slightly modified for

better readability.

9. Ibid.
10. See Hans Bender, 'An Investigation of "Poltergeist" Occurrences', *Proceedings of the Parapsychological Association*, 5, Durham, North Carolina, 1968, pp. 31–3.
11. Ibid.
12. Perry (ed.), op. cit., pp. 12–13.
13. David Fontana, 'A Responsible Poltergeist: A Case from South Wales', *Journal of the Society for Psychical Research*, 57, 1991, pp. 385–402; and, by the same author, 'The Responsive South Wales Poltergeist: A Follow-up Report', *Journal of the Society for Psychical Research*, 58, 1992, pp. 225–31. This case was also featured in London Weekend Television's *Strange but True?* programme of 28 October 1994. I have used the true names of the original witnesses as given in this rather than the pseudonymous ones in David Fontana's reports.

CHAPTER 4

1. Ronald Rose, *Living Magic: The Realities Underlying the Psychical Practices and Beliefs of Australian Aborigines*, London, Chatto & Windus, 1957.
2. Quoted in C. H. Herford, Percy and Evelyn Simpson (ed.), *Ben Jonson*, Vol. I, Oxford University Press, 1925, pp. 139–40.
3. *Proceedings of the Society for Psychical Research*, Report of the Literary Committee, 1882–3, Vol. I., pp. 124–6.
4. Mrs E. Sidgwick, 'Phantasms of the Living', *Proceedings of the Society for Psychical Research*, 1923, Vol. 33, pp. 152–60.
5. Quoted in Colin Wilson, *Beyond the Occult*, London, Bantam, 1988, pp. 259–60.
6. Letter from Krystyna Kolodziej to the author, and earlier quoted in my book *The After Death Experience*, London, Sidgwick & Jackson, 1987, pp. 98–9.
7. Aniela Jaffé, *Apparitions and Precognition*, New York, University Books, 1963, p. 165.
8. Roy Jenkins, *European Diary, 1977–81*, London, Collins, 1989.
9. Quoted in Diana Norman, *The Stately Ghosts of England*,

London, Muller, 1963, pp. 16–17.

10. From notes supplied by Miss Hughes, June 1994.

11. Sir Ernest Bennett, *Apparitions and Haunted Houses*, London, Faber, 1939, pp. 142–4. In the original the two priests are referred to only by their initials, but with the aid of Father Michael Clifton, archivist for the Roman Catholic diocese of Southwark, I have supplied their full names.

12. It is important, however, not to be too categoric. Roy Jenkins in fact received a second 'visit' from Anthony Crosland, about a week after the first.

CHAPTER 5

1. Adolf Erman, *The Literature of the Ancient Egyptians*, translated by Aylward M. Blackman, London, Methuen, 1927, pp. 170–2.

2. J. Nougayrol, 'Aleuromancie babylonienne', *Orientalia*, 32, 1962, p. 381ff.

3. Suetonius, *The Twelve Caesars*, translated by Robert Graves, Harmondsworth, Penguin, 1957, p. 178.

4. *The Letters of Pliny the Younger*, Book 7, 27, as translated by the author after the Latin text, as published in the Loeb Classical Library, London, Heinemann, 1915, pp. 70–3.

5. A. B. Mitford, *Tales of Old Japan*, Tokyo, Tuttle, 1966, pp. 268–70.

6. Arthur P. Wolf, 'Gods, Ghosts and Ancestors', in *Religion and Ritual in Chinese Society*, Stanford University Press, 1974, p. 170.

7. From Danish weekly journal *Light Reading for the Danish Public*, 8 March 1839, quoted in P. V. Glob, *The Bog People*, London, Faber & Faber, 1969, p. 76.

8. P. V. Glob, op. cit., pp. 76–7.

9. Ibid., p. 149.

10. Lewes Lavater, *Of ghostes and spirites walking by nyght, and of strange noyses, crackes, and sundry forewarnynges, whiche commonly happen before the death of menne, great slaughters & alterations of kyngdomes*. In 1929 this was republished as *Of ghostes and spirites walking by nyght*, edited and with an introduction and appendix by J. Dover Wilson and May Yardley, printed for the Shakespeare Association at the University Press, Oxford, 1929, p. 71.

11. 'A Great Wonder in Heaven Shewing the Late Apparitions and prodigious noyes of War and Battels, seen on Edge-Hill near Keinton in Warwickshire', British Museum Thomason Tracts E.85(41).

12. 'The New Yeares Wonder', British Museum Thomason Tracts E.86 (23).

13. For much of the above information concerning Edgehill and its apparitions, I am indebted to Peter Young, *Edgehill 1642*, Kineton, Roundwood Press, 1967.

14. Bodleian Library Rawlinson MS A 186, ff. 110–11.

15. Wing-tsit Chan (ed.), *A Source Book in Chinese Philosophy*, Princeton, Princeton University Press, 1963, p. 301.

16. Charles F. Emmons, *Chinese Ghosts and ESP*, Metuchen, New Jersey, The Scarecrow Press, 1982, p. 20. Emmons also included in his list 'improper worship after death', but this really relates to the Chinese custom of ancestor worship beyond the scope of our discussion here.

CHAPTER 6

1. Personal correspondence from Simon Thurley, 7 July 1994.

2. Peter Underwood, *A Gazetteer of British Ghosts*, London, Souvenir, 1971.

3. This and the subsequent quotations are from a tape-recorded interview, 27 April 1995. The names of the actual companies mentioned by 'Peter Taylor' have, however, been removed.

4. This and the quotations from Barbara McKenzie that follow all derive from Underwood, *No Common Task*, op. cit., pp. 117–20, except for slight editing, also substitution of the true names Robin and Rose for the pseudonyms 'Christopher' and 'Lily'.

CHAPTER 7

1. Quoted in Gordon Thomas, *Issels: The Biography of a Doctor*, London, Hodder & Stoughton, 1975, pp. 181–2.

2. *St Louis Medical and Surgical Journal*, February 1890.

3. Dr Michael Sabom, *Recollections of Death: A Medical Investiga-*

tion, New York, Harper & Row, 1982, p. 117.

4. Robert Crookall, *Case-book of Astral Projection*, Secauscua New Jersey, University Books, 1972, pp. 545–746.

5. Rupert Sheldrake, *Seven Experiments that Could Change the World*, London, Fourth Estate, 1994, p. 117ff. I am greatly indebted to Dr Sheldrake for much of the subsequent material in this chapter.

6. Ibid., p. 118.

7. Ibid., p. 143.

8. As reported by the Revd J. Aelwyn Roberts, this practice of burying an amputated limb was well known in Wales: 'In the slate quarry town of Blaenau Ffestiniog, where I was brought up, if a man lost a leg or an arm, or even a finger, in a quarry accident, the cut-off limb would be carefully placed in a little casket and buried in a place apart, in the churchyard, and its place would be marked in the church register. Years later . . . his body was laid to rest where the missing limb awaited him. In this way . . . he could arise whole on the Resurrection Day.' J. Aelwyn Roberts, *Holy Ghostbuster*, London, Robert Hale Ltd., 1990, p. 165.

9. Sheldrake, op. cit., p. 127, after S. H. Frazier and L. C. Kolb, 'Psychiatric aspects of the phantom limb', *Orthopedic Clinics of North America*, 1, 1970, pp. 481–95.

10. Ibid., p. 126.

CHAPTER 8

1. Celia Green and Charles McCreery, *Apparitions*, London, Hamish Hamilton, 1975, p. 80.

2. Mrs E. Sidgwick, 'Notes on the Evidence, Collected by the Society, for Phantasms of the Dead', *Proceedings of the Society for Psychical Research*, Vol. 3, 1885, pp. 69–150.

3. From an interview with journalist John Darnton, published in the *New York Times*, Thursday 21 April 1994.

4. From a letter to the author of 22 March 1994 from club secretary RN Commander J. A. Holt, MBE.

5. From a letter of 20 November 1963 from Mrs Coleen Buterbaugh in response to an enquiry from the eminent American psychologist and psychical researcher Dr Gardner Murphy. Extracts from

this letter are quoted in Gardner Murphy and Herbert L. Klemme, 'Unfinished Business', *Journal of the American Society for Psychical Research*, Vol. 60, October 1966, p. 306ff.

6. Alexander MacKenzie, 'A Case of a Haunting in Kent', *Journal of the Society for Psychical Research*, Vol. 44, 1967, pp. 131–49.

7. Brian C. Nisbet, 'Apparitions', in Ivor Grattan-Guinness (ed.), *Psychical Research: A Guide to its History, Principles & Practices*, Wellingborough, The Aquarian Press, 1982, pp. 94–5.

8. Ibid.

9. Quoted in Andrew MacKenzie, *The Seen and the Unseen*, London, Weidenfeld, 1987, p. 112.

10. Andrew MacKenzie, 'Visit to a Haunted House', *The Psi Researcher*, no. 13 (newsletter issued by the Society for Psychical Research), p. 8.

11. Quoted in Norman, op. cit., pp. 174–5.

12. Ibid., p. 178.

13. One notable exception to this is a case reported, without clear source, in Joan Forman's *The Mask of Time*, London, Macdonald & James, 1978. The informant was a retired brigadier, K. Treseder, who with a party of skiers a few miles out of Oslo was accused of trespassing by 'a tall old lady dressed in a brown herring-bone tweed suit'. The old lady harangued the skiers, all of whom saw her, then disappeared, and was concluded to have been a ghost. As I have been unable to discover anything of Brigadier Treseder I have omitted this case from consideration.

14. Mrs Bray, *Traditions, Legends, Superstitions and Sketches of Devonshire*, Vol. II, 1838, p. 298; also E. M. Leather, *The Folklore of Herefordshire*, 1912, reprinted 1970, p. 33; also Chris Barber, *Ghosts of Wales*, Cardiff, John Jones, 1919, p. 7.

15. The exception to this, apart from the example mentioned in note 13, would appear to be the dead encountered in dreams, but for our present purposes at least these are not included as 'true' ghosts.

16. Green and McCreery, op. cit., p. 80.

17. Murphy and Klemme, op. cit., p. 306.

18. Norman, op. cit., p. 170.

19. Underwood, *Nights in Haunted Houses*, op. cit., p. 15.

20. J. A. Brooks, *Britain's Haunted Heritage*, Norwich, Jarrold, 1990, p. 27.
21. Underwood, *Nights in Haunted Houses*, op. cit., p. 18.
22. John Shaw, 'Marquess buys family manor – and the ghost', *Sunday Telegraph*, 9 June 1985.
23. For background information, see D. B. Barton, *A History of Tin Mining and Smelting in Cornwall*, D. Bradford Barton, c.1967.
24. Reported by Alexander Gracie's widow, Mrs Margaret O'Reilly of Sutton Coldfield, West Midlands, in the Society for Psychical Research's *Newsletter Supplement*, January 1989.

CHAPTER 9
1. MacKenzie, *Haunting and Apparitions*, op. cit., p. 213.
2. Quoted in MacKenzie, *The Seen and the Unseen*, op. cit., p. 241ff.
3. These incidents involving children at Cleve Court are described in MacKenzie, Haunting . . . , op.cit., pp. 200–01.
4. See for instance the chihuahuas in the case of Anne Allen, Chapter 16, and the Armstrongs' Labrador Beth in Chapter 17.
5. Quoted in Underwood, *Nights in Haunted Houses*, op. cit., pp. 19–20.
6. A television report on these Dover Castle occurrences, complete with interviews with the guides and others, was screened as part of London Weekend Television's *Strange but True?* documentary on 11 November 1994.
7. Christopher Neil-Smith, *The Exorcist and the Possessed*, St Ives, James Pike, 1974, pp. 17–18.
8. Ibid., p. 82.
9. Pearce-Higgins, op. cit., pp. 175–6.
10. Norman, op. cit., pp. 23–4.
11. Ibid., pp. 21–2.
12. Mervyn Stockwood, *Chanctonbury Ring*, London, Hodder & Stoughton, 1982, pp. 174–5.
13. Quoted in William Gill, 'The Ghost Breaker', *Independent* magazine, 29 January 1994, p. 35.
14. Ibid, p. 36.
15. Pearce-Higgins, op. cit., pp. 176–7.

16. Fr Francis Edwards, letter to the *Sunday Telegraph*, 28 February 1993. See also Fr Edwards' article 'An Elizabethan Goes West', *Contemporary Review*, July 1993, pp. 43–6.

17. Eddie Burks and Gillian Cribbs, *Ghosthunter: Investigating the World of Ghosts and Spirits*, London, Headline, 1995.

18. Michaeleen Maher and Gertrude Schmeidler, 'Quantitative Investigation of a Recurrent Apparition', *Journal of the American Society for Psychical Research*, 69, 1975, pp. 341–52.

19. Michaeleen C. Maher and George P. Hansen, 'Quantitative Investigation of a Reported Haunting Using Several Detection Techniques', in G. Schmeidler (Chair), *Proceedings of Presented Papers, Parapsychological Association 33rd Annual Convention*, Durham, NC, Parapsychological Association, 1990, pp. 151–67.

CHAPTER 10

1. MacKenzie, *Hauntings and Apparitions*, op. cit., p. 212.

2. At Liz's request, for reasons of privacy I have given her maiden name.

3. Letter to the author, with slight editorial adjustments, dated 25 October 1994.

4. From a short article, 'The Veazey Street Ghost', written by Commander Bellars and kindly supplied to the author in the course of correspondence, February 1995.

5. W. Macqueen Pope, *Theatre Royal, Drury Lane*, London, W. H. Allen, 1945, p. 89.

6. Erlendur Haraldsson, report for symposium on apparitions during the Parapsychological Association's convention in Iceland, 1980, quoted in MacKenzie, *The Seen and the Unseen*, op. cit., p. 260.

7. Underwood, *Ghosts and How to See Them*, op. cit., pp. 26–7.

8. Ibid., p. 97ff.

9. G. W. Lambert and K. Gay, 'The Dieppe Raid Case. A collective auditory hallucination', *Journal of the Society for Psychical Research*, Vol. 36, 1952, pp. 607–18.

10. Graham McEwan, *Haunted Churches of England*, London, Robert Hale, 1989, p. 125.

11. Quoted in A. H. McLintock (ed.), *An Encyclopaedia of New Zea-*

land, Vol. 3, Wellington, R. E. Owen, 1966, p. 360. I am deeply indebted to New Zealander Bob Cotterall for drawing this case to my attention. In an accompanying letter he writes, 'Most Kiwis of my generation (I am 81) would trust absolutely in the veracity of Mrs Sise, of the Maori and other observers. I do.'

CHAPTER 11

1. See Murphy and Klemme, op. cit., p. 318, for the information regarding the bitter wind. The heart attack is simply inferred, since Gardner and Klemme give no details regarding the exact cause of death.

2. Ibid., pp. 306–7.

3. Ibid., p. 308.

4. Ibid., p. 307.

5. *Proceedings of the Society for Psychical Research*, Vol. 25, 1911, p. 353ff.

6. *John o'London's Weekly*, 19 November 1932.

7. From a letter quoted in Andrew MacKenzie, *Apparitions and Ghosts*, London, Arthur Barker, 1971, p. 136.

8. Philippe Jullian, *Un Prince 1900 – Robert de Montesquiou*, Paris, Librairie Academique Perrin, 1965; also published in English as *Robert de Montesquiou, a Fin-de-Siècle Prince*, London, Secker & Warburg, 1967.

9. For much of the information on Harry Martindale's experiences I am indebted to Harry Martindale himself; also to John Mitchell, author of *Ghosts of an Ancient City*, York, Cerealis Press, 1974. The latter not only provided photocopies of the relevant pages from his book (sadly out-of-print), but also furnished me with a copy of his own interview with Harry Martindale tape-recorded in 1974. See also Byron Rogers, 'Floored by ghosts in the cellar' in *Sunday Telegraph*, 7 May, 1995, Review, p. 6.

10. From my own interviews with Harry Martindale, early June 1995.

11. The information on Mrs Joan Mawson's experience is partly based on John Mitchell's book (op. cit.) and a tape-recording of his interview with her; partly also on my own telephone interviews with her, January and June 1995.

12. The case is summarised in Perry (ed.), op. cit., p. 30 (Case 10).
13. From a letter of Canon Dominic Walker to the author, 24 January 1995.

CHAPTER 12

1. The case is recorded in some detail in F. W. H. Myers, *Human Personality and Its Survival of Bodily Death*, London, Longmans, 1903.
2. On one occasion, talking about how in her lifetime as the disturbed Mary she had slashed her arm, she was about to roll up her sleeve to show the scar, then checked herself, realising: 'It's not this arm – it's the one in the ground.'
3. Statement by Michael Howard Romney-Woollard, made 15 November 1966, and lodged with Brigadier Peter Young, DSO, MC, who published it in his book op. cit., pp. 164–6.
4. Dr Kenneth McAll, *Healing the Family Tree*, London, Sheldon, 1982, p. 13ff.
5. This and the other names given in the case are all apparently pseudonyms to protect the psychiatric patients' real identities.
6. McAll, op. cit., p. 15.
7. Ibid., p. 13.
8. Anthony S. Hale and Narsimha R. Pinninti (Guy's and St Thomas's Hospitals), 'Exorcism-resistant Ghost Possession Treated with Clopenthixol', *British Journal of Psychiatry*, 165, 1994, pp. 386–8.
9. Ibid., p. 387.
10. Roberts, op. cit., p. 91ff.
11. Quoted without source in Neil-Smith, op. cit., p. 45.

CHAPTER 13

1. Paul Bannister, *Strange Happenings*, New York, Grosset & Dunlap, 1978, p. 4.
2. Anne Ross, 'Two Small Stone Heads from Hexham', *Archaeologia Aeliana*, 5th Series, Vol. I, Society of Antiquaries of Newcastle upon Tyne, p. 5ff.
3. I am indebted to Underwood's *No Common Task*, op. cit., for the

main story that follows, derived from his direct interviewing of Dr Ross when she was living in Southampton. This has, however, been checked by me with Dr Ross (who had not previously seen Underwood's published account), and certain inaccuracies duly rectified.

4. Letter to the author dated 3 December 1994.
5. Ibid.
6. Perry (ed.), op. cit., pp. 95–6 (Case 35).
7. I owe both the identification of Professor Russell, and his disclaimer of any recollection of the incident, to Dr J. M. Kaye, Keeper of the Archives at Queen's College, Oxford, in a letter to me of 25 March 1994.
8. Quoted in Brooks, op. cit., p. 74.
9. In personal correspondence with Dr Anne Ross I put to her the suggestion that she might have seen the ghost of a Celtic shaman, a pre-Christian witch-doctor who might have assumed a wolf's head in a manner seen in some prehistoric cave-paintings. But Dr Ross felt that the creature she saw was partly real animal. It is worth noting that Neil-Smith, in his *The Exorcist and the Possessed,* op. cit. (p. 72), refers to the case of a young man initiated into a wolf-cult, part of the Red Indian rites in Canada. The purpose of the cult was to acquire and use the characteristics of the wolf.
10. Edmund Lenthal Swift, article in *Notes and Queries*, 1816.
11. Green and McCreery, op. cit., p. 93.
12. Prince Albert Victor and Prince George of Wales, *The Cruise of Her Majesty's Ship 'Bacchante' 1879–1882*, Vol. I, London, Macmillan, 1886, p. 551.
13. Ibid. The admiral referred to was Rear-Admiral Richard James Meade, 4th Earl of Clanwilliam in the Irish peerage, who was taken seriously ill upon arrival in Sydney on 14 July 1881, delaying the whole squadron's departure by nearly three weeks. During this time he was promoted to vice-admiral.
14. Ibid.
15. Sir Ernest Bennett, op. cit., pp. 368–9.
16. Ibid.
17. Daniel Farson, article in the *Sunday Telegraph*, 27 December 1987.

18. Society for Psychical Research, *Newsletter* no. 26, July 1988, p. 24.

CHAPTER 14

1. Stockwood, op. cit., p. 177.
2. This can be inferred from the fact that when the skeleton was given a proper burial, the haunting promptly ceased.
3. Houblon to Pepys, Bodleian Library Rawlinson MS A 186, ff. 110–11.
4. Pope, op. cit., p. 90.
5. Ibid.
6. Underwood, *Haunted London*, op. cit., p. 60.
7. Authors have differed on the exact date of this discovery, the 1848 date deriving from William Kent's *Encyclopaedia of London*. The nineteenth-century coroner's records for the Drury Lane district are preserved in the Westminster Abbey muniments, but in searches of these by me for the years 1845 and 1846 (chosen by me because of known refurbishments in these years), also for 1848, I failed to find the appropriate record.
8. Pope, op. cit., p. 91.
9. An obituary of Francis Crute appeared in the *Torquay Times*, 18 September 1953.
10. Quoted in McEwan, op. cit.
11. Much of this information derives from a report in the *Western Morning News*, 24 January 1959.
12. Quoted in McKenzie, *The Seen and the Unseen*, op. cit., pp. 48–9.
13. Ibid., p. 50.

CHAPTER 15

1. There are occasional reports of individuals, usually anonymous, feeling themselves about to be choked by an invisible entity they have assumed to be a ghost. But these occur only among the anecdotal cases that I have avoided in this book. Where they occur, they may denote a psychological problem on the part of the person having the experience, rather than the activity of any true ghost. Furthermore I know of no one actually choked in such circumstances.

2. See Chapter 13, note 10.
3. Perry (ed.), op. cit., pp. 120–3.
4. Ibid., pp. 125–6.
5. See reports in *The Times* and other national newspapers, 26 and 27 March 1975.
6. See *The Times* and other national newspapers, reports 4–9 September 1980.
7. See reports in the *Sydney Morning Herald*, 4 and 6 February and 15 and 17 September 1993, also the *Australian Parapsychological Review*, no. 18, 1993, p. 16.
8. Pearce-Higgins, op. cit., p. 170.
9. This and the two subsequent quotations derive from Stockwood, op. cit., pp. 174–5.
10. Pearce-Higgins, op. cit., p. 188.
11. Underwood, *No Common Task*, op. cit., pp. 69–70.
12. Ibid.
13. Underwood, *Nights in Haunted Houses*, op. cit., p. 2.
14. Underwood, *Ghosts and How to See Them*, op. cit., pp. 110–14.
15. Underwood, *The Ghost Hunters*, op. cit., pp. 155–6.
16. Ibid., pp. 153–60.
17. Ibid., p. 179.
18. Underwood, *Nights in Haunted Houses*, op. cit., p. 156.

CHAPTER 16
1. MacKenzie, *Hauntings and Apparitions*, op. cit., p. 214.
2. A. B. Mitford, op. cit., pp. 269–70.
3. Paul Vallely and Michael Macintyre, 'The Long Journey to Free the Spirits', *Sunday Times* magazine, 20 January 1985.
4. II Maccabees 12: 44–5.
5. Lavater, op. cit., p. 72.
6. The case that follows appears as Case 16 in Perry (ed.), op. cit., p. 41, but has been considerably supplemented by more detailed information given by Canon Dominic Walker during an interview at my home, and in subsequent correspondence.
7. Letter from Canon Dominic Walker to the author, dated 11 December 1994.

8. Letter from Mr R. J. Comber to the author, dated 30 March 1988.
9. These cases are extremely common in the anecdotal literature on ghosts mostly avoided in this book.
10. Pearce-Higgins, op. cit., p. 181.

CHAPTER 17

1. I subsequently interviewed Mr Armstrong at his office, and obtained full corroboration of what Mrs Armstrong told me.
2. This seems to be an exact equivalent of Barbara McKenzie's observation of the Robin Hayden footsteps that, unlike living footsteps, they caused no creaking of the house's stairtreads; also the observation by my wife and I at Abercrombie House that our 'breathing' ghost caused no creaking of the floorboards, even though it was impossible for a living person to walk in or outside our bedroom without doing so.

CONCLUSION

1. Important to mention here is that although there is a considerable literature on ghosts of the living, I have quite deliberately not addressed this in the course of this book, on the grounds that tackling the issue of ghosts of the dead is quite complicated enough.
2. Geoffrey Gorer, *Africa Dances*, London, Faber & Faber, 1935, p. 235.
3. Colin Wilson, *Mysteries*, London, Hodder & Stoughton, 1978, pp. 302, 303.
4. Louis Tucker, *Clerical Errors*, New York, Harper, 1943, pp. 221ff.
5. Sloman and Schmidt, 'A burning issue: phantom limb pain and psychological preparation of the patient for amputation', *Archives of Surgery*, 113 (1978), pp. 185–6.
6. Hans Holzer, op.cit., p. viii.

INDEX

269